FACE OFF

FACE OFF

China, the United States,
and Taiwan's Democratization

John W. Garver

University of Washington Press

Seattle and London

Library of Congress Cataloging-in-Publication Data
Garver, John W.
    Face off : China, the United States, and Taiwan's democratization
/ John W. Garver.
        p. cm.
    Includes bibliographical references and index.
    ISBN 0-295-97617-9 (alk. paper)
    1. China—Foreign relations—United States.   2. United States—
Foreign relations—China.   3. Taiwan—Politics and
government—1988–   4. China—Foreign relations—1976–   I. Title.
E183.8.C5G38   1997   97–9021
327.51073—dc21   CIP

The paper used in this publication meets the minimum
requirements of American National Standard for Information
Sciences—Permanence of Paper for Printed Library Materials,
ANSI Z39.48–1984. ∞

To my beloved Penelope

Contents

Acknowledgments

A great many people in the People's Republic of China, in the United States, and in Taiwan have helped this book's development by sharing with me their views about various matters. During a five month stay in Beijing during the first half of 1995 I discussed relevant issues with many people, Chinese and American. In March 1996 I traveled to Taiwan for two weeks with the support of Georgia Tech to observe the presidential election there. Once again, I exchanged views with a wide array of people. Unfortunately, discretion prevents me from explicitly thanking most of them. Among those it may be proper to acknowledge, let me convey my thanks to Allen S. Whiting, John F. Copper, Alfred D. Wilhelm Jr., Lin Chong-pin, Parris Chang, Paul Frandano, June Tuefel Dreyer, Paul H. B. Godwin, Bates Gill, Michael Pillsbury, Earl Tilford, Wu Yu-shan, James Lilley, Su Jia-hong, Peter M. Kuhfus, Gudrun Wacker, and Gert-Johannes Hagemann. I am also grateful to the Chair of the School of International Affairs, Linda Brady, for arranging a substantial block of time free from teaching obligations, during which this book was drafted. Joy Daniell typed and retyped the manuscript with efficiency and good grace. Lorri Hagman also deserves thanks for her meticulous attention to detail in the editing of the book.

John W. Garver
Georgia Institute of Technology
Atlanta, Georgia
January 1997

Abbreviations

AMS	Academy of Military Sciences (China)
APEC	Asia Pacific Economic Cooperation
ARATS	Association for Relations Across the Taiwan Strait (China)
ASEAN	Association of Southeast Asian Nations
ASW	Antisubmarine warfare
CASS	Chinese Academy of Social Sciences (China)
CCP	Chinese Communist Party
CINCPAC	Commander in Chief, Pacific (United States)
CMC	Central Military Commission (China)
DF-31	Dongfeng 31 (China)
DPP	Democratic Progressive Party (Taiwan)
GATT	General Agreement on Tariffs and Trade
GIO	Government Information Office (Taiwan)
GNP	Gross National Product
ICBM	Intercontinental ballastic missile
IDF	Indigenous Defense Fighter (Taiwan)
IECDF	International Economic Cooperation Development Fund (Taiwan)
IMF	International Monetary Fund
IPR	Intellectual Property Rights
KMT	Kuomintang (Nationalist Party) (Taiwan)
LDP	Liberal Democratic Party (Japan)
MFA	Ministry of Foreign Affairs (China)
MFN	Most Favored Nation
MOD	Ministry of Defense (China)
MOFA	Ministry of Foreign Affairs (Japan)
MOU	Memorandum of Understanding
MSS	Ministry of State Security (China)
NDU	National Defense University (China)
NORINCO	North China Industrial Corporation (China)
NPC	National People's Congress (China)
PLA	People's Liberation Army (China)

PRC	People's Republic of China
ROC	Republic of China
SDF	Self Defense Force (Japan)
SEF	Straits Exchange Foundation (Taiwan)
SRBM	Short Range Ballistic Missile
TRA	Taiwan Relations Act
UN	United Nations
USSR	Union of Soviet Socialist Republics
WTO	World Trade Organization

FACE OFF

1 / The Significance of the 1996 Crisis

I n March 1996 the United States deployed two aircraft-carrier battle groups to the vicinity of Taiwan. This deployment, the largest concentration of naval power assembled by the United States in East Asia since the end of the Vietnam War, came against the background of unprecedentedly large and extensive military exercises by the People's Republic of China (PRC) in the Taiwan Strait designed to intimidate voters in the Republic of China (ROC) as they elected their president for the first time. As Beijing and Washington entered confrontation, both made it clear that their stakes were high and hinted their preparedness for further escalation. Such escalation was averted and tension dissipated quickly. The United States and the PRC had, however, experienced their first military confrontation since that in the late 1960s over Vietnam.

The 1996 crisis was significant for several reasons. It demonstrated an important element of uncertainty and instability introduced into U.S.-PRC relations by the emergence of a democratic Taiwan. Taiwan has long shown that a smaller power can affect, even manipulate, to its own advantage relations between greater powers. President Chiang Kai-shek's policies toward the tiny offshore islands of Jinmen (Quemoy) and Mazu (Matsu) circa 1954–55 and 1958 were classic examples of this. The transition of Taiwan's political system from what American political scientist Ed Winkler termed "soft authoritarianism" to viable liberal democracy in the early 1990s has given an entirely new dimension to this old problem.[1] Moves to alter Taiwan's international status are now linked in a direct and significant way to that island's internal political processes. Changing concepts of collective self-identity on Taiwan are now linked to the acquisition and legitimation of political power via competitive political processes. This new dynamic may make Taiwan's role far more powerful, for no longer are its catalytic actions linked to the unrealistic dreams of an aging dictator (as was the case with Chiang Kai-shek's offshore-island policies of the 1950s), but to the dynamics of a competitive democratic system. As well as possibly making those actions far less

3

amenable to discipline by the greater powers whose relations are affected, this raises the stakes for both the United States and the PRC.

The 1996 crisis suggested that differing U.S. and PRC interests in Taiwan could, if not properly managed, lead to war. Great powers do not enter into confrontations with one another lightly; willingness to do so typically reflects interests deemed weighty enough to risk war to protect. Taiwan's democratic transition in the early 1990s was part of what Samuel Huntington termed the "third wave" of global movement toward democracy, that began with the transitions in Spain, Portugal, and Greece in the late 1970s and continued through the Eastern European revolutions a decade later.[2] In East Asia, South Korea and the Philippines as well as Taiwan were included in this "wave." Many of these democratic transitions to some degree resulted from the exercise of U.S. influence over a period of several decades. Such influence varied from country to country, playing a relatively greater role in Taiwan, in which the United States had a significant political investment to protect. Protection of Taiwan's democratic process conformed to a concept of collective self-identity very popular in the United States—that national power should be used to maintain and promote democracy in the world. The stakes were thus high for the United States.

From Beijing's perspective, the stakes were nothing less than the eventual incorporation of Taiwan into the state system of the PRC. Upon reaching an understanding with the United States on Taiwan in 1971, China's leaders predicated their hope for Taiwan's "peaceful unification" with the PRC upon the island's progressive isolation. China's leaders hoped that the gradual erosion of Taiwan's diplomatic ties, combined with the steady growth of PRC political influence and military power, would eventually persuade Taiwan's leaders that they had no realistic choice but to come to terms with Beijing. China was prepared to be quite generous, promising, by 1984, continued rule of Taiwan by the Nationalist (Kuomintang; KMT) elite there. Thus would peaceful unification be achieved, or so Beijing hoped.

These calculations were thrown awry by Taiwan's democratization. Its political process became much more confused and messy, and Beijing could no longer hope to reach agreement with Taiwan's rulers with scant regard for the sentiments of the island's populace. The dreams and aspirations of the ordinary people—unrealistic though they might be from Beijing's perspective—increasingly intruded into the calculations of Taiwan's leaders. Moreover, Taiwan's transition to democracy won it friends and sympathy across a broad spectrum of political opinion in Western countries and enhanced its status. Taipei's push for expanded participation in international society was assisted by its growing economic influence and by the plummeting of Beijing's international status with the juxtaposition in 1989 of the Beijing Massacre and the peaceful revolutions of Eastern Europe. Efforts to reverse the deepening international isolation to which Taiwan had been condemned after 1971 now met with mounting success and called into question the strategy of "peaceful unification" pursued by China for over two decades. Stated differently and in more Chinese terms, the establishment of bourgeois democratic political institutions in Taiwan was part of a plot to split China's territory. The question for Beijing thus became how to respond to this nefarious hegemonist plot.

The stakes were equally great for the twenty-one million people of Taiwan, who had struggled long and bitterly for several decades to achieve political freedom and democracy, finally achieving victory in the 1990s with the presidential election of 1996, in which power at the very apex of the state was to be derived from direct, free, and competitive elections. The powerful military intimidation from the mainland that emerged at that juncture threatened Taiwan's hard-won democratic institutions.

The 1996 crisis also appears to have strongly influenced U.S. and Chinese perceptions of one another, which had been in flux since the Beijing Massacre of June 1989 and the dissolution of the USSR in 1991. The 1996 crisis probably will prove to be an important episode in that ongoing process of reevaluation. After the end of the Cold War, some in the United States argued that China was an emerging expansionist power posing a threat to U.S. interests in Asia, and consequently should be contained. Others argued that China was neither expansionist nor aggressive, but merely exercising greater influence commensurate with its growing economic power; it used its power cautiously and showed no inclination to challenge the United States militarily. Moreover, an effort to contain China would, said these opponents of a new containment policy, become a self-fulfilling prophecy. Up until early 1996, the "China threat" point of view was a minority position among the American people and their leaders. One effect of the 1996 Taiwan Strait crisis may have been to reverse U.S. opinion.

The 1996 Taiwan Strait crisis came as a shock to people in both capitals. Many in Beijing had convinced themselves that the United States would wash its hands of Taiwan or perhaps already had in order to avoid confrontation with China. Many in Washington thought China would not engage in military adventurism and risk relations across the Strait and across the Pacific, upon which its rapid economic development depended. Following the 1996 confrontation those beliefs were far less common. That greater sobriety ultimately may prove to be a good thing if it leads to more realistic decision making in both Beijing and Washington and avoidance of war. It will be bad if it leads merely to enhanced Chinese preparations for war with the United States the next time China's leaders decide to move against Taiwan.

On the Chinese side, many influential people have argued since 1989 that the United States pursued an unstated but deliberate policy of trying to contain and weaken China, rallying anti-China forces all around China's periphery.[3] These critics find evidence in the disintegration of the USSR and its replacement by successor states with more-or-less Western-style governments courted by the United States; the U.S. normalization of relations with Vietnam; U.S. support for Japan's greater international role; Vietnam's membership in and India's growing involvement with the Association of Southeast Asian Nations (ASEAN) countries; and the beginning of a U.S. security relationship with India. While trying to sow discord between China and its neighbors, Washington sought to subvert China's central government, led by the Chinese Communist Party (CCP), through economic pressure, support for "human rights," radio broadcasts, and so on. Washington used the threat of revoking Most Favored Nation (MFN) status to force China to adopt a more liberal attitude toward internal dissent, which would allow China's subversive, counterrevolutionary forces to grow strong. Washington lobbied to prevent Beijing from hosting the Olympics in the year 2000 because such an honor would raise the prestige of China's government. The purpose of all of this, many Chinese leaders believed, was to undermine China's unity, discipline, and morale. A China thus weakened would be less able to oppose American advances and would be open to U.S. penetration, exploitation, and domination, just as it had been before 1949. The United States would then, finally, achieve its objective of world domination. These Chinese "antihegemonists," if we may call them that, saw modifications in U.S. policy toward Taiwan as manifestations of U.S. hegemonism.[4]

This conservative, antihegemonist perspective did not, and does not, dominate Chinese foreign policy.[5] The mainstream point of view among

China's elite was deeply suspicious of U.S. purposes, but recognized China's need for continued cooperation with the United States and the West, and for maintenance of a placid international environment conducive to China's continued economic and technological development. It sought to avoid confrontation with the United States.

United States leaders bent over backwards to dissuade China's leaders from adopting the antihegemonist view of U.S. actions. They stated repeatedly that the U.S. sought not to contain but to engage China, and that it sought not a weak China, but a strong, stable, increasingly prosperous, and open China. They pointed to U.S. actions giving substance to those pledges of friendship toward China: the extension of MFN status and its independence from human rights reviews; more lenient guidelines regulating transfer of dual-use and military-related technology to China; and military exchanges and engagement. As we shall see, a desire to not further validate the hostile Chinese perception of the United States was a major factor shaping U.S. policy leading up to the 1996 crisis. Efforts to reassure China's leaders of the U.S. desire for friendship with China had some effect. Then came the 1996 confrontation.

This book investigates the domestic political dynamics within China, the United States, and Taiwan that gave rise to the 1996 confrontation. Although it does not attempt to assay the impact of that crisis on China's foreign policy, we can be sure that the crisis will influence the evolution of China's view of the world. It may be used to confirm the direst predictions of the antihegemonist conservatives or the points made by China's realpolitik mainstream about the heavy cost of confrontation with the United States. Either way it is important to understand the origin and evolution of the crisis.

The impact of the 1996 crisis on the rest of East Asia was significant. Throughout its forty-eight year history, the PRC has sustained a drive to enhance its military power. During the Soviet period of the 1950s, the Maoist era of the 1960s and 1970s, and the Dengist period after 1978, China's leaders have devoted very substantial resources to development of military power. Even during the most difficult period in the late 1950s and early 1960s, immensely expensive nuclear weapons and rocket programs were pushed forward. During the Mao years China constructed a vast indigenous scientific-technological base to support both industry and the military. While this base was far behind those of the United States and the USSR, it was far superior—and provided far better military capabilities—to anything possessed by China in the past.

This drive for enhanced military power continued after 1978 under Deng Xiaoping, with China increasingly able to draw on assets available around the world. As China became a major exporting power in the 1980s and 1990s, it had increased fiscal wherewithal to purchase from the Russians, the Israelis, and others the means to upgrade key areas of military technology. As foreign investment poured into China it brought with it much new technology, and in the 1990s the technological level and capabilities of the People's Liberation Army (PLA) grew rapidly.

Other Asian countries began to wonder about the underlying intentions of China's increased military power. Did China's leaders intend to use it to achieve their objectives in disputes with its neighbors? China had maritime territorial disputes with a number of Asian nations. With Japan and South Korea it disputed ownership of or "sovereignty" over the continental shelves and oceanic waters lying between China and those countries. With Japan, China also disputed ownership of several small islands lying between Taiwan and the Ryukyu archipelago. Chinese maps of the South China Sea showed a U-shaped dashed line encompassing all of the islands and waters to within sixty kilometers of the coast of Malaysia's eastern state of Sarawak and possibly including Indonesia's Natuna Islands. While Chinese officials studiously avoided saying exactly what this line meant, China incrementally and steadily expanded its holdings in the resource-rich South China Sea through claims and actions that brought it into dispute with Vietnam, the Philippines, Malaysia, Brunei, and Indonesia, which claimed islands and parts of the waters and sea floor.

Concern in East Asia over China's intentions and growing capabilities mounted throughout the early 1990s. In the East China Sea west of Okinawa, dozens of incidents occurred between Japanese fishing and merchant vessels and Chinese naval vessels. Were these examples of entrepreneurial free-booting by local Chinese commanders, reflecting decentralized authority? Or were they part of a subtle attempt to establish China's authority over waters claimed by both Japan and China? In August 1995 Chinese warplanes entered the disputed airspace above Japanese-held Sengaku Island, prompting Japanese fighters to scramble from an Okinawan air base to intercept them.[6] What was the meaning of this aerial intrusion? Japanese recalled that during the negotiation of the Sino-Japanese friendship treaty in 1978, Beijing ordered armed fishing boats into the islands to underline that China was not relinquishing its claims there. Was the Sengaku intrusion of August 1995 a signal that

China was prepared to use military force to protect the development of underwater resources near Sengaku? And why was China vigorously pushing forward with its nuclear weapons program, Japan wondered, when Russia and the United States were drastically reducing their nuclear arsenals and China's security was the least threatened since 1949?

The non-Communist nations of Southeast Asia had been comforted by the belief that although China might employ military force against Vietnam, it would not do so against them. In 1988 Chinese military forces broke a Vietnamese effort to resist the establishment of China's first permanent base in the Spratly Islands, sinking three Vietnamese ships, including a freighter, in the process. Several smaller exchanges of fire followed in subsequent years. Vietnam seemed, however, to be the sole target of Chinese military force in the region until January 1995, when the Philippines discovered that Chinese military forces had occupied Mischief Reef, claimed by the Philippines and located only two hundred kilometers west of the major Philippine island of Palawan.[7] Beijing handled the ensuing miniconfrontation cautiously—indeed, more so than did Manila. Beijing refused, however, to express regret for its action or to give assurances that Chinese military forces would not undertake similar actions in the future. China's military occupation of Mischief Reef and its refusal to pull back came as a shock to Southeast Asia. Concerns regarding China's willingness to use military force increased.[8]

Even before China's 1996 campaign against Taiwan, several Southeast Asian countries sought barriers to the possible use of military force by China. One major shift was the December 1995 conclusion of a security agreement between Indonesia and Australia. A founder of the non-aligned movement in the late 1940s, Indonesia—unlike most other Southeast Asian countries, which had bilateral and multilateral security arrangements with one another and with external powers—had long refused to align itself with any country. In December 1995 Indonesia abandoned its traditional stance by concluding an agreement with Australia providing for consultation "in the case of adverse challenges to either party or to their common security interests." Jakarta's major concern was over conflicting claims between itself and Beijing to the gas-rich sea floor northeast of the Natuna Islands. Both Australia and Indonesia denied that the new agreement was designed with China in mind. The context and timing of the agreement, however, suggest that this indeed was the case.[9]

A Memorandum of Understanding (MOU) signed by the Philippine and

British defense secretaries in January 1996 was a second manifestation of mounting regional apprehension about China. Under this first security agreement between London and Manila, the two sides would conduct joint military exercises, exchange defense information, and cooperate on other security matters. Britain would assist the Philippines in strengthening its air defenses. Again diplomatic politeness required denial that this agreement was in any way related to China. Yet, again, this almost certainly was the case.[10] All of this preceded China's 1996 campaign against Taiwan, one of the major consequences of which was increased regional fear regarding China's willingness to use military force to achieve its objectives. That, in turn, will almost certainly accelerate the trend toward a regional coalition to counterbalance China.

Will there be peace or war in the Taiwan Strait? That is a question of immense importance for China, for Taiwan, for Sino-U.S. relations, and for the peace and prosperity of East Asia generally. The 1996 crisis may prove to be an important step in a process that will take the three sides toward peace, or toward war. It may, unfortunately, be a harbinger of more crises to come.

China is in the midst of an epic transition away from communism. Czech president Vaclav Havel introduced the term "posttotalitarian" to describe the Leninist systems that emerged in Eastern Europe and the USSR after Stalin's death. The Communist Party apparatus still encadred all major institutions and dominated the economy via the system of central planning, the Gulag of labor reform concentration camps was still in place, and the memory of the terror still haunted people's minds. But the Party had abandoned its aspiration of creating a totally new nonbourgeois society, and no longer used its vast panoply of powers to midwife the birth of new social relations and values. Under the reforms presided over by Deng Xiaoping, China has moved far beyond Havel's posttotalitarian communism. The role of the central economic planning apparatus has become marginal, and market forces largely determine the economic patterns of Chinese society. State-owned enterprises (i.e., those controlled by a central government organ) now control less than half of industrial production. Of course most producers are not private individuals or firms, but some organ of subnational political authority, such as a township or village government or an office of a municipal government. What is important, however, is that relatively few resources are centrally controlled or allocated. Enterprises and elite groups increasingly find that significant sources of wealth derive from market-based economic activity rather than from compliance with central directives. This means that the Communist elite is increasingly fragmented. The Party's Leninist cadre structure is still in place, but is broken along the lines of parochial economic interest. Pluralism within the Party elite is growing. Moreover, an autonomous civil society is slowly emerging with the development of a class of genuine private entrepreneurs, professional associations, and so on. China increasingly resembles the non-communist authoritarian systems that characterized much of East Asia in the decades after World War II.[11]

What will be the effect of this epochal transition from communism on China's relations with other countries? Some scholars have suggested that transitional regimes in the process of becoming less autocratic are relatively war-prone. Certain aspects of the domestic origins of China's decision for confrontation in the Taiwan Strait in 1996 seem to fit with the dynamics outlined by these scholars.

Edward Mansfield and Jack Snyder have correlated involvement in war with stability and change in authoritarian regimes.[12] To determine involvement in war they relied on two standard data sets aggregating data on all interstate and nonstate (i.e., anticolonial) wars between 1811 and 1980. War and involvement in it were carefully defined. Mansfield and Snyder then grouped regimes into three categories: democracies, autocracies, and transitional regimes becoming either more democratic or more autocratic. The criteria for this categorization followed indicators developed by other prominent American theorists. A regime was considered to be "democratizing," to be in the process of becoming less autocratic and more democratic, if any of the following happened: recruitment of the chief executive became, in principle, more open to attainment by any member of the politically active population; institutionalized restraints on the decision-making powers of the chief executive, whether individual or collective, increased; or competitiveness in political participation (which was coded on a five-point scale ranging from "suppressed competition" to "competitive competition") increased.

When Mansfield and Snyder tabulated the correlation between regime type and the 890 instances of involvement in war between 1811 and 1980, they found that transitional states—formerly autocratic states in the process of becoming more democratic—were substantially more war prone than were either stable autocracies or mature democracies. Transitional regimes were two-thirds more likely to go to war than were stable regimes. Stable autocracies had a 1 in 6 chance of becoming involved in war over any ten-year period, while autocratic states moving toward democratization had a 1 in 4 chance. Moreover, the greater the movement toward democracy, the higher the likelihood of interstate war.

Mansfield and Snyder hypothesize that intensifying elite competition under conditions of rapid social change and weak political institutions account for this tendency. New elites emerge and vie with old ones for power. Old elites fight for survival against new elites and against rising popular democratic forces. In this intensifying contest for power, old and new elites use any resources they can muster. Appeal to the masses may be an effective weapon; indeed, a desire for mass support may partially explain the movement toward democracy in the first place. Ideological appeals are potent instruments for rallying mass support, and simplistic appeals are often quite attractive to new participants in the political process. "Ideology can yield particularly big payoffs," Mansfield and Snyder observe, "when there is no efficient free marketplace of ideas to counter false claims with reliable facts."[13] Nationalism is an especially effective ideological appeal for old elites threatened both by rapid social changes underway and by the specter of mass rebellion. By uniting the masses and the ruling elite, it obfuscates the cleavage between them.

This elite use of nationalism to mobilize mass support leads to war in several ways, Mansfield and Snyder speculate. Leaders may seek to shore up embattled prestige at home by seeking victories abroad. Conquest of lost territory, vindication of national honor, or even victory in war may become a way of rallying popular support. Improved standing in the domestic arena may become a major objective of assertive foreign policies, off-setting possible negative international consequences. Strong "national feeling" may also take on a life of its own. Called into being by elites seeking to enhance the state's ability to govern a split and stalemated political process, nationalist passions can easily become a significant pressure on the elite. Failure to act boldly enough or compromise in foreign confrontations rising out the elite's assertive policies can result in a major loss of domestic prestige. This creates incentive for forceful action and refusal to compromise.

The Taiwan Strait crisis may represent just such an action, and may be the first instance of international crisis linked to the new political dynamics of postcommunist China. If so, others like it may follow in the years ahead.

2 / Taiwan's "Drifting Away"

Two major sets of grievances underlay Beijing's decision to launch large-scale military exercises to intimidate Taiwan. One concerned U.S. policy toward Taiwan, and the other a perceived movement of Taiwan away from unification with the PRC and toward independence. Those grievances were concisely laid out in a statement by a councilor at the PRC embassy in Washington, D.C., in a special issue of the influential journal *Congressional Quarterly* in the fall of 1995. Beijing felt that recent shifts in U.S. policy toward Taiwan violated the "explicit commitments" and "solemn obligations" undertaken by the United States on the Taiwan question. In the three Sino-U.S. communiqués (the Shanghai communiqué of 1972, the normalization communiqué of 1978, and the 1982 communiqué regarding U.S. arms sales to Taiwan), the United States recognized the PRC as the sole legal government of China and acknowledged the Chinese position that Taiwan was a part of China. Within this framework, the United States promised to maintain only unofficial contacts with Taiwan. The U.S. decision of May 1995 to issue a visa permitting Taiwan president Lee Teng-hui to visit the United States was deemed a clear and major violation of the three communiqués. Moreover, successive U.S. administrations since the 1970s had "all declared that they would honor these commitments and never allow any figures who claim to be 'President of the Republic of China' to visit the United States." The Clinton administration's decision to issue a visa to Lee was an "abrupt and brazen break of promise." This action was "even less acceptable," according to the PRC embassy statement, "in view of the situation across the Taiwan Strait." There, "some people, including Taiwan's authorities, [were] trying to resist the historic trend of reunification" and were "stepping up activities" aimed at creating two Chinas, or one China, one Taiwan.[1]

Beijing's concerns about shifts in U.S. policy and about developments within Taiwan were interrelated. Without U.S. support, Beijing believed, the "splittists" within Taiwan would be demoralized and cautious; with U.S. support, they would be bold and aggressive. For the United States, the Taiwan "splittists" were mere tools useful for the containment of China. Their existence and arrogance created the opportunity for U.S. intervention. They insisted on dragging the United States into cross-Strait relations in hopes of "resisting the historic trend" toward incorporation into the PRC. Developments within Taiwan and shifts in U.S. policy were two sides of the same coin: Taiwan's developments created situations that U.S. hegemonists could utilize, yet U.S. hegemonist actions encouraged and abetted the "Taiwan independence" movement.

Beijing was concerned with a process that seemed to take Taiwan away from unification with the PRC—a complex, multidimensional process involving Taiwan's thinking about its relations with the mainland and about itself, Taiwan's growing international status, and the transformation of its political system. In all of those dimensions Taiwan seemed, to Beijing, to be moving further and further away from China, or, more properly, the PRC. The drastic measures of 1996 were, in large part, an effort to abort this process.

A contributing factor was the explosive growth and transformation in cross-Strait relations. Until the late 1980s, there had been very little contact between Taiwan and the China mainland, but beginning in 1987 restrictions on indirect cross-Strait trade and investment were gradually relaxed. By 1990 the official prohibitions on direct shipping, communication, and trade existed in name only. Powerful underlying economic factors worked to drive rapidly expanding cross-Strait economic integration. Taiwan businesses were increasingly concerned with high labor costs and land rents, tighter pollution controls, growing labor awareness and even militancy, and the steady appreciation of the New Taiwan dollar, which made Taiwan's exports more costly abroad. On the mainland, land and labor costs were cheap, labor was docile, and environmental controls were virtually nil. The Renminbi, the PRC currency, was falling in value, making mainland exports cheaper on the international market, and local governments on the mainland were willing to shower incentives on businesses setting up shop in their area. Lower operations costs on the mainland were strong economic incentives. There were also advantages from the Taiwan government's point of view. For a number of years Taiwan's labor-intensive manufacturing industries had faced increased competitive pressure from newly industrializing countries a step or two behind Taiwan. A shift of Taiwan's labor intensive "sunset industries" to the mainland helped Taiwan maintain its competitive advantage by allowing it to concentrate on higher value-added, more capital-intensive, knowledge-intensive industries. It also had the benefit of "exporting" to the mainland much of Taiwan's trade deficit with the United States.[2]

Virtually whole industries—among them footwear, textiles, electrical appliances, light consumer products, and plastics—shifted from Taiwan to the mainland within a period of several years. By early 1991 between 1,200 and 2,000 Taiwan firms had operations on the mainland, with a total investment of between $2 billion and $5 billion.* By the end of 1993 Taiwan investment may have totaled $7 billion to $9 billion.[3] This represented approximately 10 percent of all foreign direct investment in China; Taiwan had outranked Japan to stand as the second-largest foreign investor in China. Indirect trade via Hong Kong also grew, from about $955 million in 1986 to $8.7 billion in 1993.

Taipei's lifting of restrictions on access of its citizens to the mainland also led to an explosion of travel. By mid-1994 more than six million Taiwan citizens, roughly one quarter of the island's entire population, had visited the mainland. Frequent contacts and exchanges raised issues concerning trade disputes, document authentication, smuggling and illegal immigration, marital relations, and property inheritance. In early 1991 China and Taiwan established private associations to deal with these issues—the Straits [sic] Exchange Foundation (SEF) on Taiwan and the Association for Relations Across the Taiwan Straits [sic] (ARATS) on the mainland.[4]

Rapidly burgeoning cross-Strait economic integration raised the question of the overall political relationship between the two sides, which were becoming interdependent. Were China and Taiwan evolving toward the close, complementary, and mutually beneficial relationship of two diverse regions of the same country? Or were they two separate states conducting the sort of mutually beneficial exchanges that many sovereign states normally conduct? Beijing hoped that growing economic interdependence and cooperation, together with the greater familiarity and trust that came from frequent interaction would pave the way for reunification.

Beijing argued that the "one country, two systems" concept proposed by Deng Xiaoping in 1984 provided a fair and workable way for the two sides to institutionalize their growing economic cooperation. All Taiwan had to do was to acknowledge its status as a special administrative region

*Unless otherwise indicated, all references to dollars are U.S. dollars.

of the PRC. By doing that, Taiwan could guarantee for itself a very high degree of autonomy extending into the indefinite future. Only a few symbolic changes would be required. Then the labor power and re-sources of the mainland could freely combine with the managerial exper-tise, capital, and technology of Taiwan. Both sides would benefit. And China, the motherland, would rapidly grow rich and strong.

Unless Taiwan could find ways of countering these trends it stood to be assimilated by China's growing power and economy.[5] Very fre-quently in modern international affairs, economic dependence leads to vulnerability of small and weak states to coercion by large and powerful ones. In modern international society, as in many domestic societies, legal rights protect the weak against the powerful. States that have only a tiny fraction of the economic and military power of their neighbors will rely on legal norms associated with sovereignty to offset to some degree their weaker substantive power.[6] Related to this is recognition of a would-be state's legal rights by other members of international society. Legal norms provide protection only when they are recognized by oth-ers. In modern international society only entities recognized as "states" enjoy the protection of sovereignty. In the early 1990s Taiwan sought to establish itself as a member of international society so that it could enjoy the legal protection accorded by that society to its members. Conversely, by denying Taiwan such protection, Beijing sought to keep it vulnerable to coercion by the mainland's greater economic and military power.

The PRC grew greatly in stature and influence during the 1980s, and used its influence to persuade the international community that Taiwan was a part of the PRC—that Taiwan was not entitled to the legal protec-tion of sovereignty. To the extent that Beijing succeeded in this, Taiwan stood isolated before PRC attempts at economic and military coercion. To the extent that Taiwan secured international recognition of its status as a sovereign state, it enjoyed the powerful protection of the legal norms of international society.

The transformation of cross-Strait relations interacted with a discourse on collective identity among the people on Taiwan. Were they Chinese or Taiwanese? If they were Chinese, what exactly did this mean? Under the rule of Chiang Kai-shek and Chiang Ching-kuo, Taiwan had defined itself as an opponent of the PRC. The mainland was "the other." Taiwan was different. Free China was the antithesis of Red China. While Com-munist China repressed freedom, democracy, and Confucianism, Free China upheld those things, at least in terms of collective self-identity.

Chinese on Taiwan thought of themselves as "good China," as opposed to "bad China" on the mainland.

Expanding contacts with the mainland began to erode such Cold War generalities. Beijing hoped that increased contact would lead to a common Chinese identity. As people from Taiwan visited old friends, relatives, and homes on the mainland and witnessed China's ancient grandeur and modern progress, they would become increasingly aware of their Chinese roots, Beijing hoped. Undoubtedly this did happen to many visitors from Taiwan. But many others were repelled by the poverty, hide-bound traditionalism, and repression they found. Many Taiwan citizens deeply valued the individual freedom, democracy, and modernity that Taiwan was then achieving. What they found on the mainland was far from the ideals they identified with and aspired to for *their* country. Indeed, many suspected that realization of these ideals would be endangered by association with the PRC.

Prior to Chiang Ching-kuo's lifting of martial law during the last months of his life in 1987, an open discourse on Taiwan's collective identity was impossible. Advocacy of independence was prohibited and strictly punished. Following the demise of martial law and the lifting of the ban on political parties, ideas that had percolated sub rosa for years surfaced, and old taboos and orthodoxies began to be openly challenged. From the tremendous intellectual ferment and debate that ensued three main concepts of Taiwan's collective identity emerged.

Two of these concepts challenged the traditional idea, long upheld under Chiang Kai-shek and Chiang Ching-kuo, that the Chinese mainland and Taiwan should unify as soon as possible. Perhaps the best way to understand that intellectual shift is in terms of a break with traditional Chinese thought. One hoary Chinese idea brought into question by many people on Taiwan was the proposition that all Chinese should be united under a single emperor, the Son of Heaven, ruling over all under Heaven (Tian Xia). This notion stood at the very center of China's traditional political thought and was a factor in China's ability to hang together while other vast empires waxed and waned throughout history. The division of Chinese-populated territory into several states was considered an abnormality, an abomination, to be overcome as quickly as possible. Yet with modernization, many Chinese on Taiwan came to think that all Chinese should not necessarily be under the sway of a single highly centralized and authoritarian political system. Why should there not be multiple Chinese states, especially when one of those states, such as that on Taiwan, had finally and indisputably succeeded in creating a modern Chinese society? Such thinking did not necessarily lead to outright advocacy of Taiwan independence, but it did consider skeptically the claim that unification was ipso facto desirable.

One of the two concepts of Taiwanese identity that embraced such a nontraditional approach has been espoused by the KMT under Lee Teng-hui's leadership. According to that view, Taiwan *is* an ethnically Chinese state, but one that is liberal and democratic, and therefore quite separate and distinct from the Chinese state on the mainland. Moreover, this separateness should be recognized and accepted for the indefinite future. The unique circumstances and experiences of the Chinese on Taiwan, who shared a common Chinese language, culture, race, and history, allowed them to create the first truly modern Chinese society. While mainland China still languishes under neofeudal despotism, the Chinese polity on Taiwan enjoys a vibrant civil society and rule of law, liberal democracy, and an open market economy. These achievements are something of which the people of Taiwan, and indeed all Chinese, can be proud. According to this view, given these vast differences between Taiwan and the mainland, little is to be achieved and much risked by hasty unification. The Communist tyrants ruling the mainland, the adherents of this concept of Taiwan identity believe, would use "unity" to subordinate Taiwan, thus destroying its distinctive and successful institutions. Eventual unity is the objective. But progress in that direction must not endanger the distinctive polity that has emerged on Taiwan.

The second nontraditional variant of Taiwan collective identity rejects the idea that eventual unification with China is a desirable objective, instead deeming Taiwan to be a nation distinct from China and destined to assume its proper place among the community of nations. This concept is represented by the advocates of Taiwan independence who suffered repression under the rule of the Chiangs and who came together to form the Democratic Progressive Party (DPP) in 1987. According to the DPP concept of Taiwan's identity, the experience of the people living on Taiwan was fundamentally different from that of mainlanders. Because Taiwan is an island, fishing, piracy, and maritime commerce have always played a large role in its economy, and this frontier area, located across a hundred miles of rough sea, was remote from the capital's imperial bureaucratic representatives. A provincial administration was not established there until 1885, and then only under mounting foreign pressure, according to DPP historiography. This imperial neglect meant that the formative experience of Taiwan for more than two centuries was that of a loosely governed, ocean-oriented island. From the beginning of large-scale Chinese migration to the island during the closing years of the Ming dynasty in the 1630s until the end of the nineteenth century, Taiwan's experience was fundamentally different from that of continental China under the sway of Beijing's mandarinate.

In 1895, after only ten years of effective governance by Beijing, Taiwan became a colony of Japan. For the next fifty years it experienced stable and orderly growth under Japanese colonial administration, while the mainland underwent a half century of trauma that ultimately gave rise to modern Chinese nationalism: the 1911 revolution, the warlordism of the 1920s, the Japanese invasion of the 1930s and 1940s, bloody and protracted civil war, and peasant rebellion combined with brutal repression. All the while Taiwan's experience was very different. Although harsh, Japanese colonial rule was incorrupt and stable, and spurred substantial economic and social development. By Japan's surrender in 1945, Taiwan's populace was highly literate and its agriculture highly commercialized, and a solid transportation and communications infrastructure was in place. Habits of respect for law had begun to be inculcated; Japanese colonial authority was strict but not arbitrary. Between 1945 and the Communist victory on the mainland in 1949, Taiwan again came under control of the mainland Chinese government, and again the experience was most unpleasant. Those were years of spiraling corruption and repression. After 1950 Taiwan passed to American protection, and for the next forty years underwent experience profoundly different from that of the mainland. While the mainland was stifled and constricted under Communist totalitarianism and Mao Zedong's mass campaigns, Taiwan became an increasingly open society governed by the rule of law. The result of those unique histories, according to DPP historiography, was the formation of very different collective identities. This point of view extolls Taiwan's distinctive identity and sees only danger in maintaining even a residual concept of Chineseness.

The third major concept of Taiwan's identity is more traditional, and is represented politically by the New Party, which split off from Lee Teng-hui's KMT in 1994, largely over the question of Taiwan's collective identity. According to this view, Taiwan is indeed a province of China and should be unified with the mainland when China abandons communism. Adherents see the Chinese-speaking people on Taiwan as ethnically and racially Chinese, as *tong bao* (born from the same womb) with mainland Chinese. Racial awareness and pride play an important part in this point of view, as does belief that agreements could be and should be reached hastening unification with a post-Communist mainland. Like the KMT and DPP views, this view typically disdains the political arrangements prevalent on the mainland. The New Party, however, believes that the "Taiwan model" could be and should be applied to the mainland. Most fundamentally, perhaps, this perspective longs for the day when China is accorded its rightful place as one of the leading nations of the world. It desires a powerful Chinese nation-state and derives a deep satisfaction from identification with that would-be state.

The appeal of these concepts of identity vary among Taiwan's subethnic groups. One of Taiwan's deepest social cleavages is between Chinese with several generations of Taiwan-born ancestors and Chinese who themselves or whose parents immigrated with the collapse of the KMT regime on the mainland in the late 1940s. Both groups are ethnically Chinese, but speak different dialects and share differing experiences. "Mainlanders," or "people from other provinces" (*waishengren*), constitute about 15 percent of Taiwan's population and served as the key constituency for Chiang Kai-shek's harshly authoritarian KMT for several decades. *Waishengren* monopolized important KMT and government organs, the officer corps of the military, and the state enterprises that dominated Taiwan's economy until the 1960s. This privileged position was justified by the KMT's intent to invade the mainland to destroy the CCP regime that had usurped authority there. Members of the younger *waishengren* generation have been raised with corresponding beliefs. Native-born Taiwanese, "people from this province" (*benshengren*), who comprise roughly 85 percent of Taiwan's population, were the subordinate class during the long period of KMT authoritarianism. To them the KMT's "one China" doctrine served primarily as justification for KMT oppression. Because they had only vague concepts of the Chinese empire that once held sway on the continent of Asia, the New Party's vision of a racially based Great China uniting Taiwan and the mainland had little appeal to native Taiwanese. Conversely, the DPP's vision of an independent state of Taiwan had little appeal to *waishengren*, but great appeal to *benshengren*.

Waishengren and *benshengren* also differ in their valuation of foreign countries. Mainlanders tend to dislike Japan and to be extremely skeptical of the United States. Japan, of course, ravaged the mainland in the 1930s and 1940s and was largely, though indirectly, responsible for the

Communist rise to power there. The United States also is assigned major responsibility for the Communist victory through its Europe First strategy in World War II and its "weak, irresolute policy" toward the CCP from 1944 onward. In contrast, among native Taiwanese there is a good deal of respect for Japan and things Japanese, and little of the bitter resentment of Japan characteristic of mainlanders. Native Taiwanese tend to take an impartial view of U.S.-China relations prior to 1949. Indeed, Taiwan's own experience of KMT brutality after 1945 makes it easy for native Taiwanese to understand why the United States decided to wash its hands of the KMT in 1948. Throughout the post-1950 period many educated Taiwanese viewed the United States as a force constraining KMT harshness and moving Taiwan in the direction of rule of law and democracy, or at least hoped that the United States would become such a force. It is significant that in terms of orientation toward Japan and the United States, and of lack of enthusiasm for democracy, there are similarities between the New Party and the CCP.

All three concepts of Taiwan's identity are anti-Communist—that is, all disapprove of the political beliefs and practices of the CCP and do not want to see the CCP's power expand to Taiwan. All are deeply distrustful of the CCP and wary of deceptive ploys and feints that the CCP may use to mislead its opponents. There are in Taiwan advocates of the extension of CCP control to Taiwan, but they are very few in number.

Beijing watched with dismay as the discourse between these contending concepts of collective self-identity blossomed in Taiwan after 1987. Some leaders within the CCP advocated a relaxed, tolerant attitude toward such debate. Historically, however, the CCP has crushed the expression of ideas viewed as challenging its power and policies. After June 1989 the tolerant approach was condemned and orthodoxy upheld by a reinvigorated Party apparatus. From the perspective of the post-1989 CCP, the ideas expressed by the DPP and Lee Teng-hui's KMT were virulent "poisonous weeds." The proper way to deal with such "weeds" was to root them out.

Equally objectionable from Beijing's perspective was the fact that the democratization of Taiwan's political system linked concepts of collective identity to the exercise of political power. The democratic transition that remade Taiwan's politics in the 1990s traces back to the 1950s, when popularly elected assemblies were set up in the villages to administer U.S. development assistance. While the power of those village councils was very limited, they inculcated popular understanding of the workings and habits of electoral democracy. Following Chiang Kai-shek's death in 1975 and his succession by his son Chiang Ching-kuo, Taiwan made a transition to "soft authoritarianism."[7] The top positions of government were still not subject to popular election, and the KMT held a tight grip on all aspects of administration. Yet Taiwan's election system was generally fair and increasingly competitive. While the KMT continued to dominate political life, candidates "outside the Party" ran vigorous campaigns that were often strongly critical of the government and the KMT. While voting fraud occurred, it was the exception; by the early 1980s counting of the ballots in elections was generally fair.

Throughout the 1980s there was a gradual expansion of the limits of permissible debate and opposition. The lifting of martial law in 1987 greatly accelerated that process. Independent political parties quickly formed, with the DPP emerging as a strong, island-wide opposition. In the election of 1989 the DPP polled 28 percent of the popular vote. The power and democratic nature of Taiwan's Legislative Yuan (or lawmaking body) grew steadily. In 1992 changes in election laws made possible for the first time direct election of *all* legislators by the citizens of Taiwan. Previously some had been appointed. Legislators became increasingly assertive, calling ministerial officials to account and exercising control in such previously off-limit areas as the defense budget. Taboos on political debate fell. In mid-1994 the Constitution was amended to provide for direct election of the governor of Taiwan and the mayors of major cities. Further amendment of the constitution in August 1994 to provide for direct election of the president marked the culmination of Taiwan's long march to democracy.

As Taiwan democratized, politicians and parties used concepts of collective identity to distinguish themselves and rally voters. These concepts became perhaps the single most important factor differentiating political parties and their popular appeal was a key to electoral success. As in any competitive democracy, success or failure at the polls was not the function of a single factor. Corruption associated with the KMT's forty-five-year grasp on political power, environmental issues, and social issues figured prominently in election campaigns. Yet the popular appeal of concepts of collective identity became an important determinant of who exercised political power.

This rooting of political power in popular beliefs and in the free consent of the governed greatly complicated Beijing's strategy for unifying Taiwan. In the free marketplace of ideas that Taiwan became in the

1990s, the idea of unification with the PRC as a subordinate special administrative region under a central government in Beijing (i.e., "one country, two systems") had very little appeal. This was the fundamental genesis of Beijing's decision to resort to military coercion in 1995–96.

Prior to the beginning of Taiwan's democratic revolution in 1987, the political systems of the two sides of the Strait had increasingly converged. Under Deng Xiaoping's rule the CCP had abandoned its totalitarian aspirations and concentrated on economic development. As it did so it became much more like the classic East Asian developmental autocracies of the Meiji emperor, Park Chung-hee, and Lee Kwan Yew—and Chiang Kai-shek and Chiang Ching-kuo. If Taiwan remained an authoritarian system while the CCP gradually abandoned totalitarianism, the two sides would converge; if Taiwan's rulers did not depend on the consent of the governed, the possibility of a deal between those rulers and the CCP remained. Moreover, if Taiwan's rulers were mostly mainlanders who identified more with the imagined grandeur of "China," prospects for such a deal would be better. Once the actions of Taiwan's rulers became constrained by the sentiments of the island's more than twenty million citizens, a cozy deal between the CCP and Taiwan's rulers over the heads of those people became much less likely. As native Taiwanese politicians replaced mainlanders in Taiwan's government, Beijing's problems increased.

One consequence of Taiwan's democratization and intellectual ferment was that the CCP's concept of collective identity for Taiwan found few takers there. Moreover, the CCP was completely unfamiliar with and disdainful of competitive elections and free intellectual debate. From the CCP's perspective, the evolution of Taiwan's politics since 1987 represented a conspiracy of traitors determined to "split the motherland" with the support and instigation of U.S. hegemonists. An important part of the operational code of the CCP has been to repress ideas it views as pernicious.

Beijing grew increasingly apprehensive of Taiwan's direction. As PRC president Yang Shangkun told Taiwan reporters in September 1990, "When Chiang Ching-kuo was alive, messages spread hinting Taiwan's intention for reunification, [and] we felt somewhat optimistic. But now the matter is hanging around and we are anxious."[8] Throughout the early 1990s the CCP took an increasingly dark view of Lee's intentions and of his relationship to the DPP. One particularly important milestone in this process was the publication in June 1994 of an interview Lee had given several months earlier to the prominent Japanese writer Ryotaro Shiba. Within Chinese communities everywhere that interview had a great impact; in Taiwan it was termed the equivalent of a "political atomic bomb," which greatly deepened the division between Lee's KMT and the emerging New Party.

The starting point for analysis, Lee told Ryotaro, was the premise that "Taiwan must belong to the people of Taiwan" (*Taiwan bixu shi Taiwanrende*). The forty-five or so years after 1945 had been a period of oppression and darkness for the people of Taiwan. The KMT regime that came to Taiwan in the late 1940s was purely an "alien regime" (*wailaide zhengquan*) that "ruled over the people of Taiwan." There was the brutal repression of 28 February 1947. Students were required to speak Chinese (Zhongguohua) and punished for speaking their native language, Taiwanese (Taiwanhua). Twice in the interview, Lee used the Old Testament story of Moses leading the Hebrew people out of slavery in Egypt to implicitly describe his self-conceived mission regarding Taiwan. Lee did not flesh-out that metaphor. My interpretation is that "Egypt" symbolizes the condition of powerlessness and oppression endured by the people of Taiwan for long decades. Prominent analysts in Beijing, however, believed that "Egypt" symbolized China, and that Lee's self-styled mission was to lead the people of Taiwan out of China.[9] Regarding China, Lee said very little, but what he did say was not to Beijing's liking. The exact meaning of the word "China" was "unclear," Lee told Ryotaro. Too much Chinese history was taught in Taiwan's elementary schools. Children were required to learn the names of China's emperors, and so on. It would be better if they studied more about Taiwan's history and geography. Regarding relations between Taiwan and the mainland, Taiwan's democratization created a major problem for Beijing, Lee told Ryotaro. No longer could Beijing hope to reach a settlement with a group such as the previous KMT, ignoring the wishes of the people of Taiwan.

These views were quite similar to those of the DPP. They may, in fact, have been part of a calculated effort by Lee to appeal to DPP voters. This did not please the CCP whose analysts had watched DPP development closely. They concluded that the DPP's deep factional divisions and radical program rendered it relatively ineffective—no more than a nuisance to the KMT.[10] Cooperation between the KMT under Lee Teng-hui and the DPP was a far more dangerous matter.

Especially troubling to the CCP was the old friendship between Lee

Teng-hui and Peng Ming-min, the senior statesman of the Taiwan independence movement. Peng had emerged in the early 1960s as Taiwan's most prominent, outspoken advocate of independence, and was arrested for this in 1964. Intense U.S. pressure forced his release into exile, and for the next fifteen years he organized and lobbied in North America, Western Europe, and Japan for Taiwan independence. Both Lee and Peng are native-born Taiwanese, are Presbyterian Christians by faith, learned Japanese language in their homes and schools long before they learned Mandarin Chinese, and studied in Japanese universities before 1945. After 1945 both studied at National Taiwan University in Taipei, coming under the influence of pro-independence teachers there. In Beijing's reconstruction of things, Lee and Peng became close friends during their student years, sharing many political views but differing in tactics. While Peng favored straightforward advocacy of Taiwan independence, Lee "concealed his intentions of advocating 'Taiwan independence' and worked for the KMT for a long time, rising to the 'pinnacle' of power in Taiwan."[11]

According to Beijing, after Lee became vice president of the Republic of China in 1984, he had a trusted lieutenant establish secret contact with Peng. As Lee consolidated power in his own right, he courted Peng, in April 1990 sending him a "sincerely worded invitation" urging him to return to Taiwan from the United States.[12] Beijing interpreted Lee's 1992 dismissal of mainlander general Hao Pei-tsun as premier and his replacement with native Taiwanese Lian Chan as a sop to Peng. Lian had been a student of Peng's at Taiwan National University. Lee then sent Lian to Washington to urge Peng's return to Taiwan. Lian went so far as to warmly embrace Peng in a public auditorium during that trip. When Peng finally returned to Taiwan in late 1992, Premier Lian Chan twice attended parties welcoming his return and drank toasts with him.[13]

In mid-1994 Lee approached DPP chairman Hsu Hsin-liang in a bid for an understanding over the question of independence—or so Beijing interpreted the event.[14] Lee told Hsu that he had already adopted many key measures advocated by the DPP, such as a push to join the United Nations (UN), International Monetary Fund (IMF), and World Bank; and direct election of the president. Most important, Taiwan had already brought to an end the "accumulation" of forty years—a euphemistic reference to the long political domination by mainlanders. Regarding the question of Taiwan's future road, Lee said he was "very clear." However "the Chinese Communist factor" could not be overlooked. "Therefore it is necessary for mainland policy to be a little vague. It cannot be too open." Regarding the name used by Taiwan to apply to the UN, if it insisted on "Republic of Taiwan," this would "certainly encounter a military response from the Chinese Communists." Moreover, application in the name of a country that already existed, the Republic of China, had a greater chance of success. Therefore, both avoiding military conflict with the mainland and rallying international support for Taiwan pointed toward keeping Taiwan's existing formal name.

In the CCP estimate, Lee's appeal to Hsu indicated that his objectives were identical to the DPP's; Lee and the DPP differed only in tactics. In the words of a commentary by Beijing's Xinhua News Agency, Lee Teng-hui and Peng Ming-min were "absolutely identical in attempting to divide the motherland." Peng's "undisguised independence of Taiwan" had already identified with Lee's "disguised independence of Taiwan." The ideas of both were from the same source, root, and stream. "All the Chinese people, including the compatriots in Taiwan," would "never agree with them" and they were "doomed to failure."[15]

Since the basic purpose of Lee Teng-hui's "disguised independence" was prevention of mainland military pressure on Taiwan, the best response, Beijing concluded, was application of military pressure. This would demonstrate that Lee's duplicity was not succeeding in fooling China. Striking a blow at Lee's "disguised independence" would expose its true nature while punishing it. It would teach the "disguised independence" traitors a lesson.

3 / Taiwan's "Pragmatic Diplomacy"

I n one sense, Beijing's military intimidation of 1996 was directed at the intellectual and political trends described in the last chapter. Those trends had given rise, however, to particular diplomatic activities on the part of Taiwan—aimed at securing for Taiwan protection of the legal norms of the international community—that provided the proximate targets for Beijing's protests and threats.

The specific actions that offended Beijing can be subsumed under the term "pragmatic diplomacy." The starting point was the ROC decision to no longer contest the legitimacy of the PRC's rule of the mainland. When Lee Teng-hui succeeded Chiang Ching-kuo as Taiwan's paramount leader in January 1988, the formal position of the ROC was that *it* constituted the legitimate government of all of China, including the mainland. Taiwan was indeed a province of China—that is, the ROC, whose territory included mainland China as well as Taiwan—and China's legal government happened to reside in Taiwan.

That traditional position began to change in the 1990s, driven by the expansion of economic relations with the mainland and intensifying political competition within Taiwan. In April 1991 Lee's government terminated the 1948 National Mobilization for Suppression of Communist Rebellion, which had provided the legal basis for the KMT's authoritarian rule over Taiwan. This action ended, at least from Taipei's perspective, the civil war that had existed across the Strait for four decades. The month before the 1948 law was terminated, the Mainland Affairs Council, an organ of Taiwan's government set up to handle expanding relations with the mainland, issued new Guidelines for National Unification. After elaboration in the following months, those guidelines formally abandoned the ROC's claim to sovereign jurisdiction over the mainland and recognized the jurisdiction of the PRC there. They spoke of "one China" defined by common historical, geographical, cultural, and ethnic factors. Within that "one China," however, there existed "two political entities," between which the eventual political unification of China would be achieved on the basis of "parity."

27

Beijing was disturbed by the assertion of "two political entities" in Taipei's new guidelines. But at least the guidelines spoke of "one China" and of the objective of "national unification." The most troubling aspect from Beijing's perspective was the demand for "parity." Two "political entities" with distinct territorial jurisdictions could conceivably be fit into the framework of "one country, two systems" advocated by Beijing. "Parity," however, contradicted the subordination implicit in the "one country, two systems" doctrine. Most important at the time the guidelines were issued in 1991 was the fact that, by recognizing PRC jurisdiction on the mainland, the guidelines paved the way for increased cross-Strait economic cooperation. The guidelines provided the political-legal basis for Taiwan's establishment of the SEF, and that organ in turn handled the host of mundane problems arising from the new and expanding economic and cultural relationship, making possible the blossoming of cross-Strait economic relations.

More disturbing was the redefinition of "one China" implicit in Taipei's new thinking. Under Chiang Kai-shek and Chiang Ching-kuo, "one China" had referred to a state organization, the Republic of China, which, the Chiangs insisted, exercised sovereignty over the entire mainland. Ironically, this claim was acceptable to Mao Zedong, perhaps in part because of its very implausibility. Under Lee Teng-hui, "one China" referred no longer to state organization, but instead to a set of shared characteristics that create a sense of Chinese ethnicity: language, history, customs and rituals, and so on. Emphasis on these factors coincided with the cultural nationalism that emerged in China after the Beijing massacre and differed sharply from the symbols of Taiwanese distinctness advocated by the DPP, and for these reasons was not entirely unacceptable to Beijing. It had the drawback, however, of making possible the embrace of multiple state organizations within the framework of "one China."

Throughout 1992 the SEF and ARATS discussed the concept of "one China" in preparation for a meeting of their respective heads to conclude agreements dealing with matters such as repatriation of illegal migrants, verification of documents, compensation for lost mail, and so on. Since these matters required contact between official organs of the two sides, they inevitably raised the question of the nature of contact. Would interaction be between a local government and a central government, or between two equal governments? Beijing's "one country, two systems" approach required the former, and Taipei's "Guidelines for

National Unification" the latter. Eventually agreement was reached, with contact between SEF and ARATS defined as "nongovernmental, practical, economic, and functional in nature," sidestepping the question of equality versus subordination of respective official organs. Each side agreed to accept in practice the official documents and acts of the other side, but refrained in their written agreements from specifying what this meant for "one China." Each was allowed to verbally and separately express its views on the meaning of "one China," which for Beijing meant the PRC including Taiwan as a high-autonomy special administrative region, and for Taipei meant two equal "political entities" moving gradually toward eventual and peaceful unification within the context of a single Chinese nation shaped by language, race, and culture. This agreement to semantically disagree opened the way for an April 1993 meeting of the heads of ARATS and the SEF in Singapore at which a series of agreements dealing with mundane details of cross-Strait relations were signed.[1]

In July 1994 the Mainland Affairs Council of Taiwan's Executive Yuan issued a long statement on cross-Strait relations that became known as the "White Paper." This statement moved Taiwan's legal formulation of cross-Strait relations a step further away from Beijing's. Whereas the 1991 "Guidelines" mentioned "two political entities" and claimed parity for them, the "White Paper" spoke of "sovereign independence." It was an "incontrovertible historical fact," the "White Paper" said, that the ROC "has always been an independent sovereign state." The "reality" was that China was divided "for the time being" into "two political entities" with jurisdiction over separate territories. Those entities would interact on the basis of equality and mutual respect. The "White Paper" rejected the "one country, two systems" doctrine because it required a subordinate relationship in which Beijing, as a central government relating to a local government, would "hold the right of explanation and the right of final decision." The "White Paper" concluded that "the 'two systems' can only be an expedient measure for putting Taiwan at the mercy" of the CCP. Regarding unification, the parties "should not be overanxious and act hastily." The requisite conditions for ultimate unification included the mainland's abandonment of the option of using force against Taiwan and its implementation of liberal, democratic political institutions.[2]

Needless to say, Beijing rejected Taipei's "White Paper," the purpose of which, Beijing said, was to "create two Chinas under the banner of one

China." Taipei's opposition to the "one country, two systems" plan was "unprincipled" and "unhelpful." Further deferment of the issue of sovereignty would only help the advocates of Taiwan independence who "want to take advantage of the situation to divide the national territory." The purpose of the "White Paper" was to enhance Taiwan's standing in the international arena. It was, Beijing noted, part of Lee Teng-hui's "pragmatic diplomacy."[3]

Paralleling Taiwan's rethinking of its relationship with the mainland was its effort to gain greater international recognition which was related to the discourse on collective identity. The people of Taiwan were increasingly proud of their accomplishments. By 1990 average per capita income had reached $6,900—about midway between that of Hong Kong and South Korea, and firmly in the mid-level range of development.[4] Taiwan's "economic miracle" was increasingly matched by a "political miracle" of transition to a vibrant, substantial, and stable liberal democracy. Some intellectuals even spoke of a "cultural miracle" that had achieved the long-sought combination of Confucian tradition with modernity to produce a sophisticated hybrid, yet ethnically Chinese, society. The people of Taiwan desired others around the world to acknowledge their country's successes, and they supported politicians who promised to secure such recognition.

Greater international recognition also was linked to Taiwan's security in the face of threats from the mainland. To the extent that Taiwan could secure recognition of itself as a member of international society, the costs to Beijing of an attack on it would increase. Beijing might still be willing to assume those costs, but it would have to face international opprobrium, and Taiwan would be less likely to stand alone. Beijing's awareness of this was a major reason for its opposition to Taiwan's pragmatic diplomacy.

Achieving Taiwan's membership in the UN General Assembly was a centerpiece of pragmatic diplomacy. The DPP had advocated such an effort since the late 1980s, and in September 1991 launched a campaign for UN membership under the name "Taiwan" or the "Republic of Taiwan." In October 1971 during the UN debate, Chiang Kai-shek's government had refused to support a US-Japan sponsored proposal for "dual representation." The DPP considered this part of the KMT's "betrayal" of Taiwan, and in 1992 incorporated the socially popular call for UN membership into its party platform. Sensing the popularity of this demand, Lee Teng-hui moved to co-opt it.

In September 1993 Taipei announced its new goal of joining the General Assembly as the "Republic of China" under the "divided state" formula that had allowed the two Germanys and the two Koreas to join. Seven Latin American countries (El Salvador, Guatemala, Nicaragua, Costa Rica, Honduras, Panama, and Belize) petitioned to have the General Assembly debate the issue of ROC representation, and in a letter to Secretary General Boutros Boutros-Ghali supported Taiwan's appeal. Twenty-three members endorsed Taiwan's case in the General Assembly, marking the first time since October 1971 that the issue had been raised.[5] In 1994 twelve UN members submitted a second request for UN reconsideration of ROC representation. As in 1993, the General Committee, which sets the General Assembly's agenda, did not act on the petition. The push easily failed because of Beijing's opposition and lack of support from any of the major powers.[6] When in 1995 Taiwan again pushed to enter the UN, the effort was backed by a Foreign Ministry "White Paper" detailing the ROC's historical involvement with the UN. In preparation for its bid, Taipei said that it might donate $1 billion to the UN if it were allowed to become a member. This time Taiwan gained the support of twenty-nine countries.[7]

Taiwan's UN campaign was enhanced by its economic power. Its substantial foreign aid program helped persuade countries to befriend Taiwan in the UN and substantial sums were spent on publicity. More than forty times in 1994 and 1995 Taiwan's Government Information Office (GIO) placed a large display ad in such publications as the *New York Times*, the *Washington Post, Newsweek, Time,* the *Wall Street Journal,* and *Foreign Affairs.* The GIO wrote op-ed pieces for newspapers and sponsored conferences around the United States on Taiwan and the United Nations, and its director general, Jason C. Hu, appeared on CNN's *Firing Line* to debate the issue with former secretary of state Henry Kissinger.[8]

Taiwan also began expanding its high-level contacts around the world. In January 1994 Premier Lian Chan made a "vacation trip" to Singapore and the Philippines, where he met with top officials—in a purely "private" capacity, of course. The next month President Lee Teng-hui, with forty officials and businessmen in tow, made a "private holiday" trip to the Philippines, Indonesia, and Thailand. In the Philippines and Indonesia, Lee met "privately" with Presidents Ramos and Suharto. He failed to meet with Tailand's prime minister because of pressure from Beijing. He did, however, see Tailand's King Bhumibol Adulyadej.

In addition to raising Taiwan's international stature, such "vacation diplomacy" was part of a government effort to direct Taiwan investment to Southeast Asia and away from mainland China.[9] The massive investment of Taiwan capital in the mainland during the early 1990s made Taipei increasingly worried about the political risks associated with such over-reliance. The ways in which Beijing could manipulate Taiwan's economic dependence were many, and the effect on Taiwan potentially devastating. Taipei responded by adopting a "Go South Investment Policy" to encourage Taiwan businesses to look toward Southeast Asia. Bilateral investment protection agreements were signed with Vietnam, Malaysia, Singapore, Indonesia, and the Philippines. Joint task forces were set up to promote development of industrial zones modeled after those of Taiwan in the 1960s and 1970s and mainland China in the 1980s and 1990s, in which Taiwan firms might invest. Taiwan's International Economic Cooperation Development Fund (IECDF), which administered the country's foreign aid, extended loans to support the development of those industrial zones and associated infrastructure. Fifty-five million dollars in loans went to Vietnam. Thirty million dollars went to Indonesia for rural development projects and the development of Batam Island. Another $24 million was committed to Vietnam to develop a Hanoi industrial park and associated highway transportation.[10]

Lee Teng-hui's and Lian Chan's "vacations" in Southeast Asia were part and parcel of the "Go South" policy. They endeavored to persuade regional leaders that incentives such as preferential tax rates and access to domestic markets would be necessary to offset the advantages offered by mainland China. Following Lee's "vacation" in Southeast Asia, Taipei adopted additional measures to encourage investment southward and to secure permission for Taiwan financial institutions to establish branches in Southeast Asian host countries to serve Taiwan businesses. An overseas investment insurance system was approved. Chinese language schools were to be set up in Southeast Asia for the children of Taiwan investors. Agreements avoiding double taxation were to be signed, and Taiwan banks were to be encouraged to open branches in Southeast Asia. Meanwhile enterprises owned by the KMT and Taiwan's government led the way in opening new fields in the region. Following Lee's visits to the Philippines, Indonesia, and Thailand, Taiwan investment in those countries doubled.

Taiwan's "pragmatic diplomacy" was a challenge to substantial PRC economic interests, as well as to Beijing's strategy of coercing Taiwan into accepting the "one country, two systems" arrangement. Because

Taiwan investment had been a major factor in the explosive growth of coastal China during the 1990s, direction of investment away from China to Southeast Asia would hinder China's development. Expanding cross-Strait economic cooperation was to have been an engine of unification, fostering common Chineseness and eroding mistrust. Not least, by diversifying Taiwan's overseas economic partners, "pragmatic diplomacy" lessened the vulnerability of Taiwan to economic coercion by Beijing.

Significantly, Lian Chan's and Lee Teng-hui's Southeast Asian "vacation diplomacy" of early 1994 drew no strong PRC response. Polemical condemnations issued from the CCP's propaganda apparatus, but there were no high-profile diplomatic protests and no sanctions against the Southeast Asian governments that hosted Lian and Lee. This passivity was seen by critics of the Ministry of Foreign Affairs (MFA) as a major diplomatic mistake, particularly after Lee's visit to the United States.

The polemics issuing from Beijing condemned Taipei's new policy directions. The notion of the existence of a "political entity" on Taiwan alongside and equal to the "political entity" on the mainland was held to be "absurd." Lee Teng-hui's "pragmatic diplomacy" was a conspiracy to "split both China's territory and sovereignty"—"a tactic used by the Taiwan authorities" to get Taiwan "recognized as an independent sovereign state by the international community." Lee Teng-hui's efforts to "split China" via "pragmatic diplomacy" caused cross-Strait relations to deteriorate abruptly in 1995. Such efforts were "unrealistic." Beijing reiterated that "the Taiwan people's international interests can only be taken care of through appropriate arrangements made on [the] premise of one China."[11]

Beijing's criticism found a resonance within Taiwan with the Chinese nationalist faction in the KMT, which saw Lee's pragmatic diplomacy as violation of the "one China" principle long upheld by the KMT under the Chiang regimes. A substantial group of those Chinese nationalist cadres left the KMT to form the New Party.[12] The KMT emerged from the split more Taiwanized than ever and made UN membership a central component of its diplomacy.

Through its lobbying efforts on behalf of UN membership and diplomatic recognition, Taipei was bidding up the cost to Beijing of retaining influence in various capitals. Since it began giving foreign aid in the 1950s, Beijing's foreign aid program had been used to achieve targeted political objectives, not the least of which were achieving UN membership for itself and isolating Taiwan. Beijing thought it had won those battles long ago, and had spent large amounts of money in the process. Then the whole battle seemed to start again. Not only was Taipei much wealthier than Beijing in this new round of competition, but it also had substantial ideological cachet. In the midst of the collapse of Soviet and East European communism, Taiwan was an apparently lovable new democracy, while the PRC was one of the few unrepentant Communist-led states still around. If Taiwan's wealth and prestige were combined, it would be quite difficult for Beijing to defeat Taiwan politically, and expensive too. A shift of the contest to the military realm would give Beijing a much greater advantage.

4 / Beijing's Objections
to U.S. Policy

B eijing believed that the true danger of Lee Teng-hui's nefarious scheme of "disguised independence" came from the United States. Without U.S. encouragement and support, Lee's "splittist" conspiracies would come to naught. With it, they would be very dangerous. Hegemonists in Washington, D.C., were supporting Lee's "splittism" as part of their strategy of weakening and containing China, many influential people in Beijing believed, and Lee was their puppet.

Chinese discontent with U.S. Taiwan policy began with President George Bush's 3 September 1992 decision to sell 150 F-16 fighter planes to Taipei. A few weeks later the U.S. Defense Department announced the sale of twelve advanced antisubmarine helicopters. The French government soon followed by agreeing to sell Taiwan sixty Mirage 2000-5 fighters. Those sales represented a significant gain for Taiwan's effort to maintain superiority over the air approaches to Taiwan and were an obstacle to Beijing's strategy of gradually shifting the cross-Strait military balance in the PLA's favor. Beijing calculated that as the PRC gained clear military superiority over Taiwan and as Taiwan's international isolation deepened, Taiwan's leaders would realize that avoidance of war required coming to terms with Beijing. Added inducements would be the high degree of economic integration between Taiwan and the mainland, and Beijing's promise of continued autonomy for Taiwan as long as its leaders agreed to the "one country, two systems" plan. A shift in the cross-Strait military balance was a key premise of that strategy.

Beijing believed that its 1981–82 confrontation with the United States over the early Reagan administration's arms sales to Taiwan had secured the international conditions for such a shift. In the August 1982 communiqué the United States stated that it "does not seek to carry out a long-term policy of arms sales to Taiwan," and that arms sales to Taiwan "will not exceed, either in qualitative or in quantitative terms" the level supplied in "recent years." Moreover, U.S. sales would "reduce gradually" "leading over a period of time to a final resolution."[1] But U.S. arms sales in 1992 cast doubt on the very premise of Beijing's strategy. Only a decade after its conclusion, the United States seemed to be deviating from the 1982 communiqué.

The U.S. arms transfers circa 1992 threatened to offset recent, impressive PLA improvements. Beginning in 1989 China had begun budgeting substantial increases in military spending, a major portion of which went to modernize the PLA's air and naval capabilities. Much of that modernization was in cooperation with former Soviet munitions producers. One major advance came with the 1991 purchase of twenty-four Su-27 fighters, a high-performance air superiority fighter comparable in mission and performance to the F-15. That and other acquisitions from the former USSR substantially strengthened China's capabilities vis-à-vis Taiwan.[2] A combination of increased military spending and expanded military technical cooperation with Moscow accelerated Chinese military development, promising to shift the cross-Strait balance decisively in the mainland's favor. Taiwan attempted to offset this through development of a new fighter aircraft, but prototypes of the Indigenous Defense Fighter (IDF), launched in December 1988, failed to live up to expectations. In 1992 U.S. aircraft were purchased to fill the critical gap in Taiwan's defenses.

Beijing's response was subdued. The Ministry of Foreign Affairs summoned U.S. ambassador Stapleton Roy to deliver its "strongest protest." The Chinese government "solemnly demands," the protest said, that the U.S. government "revoke its erroneous decision." Until it did, China would not participate in previously scheduled five-power meetings over arm's control issues. Persistence of the United States in its "erroneous decision" would have a "negative impact" on and "seriously jeopardize" U.S.-PRC relations.[3] Similar protests were made by National People's Congress (NPC) representatives, *Renmin ribao* (People's Daily) and other authoritative bodies. Beijing also began linking U.S. arms sales to Taiwan with U.S. concerns over PRC sales of arms and technology to Pakistan, Iran, and other countries. Until the United States agreed to discuss U.S. "arms proliferation" in Taiwan, Beijing was not prepared to talk about Chinese sales to various countries.[4]

France had been punished far more sternly for arms sales to Taiwan than had the United States; its consulate in Guangzhou was closed and Beijing threatened to exclude major French construction bids. The PLA urged a much stronger reaction to the 1992 U.S. F-16 sale decision, but its demands were overruled by Deng Xiaoping. Deng's decision did not seem to bring positive results, and many PLA leaders concluded that the 1992 F-16 sale was not an isolated case but part of a shift in U.S. policy toward Taiwan, which was partly a result of China's weak response.

Many PLA leaders were convinced that U.S. leaders represented a wily and duplicitous hegemonist enemy, professing friendship for China while renewing MFN status, for example, but using MFN as leverage to secure various objectives intended to weaken China. President Bush, for example, used renewal of MFN in 1992 to secure China's acquiescence to U.S. actions fundamentally injurious to China's peaceful unification with Taiwan. Several years later, in 1994, President Clinton used a similar tactic—delinking MFN from an annual review of China's human rights status, and then using this action to pressure China to acquiesce to the U.S. Taiwan Policy Review and decision to allow Lee Teng-hui to visit the United States.

During his 1992 campaign Clinton attacked Bush for his extension of MFN status to China. Bush even went so far as to veto a Congressional majority on this issue in March 1992, and succeeded in blocking a two-thirds Congressional override of that veto by only eight votes. Candidate Clinton's criticism was sharp. Rather than "coddling the tyrants of Beijing," he said, Bush should have used extension of MFN as an instrument to pressure human rights concessions from Beijing. Human rights would have a much higher priority in the China policy of *his* administration, Clinton said.

During the first eighteen months of the Clinton administration, relations with China were dominated by a series of confrontations over market access, protection of intellectual property rights, the terms of China's entry into the General Agreement on Tariffs and Trade (GATT) and the World Trade Organization (WTO), and human rights. The Taiwan issue lay quiescent. President Clinton quickly learned that he could chose between human rights or continuing trade with China. Trade was linked to another of Clinton's priorities: jobs for American workers. His eventual choice of jobs and resultant decoupling in May 1994 of human rights and MFN was a politically costly decision that contributed to his image as a "flip-flop president" without principles. That image, in turn, was one factor in the Republican seizure of Congress in November 1994. When Clinton delinked MFN and human rights, he hoped for reciprocation from China, but that was not to be. The month of his MFN decision an incident occurred that colored subsequent debate in the United

States. A plane carrying President Lee Teng-hui on a state visit to Central America stopped enroute for refueling in Hawaii. During his stop Lee was refused a transit visa to allow him to leave his plane, stretch his legs on U.S. soil, and spend the night in a hotel bed. He was forced to sleep overnight on his plane. That strict application of U.S. law was seized upon by supporters of Taiwan.

In 1994 the United States began to modify longstanding policy regulating U.S. relations with Taiwan. Although the F-16 sale of 1992 represented a significant departure, the Bush administration had not tinkered with formal policy. In early 1994 movement began toward what became known as the Taiwan Policy Review, which resulted in adjustments in U.S. policy in the fall of that year. Evaluation of the dynamics behind this process is critical because many Chinese leaders concluded that these adjustments were the result of an anti-China containment policy secretly adopted by the highest levels of the U.S. government.[5] My view is that this common Chinese belief is a misperception of policy adjustments that resulted from U.S. public opinion regarding China and Taiwan, the sharing of foreign policy powers by the executive and legislative branches of the U.S. government, and partisan maneuvering against a presidency weakened by the deepening debacle of its health care reform proposal during the course of 1994.

The U.S. public's common image of China was not good. Following the Beijing massacre in 1989, the number of Americans having a favorable opinion of China had fallen by 45 percentage points to 58 percent, the sharpest such drop since the 1940s.[6] In the aftermath of the Beijing massacre, China's standing in U.S. public opinion was roughly comparable to that in 1972 just after Richard Nixon's first visit to China. The Beijing massacre had wiped out nearly two decades of gains in positive sentiments. While China had become odious to ordinary Americans, Taiwan's standing was rising. The value of Taiwan's staunch friendship with the United States and its anticommunist stance had been offset during Chiang Kai-shek's years by his efforts to entangle the United States in conflict with Red China and by the harsh authoritarian dictatorship of his regime, but such efforts diminished after Chiang's death in 1975, and Taiwan's transition to democracy in the late 1980s and 1990s further improved Taiwan's standing in American public opinion. While only a small minority of Americans were aware of the changes underway in Taiwan, it was they who wrote newspaper articles and editorials, magazine and journal articles, and letters to the editor, functioning as opinion leaders. Taiwan quickly became a "good" country, pro-U.S. and economically prosperous because of cooperation with the United States and, finally, liberal and democratic.[7]

Though mainland China's stock in the U.S. was falling and Taiwan's was rising, the Clinton administration insisted on treating Taiwan as a pariah because of the objections of the odious "tyrants of Beijing," or so Clinton's congressional critics charged. Taiwan's president was not even allowed to put his feet on U.S. soil at the Honolulu International Airport! The U.S. government excluded few people from private visits to the United States—only known criminals and terrorists. And yet Taiwan's leaders were excluded because of Beijing's objections! This confounded many Americans, and many in Congress were sensitive to these popular sentiments. They had won office, after all, by catering to such views. Moreover, they were acutely aware of their constitutional responsibilities in the area of foreign affairs. Clinton's first year in office had seen a series of executive-legislative struggles over foreign policy, one of the most heated of which had concerned China's MFN status. Clinton was politically vulnerable on China.

In April 1994 Congress's Foreign Relations Authorization Act for 1994 and 1995 was signed into law by President Clinton in spite of his objections to it. The law directed the president to undertake a significant upgrading of U.S. relations with Taiwan and directed the State Department to allow U.S. citizens born in Taiwan to list "Taiwan" rather than "China" as their place of birth.[8] It expressed the "sense of Congress" that the president should send cabinet-level officials to Taiwan "to promote U.S. interests" and that the president should "make clear" U.S. support for Taiwan in international organizations of which the United States was a member. Most egregious of all, from Beijing's perspective, was the law's provision that Section 3 of the Taiwan Relations Act (TRA), providing for U.S. sale of defensive weapons to Taiwan, "takes primacy over statements of U.S. policy, including communiqués" and "policies based thereon." The relevant communiqué was the 1982 arms sales communiqué.

Clinton's objections to the Foreign Relations Authorization Act included his concern that upgraded relations with Taiwan would lead to deterioration of Sino-U.S. relations. Veto of the bill, however, would have entailed taking an extremely unpopular stance just as the administration was gearing up for what it hoped would be the centerpiece of its first term in office, reform of the health care system. A congressional override of a presidential veto was quite possible. The powerful commercial interests that supported presidential confrontations with Congress over MFN would not be mobilized over the "upgrading" of U.S. relations with Taiwan. Congressional override of a presidential veto would have weakened an already embattled president just as he embarked on the central political fight of his first term in office.

Once the bill became law the president was constitutionally obligated to enforce it. That failure to do so was grounds for impeachment was an important point that Chinese leaders—who were imbued with an ethos of rule of men rather than rule of law—found incomprehensible. It was much easier for them to believe that the U.S. president was following a secret strategy.

Throughout the summer of 1994 the U.S. administration deliberated how to respond to the law mandating upgraded relations with Taiwan— a process that became known as the Taiwan Policy Review. Meanwhile, there were reports that the United States should, or was, considering using Taiwan to punish Beijing. According to those reports, threatening revocation of MFN was like threatening nuclear attack in that it lacked credibility. Furthermore, broad economic sanctions would devastate U.S. business interests. After the mobilization of those interests during the MFN debates of 1992 and 1993, Beijing understood this very well and concluded that the threatened cancellation of MFN was bluff. The United States therefore needed a more credible instrument to pressure Beijing, and Taiwan and Tibet might be the solution. In the words of one prominent media analyst, "If Washington were to make clear that it would react to Chinese abuse of human rights by moving closer to Taiwan and the Dalai Lama, the Communists might ease up a bit on repression—just as in past years they did to avoid a cutoff of MFN, when the threat seemed more credible."[9] The notion of using Taiwan to punish Beijing quickly became known as "the Taiwan card."

The results of the Taiwan Policy Review were announced on 7 September 1994. It did not go as far as congressional leaders of both parties had hoped, and was quickly criticized as inadequate.[10] It did, however, allow more direct contact between the United States and Taiwan officials, specified U.S. support for Taiwan's entry into GATT and the WTO, and permitted a geographical reference, "Taipei," to appear in a new name for Taiwan's representative office in the United States. The name for Taiwan's unofficial "embassy" in the United States was changed from "Coordinating Council for North American Affairs" to "Taipei Economic and Cultural Affairs Office."[11] Following the announcement of the Taiwan Policy Review, Deputy Secretary of State Peter Tarnoff traveled to Beijing to reassure PRC leaders that the modifications did not change U.S. policy toward China or toward the Taiwan question.

With the announcement of the Taiwan Policy Review, Ambassador Roy was again summoned by the Ministry of Foreign Affairs in Beijing to receive a "strong protest." The United States was "taking steps" to create "two Chinas, or one China, one Taiwan," the MFA said. That would "not only stall, but lead to the deterioration" of Sino-U.S. relations. United States actions "brazenly interfered in the internal affairs of China" and "seriously violated" the three joint communiqués. "We demand that the U.S. Government approach the question of Taiwan with every seriousness and caution," the Chinese protest said. In spite of those tough words, "Western diplomats" interviewed by the *New York Times* correspondent in Beijing noted that China still sought a visit by Clinton to China.[12] Hard-line Chinese critics of Deng's weak U.S. policy undoubtedly noted the same thing, as well as the fact that hostile foreign powers had observed it.

In January 1995 Chinese president Jiang Zemin tried to recapture the initiative in cross-Strait relations by issuing a proposal on "Continuing to Promote the Reunification of the Motherland."[13] Jiang's Eight Points (Jiang Ba Dian) were a response to the "drifting away" of Taiwan over the previous several years and an attempt to reverse that process. Taiwan's tepid response to the proposal was an important factor in the subsequent PRC decision to apply coercive military pressure.

The proposal contained nothing new, but was moderate and generous in tone. Its core was a reiteration of what Beijing viewed as the conciliatory "one country, two systems" proposal. Unification under its framework would not mean that the mainland would "swallow up" Taiwan. After unification, Taiwan's social and economic system would not change. Rather,

> as a special administrative region Taiwan will exercise a high degree of autonomy and enjoy legislative and independent judicial power, including that of final adjudication. It may also retain its armed forces and administer its party, governmental, and military system by itself. The central government will not station troops or send administrative personnel there. What is more, a number of posts in the central government will be made available to Taiwan.

Left implicit, but clearly so, was that the government of the Taiwan special administrative region was to be a local one subordinate to the central government of the PRC in Beijing. That raised a number of considerations. Perhaps the most important was that any government in Taipei that accepted such a proposition would immediately encounter strong opposition from an overwhelming majority of Taiwan's electorate and could not expect to rule on the basis of consent of the governed. Such a government would necessarily be an authoritarian one that ruled perhaps in the best interests of the people, but without their consent. Jiang's proposal may have recognized that when it said:

> What the entire Chinese people should watch out for is the growing separatist tendency and the increasingly rampant activities of the forces working for the "independence of Taiwan" on the island in recent years. Certain foreign forces have further meddled in the issue of Taiwan interfering in China's internal affairs. All this not only impedes the process of China's peaceful reunification, but also threatens peace, stability, and development in the Asia-Pacific region.

In other words, if the Taiwan government continued to tolerate pro-independence speech and activities, the mainland would more likely use force against Taiwan. Similarly, "foreign meddling in China's internal affairs," such as the 1994–95 Foreign Relations Authorization Act and the Taiwan Policy Review, was considered by Beijing to encourage pro-independence forces to believe that they had U.S. support and to embolden them, thereby compelling Beijing to resort to force.

After declaring, "Now it is high time to accomplish the reunification of the Motherland," Jiang laid out his Eight Points. First, Taipei should adhere to the principle of one China and cease all words or actions aimed at "creating an independent Taiwan," splitting the country into two "separate regimes," or allowing "two Chinas over a certain period of time." In short, Taipei should abandon its post-1987 "drift." Second, Taipei should stop expanding its "international living space." Such activity was contradictory to reunification, and "could only help" the forces working for Taiwan independence. Third, the two sides should hold negotiations "on the peaceful reunification of the Motherland under the premise that there is only one China." Under that premise Beijing was willing to discuss all issues of concern to Taipei. Critical to Beijing was the notion that those would be internal talks, among Chinese, about China's domestic affairs. Ideally, those would be discussions between China's central government and a local government, but conceivably the two sides could find a way to sidestep that point.

Jiang's fourth point was subsequently one of the most widely quoted: the two sides should strive for peaceful unification, "since Chinese should not fight Chinese." He then added, "Our not undertaking to give up the use of force is not directed against our compatriots in Taiwan, but against the schemes of foreign forces to interfere with China's reunification and to bring about the 'independence of Taiwan.'" Those words had a dual meaning. They were directed against the advocates of Taiwan independence within Taiwan who were, after all, well organized, articulate, and well connected and had a substantial base of popular support. Those forces were, by definition, not "compatriots," but had lost their Chinese national character and become dupes of the anti-China schemes of U.S. hegemonists. Jiang's words were also a warning to the United States. Continued U.S. "encouragement" of Taiwan's pro-independence elements might lead Beijing to adopt nonpeaceful means of addressing the Taiwan problem.

Point five called on Taipei to agree to direct cross-Strait telecommunications, postal service, and trade. Point six called for Taipei to carry forward the fine traditions of Chinese culture. One relevant subtext of that seemingly innocuous provision was the effort of Taiwan's proindependence forces to substitute "Taiwanese" for "Chinese" culture (e.g., by rewriting textbooks to give greater coverage to Taiwan's history and less to China's). Of course, since about 1990 Beijing had stressed cultural nationalism to rally Han Chinese around the beleaguered CCP government. Point seven of Jiang's program provided that PRC organs abroad should help Taiwan compatriots and called on them to avail themselves of such help. It also promised that "all personages from various circles [within Taiwan] who have contributed to the reunification of China will go down in history for their deeds." Implied was the possibility that they might also go up to Beijing to fill one of the posts in China's central government that point one promised would "be made available to Taiwan." Also implicit was the threat that those who opposed reunification would be punished as traitors.

Jiang's final point welcomed visits and talks between leaders of the two sides of the Strait, but stipulated that such communication "does not take an international occasion to accomplish." The background to this was a statement by Lee Teng-hui to the *Asian Wall Street Journal* in early October 1994 that he hoped to meet with Jiang Zemin at the upcoming Asian Games in Hiroshima or the Asian Pacific Economic Cooperation (APEC) summit in Bogor, Indonesia. (Beijing had vetoed Taiwan participation in the September 1994 Asian Games.) Speaking in Singapore just before the APEC summit in November, Jiang announced that he was willing to meet with Lee to discuss how to gradually achieve the goal of unification between Taiwan and the China mainland. Such a meeting should take place, however, as a meeting about internal affairs between Chinese people. Taipei rejected that, insisting that any meeting take place at an international event.[14]

Taipei had two central concerns regarding Jiang's Eight Point Proposal. One was that once Taipei agreed that the issue of cross-Strait relations was purely an internal affair of China, however defined, Beijing would use this agreement to make less likely U.S. support for Taiwan in the face of mainland pressure. After all, Beijing would say, since both parties to the dispute had agreed that what was involved was an internal affair of the Chinese nation, on what standing could foreign governments involve themselves? The second concern was more immediate: agreement between Taipei and Beijing that Taiwan was "a part of China" would alienate and probably mobilize a large portion of the Taiwan population who ardently opposed such a proposition. Such a development would benefit neither Lee Teng-hui's election strategy, the increasingly fragile cohesion of the KMT, nor even stability in Taiwan.

In politics, self-perception is often as important as the view of others. Beijing saw Jiang's Eight Point Proposal as extremely generous and lenient. Most CCP cadres would probably reject the critical deconstruction of Jiang's Eight Points presented above. In the months after the promulgation of the proposal, PRC media worked assiduously to convince everyone concerned that it was an important, new initiative requiring a positive response. There were, of course, instrumental purposes to this propaganda. It aimed to create a climate of opinion that might both abort Taiwan's "drift" and prepare political conditions for resort to more forceful, military resources should "drift" continue. Service of instrumental purposes and sincere belief were not mutually exclusive. When Taiwan's leaders did not embrace Jiang's proposal, PRC leaders were genuinely angry. Such obstinance confirmed to them that Lee and his cohorts were die-hard traitors who had to be dealt with by forceful means.

Taiwan's response to Jiang's proposal came in an 8 April speech by Lee

Teng-hui to the National Unification Council, an organ of Taiwan's government charged with setting policy toward the mainland.[15] Lee referred repeatedly to the goal of national unification, but insisted that could only come about "in gradual phases [guided by] the principles of reason, peace, parity, and reciprocity." The two sides of the Taiwan Strait were to be equal, at present, and were not to use force or the threat of force against one another. The prerequisite for movement toward reunification, Lee said, was acceptance by the mainland authorities "of the reality that the government of the Republic of China has been in existence for 84 years and that it exercises sovereign authority and effective jurisdiction over Taiwan, Penghu, Kinmen [Jinmen], and Matsu [Mazu]." China and Taiwan should "normalize relations" on the basis of "the reality that the two sides are governed respectively by two governments." Moreover, "the two political entities" that ruled over the mainland and Taiwan were "in no way subordinate to each other" and had "separate governmental jurisdictions." It followed that the two sides should join international organizations "on an equal footing." Leaders could meet each other on "international occasions." To create conditions favorable to unification "the mainland authorities" should "demonstrate their goodwill by publicly renouncing the use of force and refrain from making any military move that might arouse anxiety or suspicion on this side of the Taiwan Strait." Lee called for increased cultural and economic exchanges between the two sides, but called the issues associated with direct contacts "very complicated" and said that "the agencies concerned have to make in-depth evaluations and careful plans."

Lee Teng-hui's Six Point Proposal was the first direct response by a Taiwan leader to a PRC proposal. Leaders and analysts in China studied it carefully. Several months later a Xinhua commentary condemned the "Taiwan authorities" for "disregarding" the common aspirations of the people on both sides of the Strait. The "one country, two systems" plan had "won popular support from the overwhelming majority of Chinese at home and overseas and peace-loving people in the rest of the world"; Taiwan authorities should adopt that reasonable plan, rather than "creating troubles."[16] In January 1996, on the first anniversary of Jiang's Eight Points, Chinese premier Li Peng condemned "certain leaders of the Taiwan authorities" for "continuing to stick to their stand of splitting the motherland." According to Li, "these perverse acts met with resolute opposition from the Chinese people, including the people of Taiwan." Avoiding mention of Lee's Six Point Proposal, Li said the vari-

ous "perverse" activities of "the Taiwan authorities" had as their "fundamental purpose" separating Taiwan from China and carrying out "Taiwan independence."[17]

Both Jiang's Eight Points and Lee's Six Points were moderate in tone
and stressed the need for increased contact. Common ground could
conceivably have been discovered via further talks on direct communications across the Strait, meetings of high-ranking officials, and mutual
visits by leaders. Even general agreement on the principle of one China
and the ultimate goal of unification might have been possible. On three
interrelated core issues, however, the differences were stark. Jiang demanded that Taiwan accept a status subordinate to Beijing, while Lee
insisted the two sides be coequals. Jiang demanded that Taiwan suspend
its "pragmatic diplomacy," while Lee insisted that Beijing stop opposing
Taiwan's efforts to expand its international relations. Finally, Jiang insisted on Beijing's right to use force against Taiwan, while Lee demanded
that Beijing renounce that right. The two sides might have set aside
those differences and explored common ground via talks, but hard-
liners in Beijing rejected that approach, feeling that further talks would
only be taken by the splittists and foreign hegemonists as weakness, as
Chinese acquiescence to "two Chinas, or one China, one Taiwan." Agreement to talk would only encourage further offensive actions by anti-
China forces. Firmness, including military action, was called for.

5 / The Taiwan Issue in
Chinese Domestic Politics

n the PRC, as in the United States and in Taiwan, there were strong
links between the Taiwan issue and domestic politics. In China the
Taiwan issue was linked to deep divisions within the CCP over the
course of China's post-1978 reforms; to declining belief in Marxism–
Leninism–Mao Zedong Thought and emergence of nationalism as a new
source of state legitimacy; to the transition of political power from the
generation of elders who founded the PRC to successors lacking the authority deriving from participation in epic state-forging struggles; to the
struggle within the CCP elite to consolidate a new paramount leader as
successor to Deng Xiaoping and Mao Zedong; and especially to the increasing role of the PLA in China's political process as members of the CCP
elite maneuvered for the mantle of Deng and Mao while seeking to
avoid popular uprisings of the sort that resulted in the collapse of the
Communist regimes in Eastern Europe. The linkages between the Taiwan issue and questions of domestic power and policy were deep and
complex.

During the 1980s there was mounting elite opposition to the reforms
that were swiftly moving China away from a planned and self-reliant
economy toward a market economy open to the world. According to
American political scientist Richard Baum, the reform coalition that supported Deng Xiaoping's rise to paramount power in 1978 involved dispa-
rate groups. Some reformers, represented by Hu Yaobang, favored full
development of a market economy integrated into the world economy,
and were even willing to countenance a degree of political pluralism to
achieve those ends. Hu Yaobang was secretary general of the CCP from
1981 to 1987. The early 1989 commemoration of his 1988 death touched
off the powerful movement that culminated in the Beijing massacre.
Others, represented by veteran leader Chen Yun, favored a much more
limited role of markets within a system of continued dominance by
central planning and state enterprises. These more conservative reform-

ers viewed any political liberalization as anathema. In the early years of reform these divergent perspectives were united in opposition to the Maoists and neo-Maoists led by Hua Guofeng. Mao had chosen Hua as his successor when Deng Xiaoping was purged for the second time in April 1976. Hua led the purge of extreme Maoists, but insisted on continuation of the Maoist development model. As the process of marketization deepened and accelerated in the mid-1980s, tension mounted between the divergent liberal and conservative reform perspectives.[1]

Taiwan was linked to this intensifying factional debate within the reform camp. One aspect of the conservative critique was that integration into world markets and other global economic institutions would lead to dependence on the United States, which, with its Western allies, had set up and dominated them. Extensive Chinese involvement in such institutions would make China vulnerable to U.S.-Western pressure. Sooner or later the United States was certain to use China's greater dependence to extort China. When the Taiwan issue erupted in 1992 with President Bush's decision to sell F-16s to Taiwan, the dire warnings of the conservative reformers seemed validated. Here was the U.S. president asking for Chinese acquiescence to a blatant violation of the 1982 communiqué on the ground that he had opposed efforts to withdraw MFN status for China! In other words, because China needed continued access to U.S. markets, it should turn a blind eye to the sale of high-tech weapons to Taiwan.

There was another, more ideologically rooted link between the conservative critique and Taiwan. Among the main forces of the conservative camp were leading functionaries in the ideological apparatus, men such as Deng Liqun and Hu Qiaomu.[2] These ideologues believed that the United States was pursuing a secret, long-term strategy to weaken China because it stood as the last major obstacle to U.S. achievement of world hegemony. One manifestation of this strategy was the U.S. effort to subvert socialism and communism via "peaceful evolution." Much of the liberal reformers' program was in line with this imperialist plot, Deng Liqun said. Another dimension of the plot was an effort to split China's territory. Tibet and Taiwan were the main targets of this campaign.

The 1989 upheaval in China had already swung power dramatically in the conservative direction. Such key liberal leaders as Zhao Ziyang, Hu Qili, and Tian Jiyun had been purged or demoted.[3] Strict controls over political and cultural affairs were reimposed. A strident propaganda campaign and concomitant efforts at ideological education were begun.

Most initiatives for further economic reform were put on hold and some earlier economic reforms were actually rolled back. The collapse of the Communist regimes in Eastern Europe and the USSR added further fuel to the conservative effort.[4] As conservative influence reached its peak with the disintegration of the USSR in late 1991, the Chinese media launched a wave of attacks on "Western hostile forces," a code word for the United States.[5] Not until early 1992 was Deng Xiaoping able to rally the demoralized liberal reform forces.[6] Even after engineering a renewal of the drive for market-oriented reform and openness, Deng remained vulnerable on the Taiwan issue. The great danger for Deng and the promarket group was that Taiwan would provide a rallying point for opposition to them, if not to their economic policies. They had to guard their flank by showing no weakness on the Taiwan issue.

China's transition from Marxism–Leninism–Mao Zedong Thought to nationalism as a basis of political legitimacy also made the Taiwan problem more sensitive. Throughout the 1980s Marxism declined worldwide as a credible ideology. China's "opening to the outside world" made its citizen's more aware of the high levels of prosperity and freedom commonplace elsewhere. Within China experimentation with market economics demonstrated the creative powers of capitalism. The CCP's response to ideological questioning was to wage repeated campaigns against "spiritual pollution," "bourgeois liberalism," and other such maladies, but each successive campaign became less effective. The upheaval of 1989, when wide sections of the Beijing populace called for political reform only to be met by brutal repression, further reduced the appeal of the Marxism-Leninism. Shortly afterward Communist rule collapsed in Eastern Europe. Then the USSR itself disappeared. By the early 1990s there was a vast gulf between the formal ideology used to justify continued CCP rule of China and belief in that ideology by the urban and educated populace.

One major response of the CCP to that "crisis of faith" was to use nationalism to fill the void.[7] The new justification of CCP rule was not construction of socialism and communism, but development of power and wealth for China. Educational and propaganda organs began to stress "patriotic" indoctrination. Patriotism (*aiguo zhuyi*) became China's new political orthodoxy, its new standard of political correctness. The central aim of this doctrine was to wipe out a century of "humiliation" and establish China as a front-ranking country in the world. In that context, movement toward the incorporation of Taiwan into China, into the PRC, would be a major gain for the leader achieving it. Allowing Taiwan to "drift away" would dam a leader's political aspirations.

The transition from the so-called "second generation" of CCP leaders to the "third generation" further enhanced the sensitivity of the Taiwan issue. The "second generation"—such people as Deng Xiaoping, Ye Jianying, and Chen Yun—had played important roles in the epic, nation-founding struggles of the 1930s through 1970s.[8] By the early 1990s power was passing from that group to a "third generation"—including Jiang Zemin, Li Peng, Qiao Shi, and Zhu Rongji—who simply did not have the prestige and authority of their elders.[9] Most members of the founding generation had shifted among party, government, and military as the requirements of the struggle necessitated. Most of the "third generation" were technocrats who had risen within the confines of a fairly narrow career track before reaching the apex of power. Their lesser authority meant that others were more willing to challenge them. Whereas Mao Zedong or Deng Xiaoping at the height of power could dispose of the Taiwan issue as they wished without much fear of criticism, this was not the case for those trying to fill their shoes.

The struggle to succeed Deng Xiaoping as paramount leader further increased the pluralistic tendencies of Chinese politics and the sensitive nature of the Taiwan issue. In analyzing the role of the struggle to succeed Mao Zedong in the reform of China's economy in the late 1970s and early 1980s, American political scientist Susan Shirk concluded that succession struggle corresponded with policy innovation as would-be-successors tried to build adequate bases of support by catering to the interests of various groups, including relatively disenfranchised elites. The absence of a clear paramount leader meant that lower-level interests had opportunities to promote their views while would-be paramount leaders had an interest in responding to those views.[10]

By 1995 Deng Xiaoping clearly was in physical decline. He was no longer involved in the day-to-day affairs of government, party, or military, and seldom intervened in issues of high policy. Deng's anointed successor (his third after Hu Yaobang and Zhao Ziyang) was Jiang Zemin. Jiang's need to consolidate power to retain his position as paramount leader meant that he had to pay attention to the views of influential would-be supporters, several groups of which held the Taiwan issue close to their heart. Chief among these was the PLA. Failure to deal firmly enough with the challenge of Lee Teng-hui's "splittism" and American "hegemonism" would cost Jiang heavily in terms of PLA support.[11]

Recovery of Taiwan ranked relatively high in the PLA scheme of things for several reasons. First was the relatively nationalistic institutional culture of the PLA, which viewed itself as the keeper of the flame of the Chinese nationalist faith. The recovery of Taiwan had long been a core issue on the nationalist agenda. Second, since the late 1980s the PLA had seen its strategic objective as effective control over the waters within the "first island chain" off the Asian continent. Taiwan was a central component of that chain. A longer-term objective was to gain control over the seas up to a "second island chain" delineated by the Marianas in the Western Pacific.[12] Achieving both objectives would require eliminating Taiwan as a platform for potentially hostile forces.[13] Third, among the lower ranks of the officer corps, major operations to recover Taiwan would give a new generation of ambitious up-and-comers the chance to earn their laurels in combat.[14] The PLA's last major combat operation was the 1979 punitive war against Vietnam, long before most of the better-educated urbanites who were recruited into the officer corps during the 1980s entered service. The older generation of officers won their laurels in the war against Japan, the civil wars against the KMT, or Korea. A large-scale, modern, and successful campaign to take Taiwan would give the next generation of PLA leaders a chance to prove their mettle, demonstrating their competence for high rank. Finally, resentment over the PLA's own role in the Beijing massacre of June 1989 commingled with resentment over weak policies toward Taiwan. Within the PLA many held the civilian leadership responsible for ordering them to fire on the people and were aware that that decision was ultimately Deng Xiaoping's. Chinese nationalism reserves its strongest opprobrium for Chinese leaders who have repressed Chinese people while capitulating to foreign imperialism. This is not to say that the PLA was disloyal to Deng. Rather, such considerations led to realization that even the greatest leaders make mistakes, and to a belief that true loyalty requires criticism of such errors.

In late 1992 the PLA began lobbying for a tougher response to perceived U.S. transgressions against China.[15] Earlier in that year President George Bush had informed Chinese leaders that he would support extension of MFN status for China, but hoped that China would make some concessions on human rights. That would help Bush win back some of the votes in the upcoming presidential elections that he expected to lose for supporting MFN for China. Before the decision to sell F-16s to Taiwan was publicly announced on 2 September 1992, Bush's representatives again briefed Chinese leaders and pleaded for a restrained response from China on the grounds, inter alia, that Bush was a friend of China and faced a difficult election in November. They also explained Bush's decision in terms of his need to carry votes in the state of Texas, where the F-16 was made. Deng Xiaoping reportedly bought Bush's pitch, and decided that it was better for China if Bush remained in power and that China should help him do so. According to Deng, if things happened that China did not want to happen, it could make some limited concessions to the United States. In diplomacy it was not possible to always advance and attack. Rather, it was occasionally necessary to retreat and defend oneself, making small sacrifices in order to preserve the main things.[16] In this case, the main thing was probably broad U.S. support for China's development.

Military leaders were highly critical of the decision to avoid political confrontation with the United States over the F-16 sale and called for a tougher, more tit-for-tat policy punishing Washington. China's acquisition of Soviet military technology from the former USSR promised to shift the military balance in the Taiwan Strait, but that relative gain might be wiped out by U.S. arms sales to Taiwan. By shifting the balance back in Taiwan's favor, Bush had helped Taiwan's proindependence forces, regardless of what his subjective intentions might have been. Many top PRC military leaders felt that such actions were intolerable and required strong retaliation. Specifically, they called for action on trade issues to punish the Bush administration. Suspending wheat purchases for example, would cause direct losses to U.S. agricultural exports, thus costing Bush votes in the Midwest. Other leaders opposed economic retaliation (although they did not necessarily oppose *threatening* it), on the grounds that it could well touch off a trade war that would hurt China much more than the United States. Ultimately the issue was decided by Deng Xiaoping: there would be no economic retaliation against the United States. China responded to the F-16 sale with "great noise and gestures but little real action," in the words of a common Chinese saying.

While advocating a more confrontational response to U.S. transgressions on Taiwan, PLA leaders did not necessarily favor *military* confrontation with the United States, which differs substantially from political confrontation, even one with military undertones. It seems that PLA leaders advocated a more confrontational approach beginning in 1992, but did not think it likely that it would escalate to direct PRC-U.S. military conflict.

In the aftermath of the F-16 sale, several military units reportedly submitted reports to the CCP's Central Military Commission (CMC) General Office. In response to those reports, the CMC convened an expanded meeting to discuss a report drawn up by the General Staff Department. The navy and the air force also submitted reports expressing their war readiness and proposing measures to further heighten preparedness, while the State Commission on Defense Industry called for a speed-up of defense research, development, and production. The atmosphere of the CMC meeting was apparently heated, with most of the participants urging the adoption of a new, tougher policy toward the United States and Taiwan. The General Staff Department report proposed a series of measures, which included initiating an ideological education campaign against U.S. hegemonism, reestablishing the Fuzhou military region, and issuing a warning to Taiwan about its "war preparations and disruption of cross-Strait peaceful relations."

Deng Xiaoping's representatives to the CMC conference tried to calm the militant passions. In his conclusion summarizing the conference, Yang Shangkun (then CMC first vice chairman) related Deng Xiaoping's "instructions," which included five points. First, the focus of all work would remain on economic construction except in the event of a large-scale invasion of China, and the entire PLA should escort the implementation of the basic line of reform and opening to the outside world. Second, military modernization would focus on quality. Third, China should remain calm in responding to the recent U.S. move, which was part of Bush's reelection tactics and not stirred up by the Taiwan authorities. Fourth, although the United States had indeed violated the August 1982 joint communiqué, it had damaged its own international reputation by doing so and China had gained the initiative. Here Deng implied that since Washington had injured itself, there was less need for China to punish it. Fifth, the Party's basic policy toward Taiwan should not be changed.[17]

The Propaganda Department's proposal to initiate an intense educational campaign against "U.S. hegemonism and power politics" was approved, but only after the most strident aspect (i.e., the assertion that "the main struggle in the world today is between hegemonism and opposition to hegemonism") had been deleted by Politburo Standing Committee member and propaganda chief Li Ruihuan.[18] Chen Yun also reportedly criticized Deng Xiaoping for his understanding attitude toward Bush's political difficulties. On the basis of Marxist-Leninist principles, Chen was opposed to making political deals with the Western bourgeois class.[19]

Deng's decision represented an endorsement of the Foreign Ministry proposal of a lower-key response to the F-16 sale. The MFA report on the matter asserted that in making decisions China needed to give priority to economic interests. Bush's F-16 decision arose primarily from considerations of electoral advantage and, in any case, could not be reversed. If China retaliated with trade sanctions, a cycle of mutual retaliation could unleash a trade war in which China would lose most. Moreover, damage to Bush's reelection prospects was not in China's interests. Bush was an old friend while his rival, Bill Clinton, had staked out a position as a harsh critic of China. Given this, China should adopt a tough stance in terms of propaganda, but normal Sino-U.S. trade relations should not be affected. China should do everything it could to avoid the deterioration of Sino-U.S. economic relations. The MFA report was approved by Deng and the Politburo Standing Committee.[20]

The military continued to lobby for a more forceful response to U.S. actions. In November 1992 CMC vice chairmen Liu Huaqing and Zhang Zhen plus CMC member and minister of defense Chi Haotian reportedly wrote a memorandum to the CCP Central Committee proposing that strong and practical measures be taken in response to U.S. and West European aircraft sales to Taiwan. "Defending national sovereignty and independence should take precedence over all others and over transient economic interests," the jointly signed document said. It continued: "The Chinese nation has already stood up and should play a definite role in safeguarding world peace." When the letter circulated among the top leadership, it won the support of Chen Yun and Peng Zhen. Five senior generals—Qin Jiwei, Hong Xuezhi, Yang Dezhi, Liao Hansheng, and Zhang Aiping—added their voices to the call for an uncompromising, tit-for-tat struggle against hegemonism and intervention in China's internal affairs.[21]

The debate resumed early the next year. In April 1993 a work conference on Taiwan was convened by the director of the CCP's Taiwan Affairs Office, Wang Zhaoguo. Yang Shangkun delivered "instructions" outlining a conciliatory approach toward Taiwan. The CCP should not be too rigid, he said, but should be ready to make further concessions and even be willing to state clearly that it would not use force as long as Taiwan did not pursue independence.[22] It was not clear whom these "instructions" were from—Jiang Zemin or Deng Xiaoping—or at what point in the conference proceedings they were presented. It seems, however, that a large group of generals from military regions, group armies, and military academies signed a petition to CMC chairman Jiang Zemin at this juncture advocating a firmer approach. The document was drafted by Chief of General Staff Zhang Wannian, director of the General Political Department General Yu Yangbo, and director of the General Logistics Department General Fu Quanyou. It called for the convocation of an enlarged Politburo meeting to consider changes in China's policy toward U.S. policy, which, the signers felt, was impairing the dignity of the Chinese nation and undermining the morale of the PLA. The letter reportedly asserted that since the establishment of diplomatic relations between the two countries, the United States had never ceased interfering in China's internal affairs. Particularly since the disintegration of the USSR, the United States had regarded China as its major strategic enemy and openly sought to overthrow the PRC government. Other specific grievances included U.S. violation of the three Sino-U.S. joint communiqués, the sale of sophisticated weapons to Taiwan, and inciting the Taiwan authorities to advocate "one China, one Taiwan," and "two Chinas." It was necessary to resolutely and forcefully hit back at acts of interference, subversion, and military provocation by the U.S. hegemonists. In this regard, all soldiers and officers of the PLA were ready to take the orders of Comrade Deng Xiaoping and the Central Committee, the letter said.[23]

According to the same source, another document signed by a large group of generals, including senior "advisors" Zhang Aiping, Yang Dezhi, Yang Chengwu, Qin Jiwei, Wang Enmao, Song Renqiong, Sai Fuding, Xiao Ke, and Song Ping, soon went directly to Deng Xiaoping. This memorandum, reportedly entitled "Take Action and Oppose the Hegemonists' Political and Economic Blackmail and Challenges against China," was delivered personally to Deng's residence on the eve of May Day 1993 by Song Renqiong, Qin Jiwei, Wang Enmao, and Zhang Aiping. Those four elderly generals reportedly shed tears as they implored Deng to strengthen China's policy toward the United States. If China continued to make concessions and compromises in the face of hegemonist blackmail and pressure, the generals argued, China might follow the path of the USSR, with state disintegration and social turbulence. It might once again be reduced to the status of a semicolony and its current rulers condemned by history. Reform and opening to the outside world were definitely correct, the letter said, but such policies could not be carried out on the basis of dependency upon a certain hegemonist power. China had to rely on its own national strength and resist any hegemonist challenge. Chen Yun again lent his weight to military criticism of Deng's "weak" U.S. policy. While the two letters from the generals were circulating, Chen reportedly submitted a report to the Central Committee and the State Council. The last of eight points in the report dealt with foreign policy, criticizing China's "passive" policy of tolerance and concession in the face of hostile ideological infiltration by Western hegemonists and interference in China's sovereignty under the pretense of economic interest.[24]

Deng again stood firm in the face of military pressure. At the end of April 1993, in the aftermath of the first meeting of high-level Taiwan and PRC representatives in Singapore earlier that month, Deng made "important comments" on cross-Strait relations. China would adhere, he said, to the general principle of peaceful reunification and the belief that the two sides of the Strait could not long continue to confront one another over party interests and ideological differences. On the basis of this principle, Beijing could make concessions to Taiwan, and be modest and patient. The condition of this moderate approach, however, was that Taiwan "endorse the general principle of one China" and "not do anything detrimental to this general principle."[25]

Early in May 1993 the Politburo decided to adopt a more active and assertive response to U.S. pressure associated with the renewal of MFN status for China. When informing the State Council of the decision, which had been made "after repeated discussions," Jiang Zemin engaged in a bit of self-criticism, saying that the adjustment in policy "came a little late, and we have paid a little higher price for this." At a CMC meeting Jiang genuflected to the wisdom of the PLA hardliners, saying, *"Now it turns out that our generals have more insight into strategy and policy toward the United States.* We do not want confrontation, but never will we yield to confrontation that is forced on us. We have the strength and confidence [to meet] economic, political, and military challenges"[26] (emphasis added). Jiang Zemin conveyed Deng's "latest instructions" to a regular meeting of the Politburo on 14 May 1993. Deng, or perhaps Jiang, began by acknowledging the criticism of his policies toward the United States, saying:

> It now seems that our policy toward the United States needs to be examined. It is true that we cannot be dependent on a certain big

power. . . . If we are dependent on a big power, we will be easily subjected to interference, control, and blackmail by means of political factors.

After that nod to his critics, however, he proceeded to insist on continuation of the present policy, at least for the time being:

The central authorities have a plan to extricate ourselves from passivity within two to three years. This step is correct. We are sober-minded. The problems of deviation to the right and worshipping the United States do not exist in our relation with the United States; thus it will be unsuitable to criticize and blame it for the high plane of principle.[27]

Two days later at an expanded Politburo meeting attended by veteran generals, Deng again defended his U.S. policy. China's overall policy toward the United States was correct, he insisted, and was not flawed by rightist deviation, as some alleged. Nor was it correct to say that China's policy toward the United States was passive.

In spite of Deng's apparent personal intervention, a year later military circles renewed their lobbying for changes in U.S. policy. In April 1994 the General Staff Department and the Policy Research Office of the CMC submitted to the Politburo Standing Committee a report exploring the possibility of establishing a global united front against hegemonism. The Central Committee Secretariat then convened a meeting chaired by Politburo members Deng Guangen, who was in charge of ideology, and Chief of General Staff Zhang Wannian. Foreign Minister Qian Qichen, who was also a Politburo member, vice premier, and ostensibly in charge of China's foreign relations, was conspicuously absent from the conference.[28]

Qian emerged during 1994 as the target of military criticism of China's "weak" U.S. policy. In March the PLA delegation to the Second Session of the Eighth National People's Congress put forward eight suggestions regarding the foreign relations work of the MFA. Senior elder Generals Li Desheng and Yang Dezhi personally called on the PLA delegation at their guesthouse and persuaded them to drop the matter. The attack resumed two months later at the Seventh Session of the NPC Standing Committee, when six members submitted a proposal to the Presidium requesting that Qian Qichen be invited to brief the session on the government's current policies toward the United States. That proposal was endorsed by fifteen NPC Standing Committee members before the Politburo intervened to squelch further action. Qiao Shi informed the NPC Standing Committee that policies toward the United States had been decided upon by the Central Committee. Moreover, there had been no compromise or bargaining on matters of sovereignty and principle. Qiao also pointed out that Deng Xiaoping held a high opinion of the work of the MFA and of Qian Qichen. Again, top-level intervention squelched further action.[29]

Military pressure continued, however. On 25 May 1994 National Defense University (NDU) and the Academy of Military Sciences (AMS) jointly convened a conference on "China's Foreign Policy and Policy Toward Taiwan." The conference listed over thirty mistakes made by the MFA including tolerance of U.S. interference in China's internal affairs and failure to respond strongly to the U.S. sale of sophisticated weapons to Taiwan. The conference concluded that in handling foreign affairs the MFA had committed serious rightist errors, for which Qian Qichen should be held accountable. In the name of its participants, the conference leaders drafted a letter to the Central Committee and the State Council calling for Qian's resignation as foreign minister. At the last minute the letter was withheld by NDU chancellor Zhu Dunfa and AMS president Zhao Nanqi on orders from the CMC. Zhu and Zhao also informed the conference participants that the MFA resolutely implemented the policies and principles of the Central Committee.[30]

Barely a week later, on 2 June, the Ministry of Defense, the General Logistics Department, and the Party Committee of North China Industrial Corporation (NORINCO, one of China's major PLA-linked arms merchants) jointly urged a stronger response to the recent U.S. decision to continue sanctions against Chinese weapons exports and to continue restricting U.S. export of high-tech goods to China while granting it MFN status. The MFA's responses on these U.S. actions were "incomplete" and could not reflect the government's policy toward the United States, the critics asserted.[31] A large group of generals once again weighed in on the issue. Some several dozen generals, including Qin Jiwei, Hong Xuezhi, Chi Haotian, and Zhang Wannian, reportedly signed a letter to the Politburo urging that China not compromise on matters of principle in dealing with the United States. They laid out the same litany of complaints as had the NDU-AMS conference the previous month. Jiang Zemin then reportedly convened a meeting of thirty veteran and newly appointed generals at which he praised the patriotic motives of the generals and promised that China would never compromise its principles in the face of confrontation imposed by the United States. Deng Xiaoping took special note of the letter, saying that he hoped communications among the Party, government, and military would be strengthened and that the military, in particular, would at all times submit to Party leadership.[32]

Again, top-level intervention squelched further dissent. On 8 June Jiang Zemin pointed out at a regular Politburo meeting that China's foreign policies were decided upon by the Politburo and approved by the Central Committee, and that the MFA had firmly implemented these policies. Comrade Deng Xiaoping had time and again praised Qian Qichen as a gifted and intelligent diplomat with principles and an easy manner. There were few like him in the MFA and more should be fostered. Liu Huaqing, Zhang Zhen, and General Wang Ruilin (then deputy chief of staff and former head of the Deng Xiaoping Office) also visited various military units to convey the views of Deng and the Central Committee on these issues.[33]

Confronted with the strong military lobbying effort for a tougher policy toward the U.S. and Taiwan, Deng Xiaoping sought Chen Yun's support. During a meeting in Shanghai on 24 July 1994 attended by the five members of the Politburo Standing Committee, Deng and Chen reached an eight-point agreement. Several points touched on Taiwan. (The first several points dealt with economic policy, suggesting a trade-off between internal and external policies.) Contrary to what military critics had called for, China would continue to adhere to the principle of peaceful reunification with Taiwan while, of course, firmly opposing and "smashing" Taiwan separatism. The Party's central task of economic development would not be departed from except in the event of a large-scale foreign invasion of China. The day after he reached that understanding with Chen, Deng met again with the Politburo Standing Committee plus senior advisors Wan Li, Song Ping, Yao Yilin, Yang Shangkun, Bo Yibo, Li Desheng, Hong Xuezhi, and Qin Jiwei. A short while later senior leaders of the military regions and armed services flew to Shanghai to meet with Deng in the company of the senior military advisors. It was Wang Ruilin who read out written remarks on Deng's behalf. Wang's first point was that the armed forces must unconditionally and at all times submit to the Party's leadership. It was absolutely necessary, Wang said on Deng's behalf, to correct the situation in which the gun commands the party. The second, third, and fourth points were that the central task of the army in peacetime was to guarantee reforms while striving to modernize its own capabilities. The final point was that China would continue to oppose hegemonism, Taiwan independence, foreign aggression, armed intervention, and provocative acts.[34]

Following that understanding between Deng and Chen Yun, plus an ultimately unsuccessful push by Lee Teng-hui to extend to Japan his "vacation diplomacy," the Central Committee, the State Council, the CMC and its Research Office, and the Central Policy Research Center convened a large, seven-day conference in August 1994 to discuss strategy toward Taiwan. That conference seems to have been a carefully orchestrated attempt by the Politburo Standing Committee to respond to military pressure for a tougher approach to the Taiwan issue, while building a military consensus around a continuing policy of patience, forbearance, and nonuse of force by promising a more militarily assertive policy in the indefinite but not too distant future. The August 1994 meeting was presided over by General Li Jing, deputy chief of the General Staff Department, and Generals Wang Ruilin and Zhu Dunfa. The meeting was reportedly addressed and/or attended by CMC vice chairman Liu Huaqing and Zhang Zhen, Chief of General Staff Zhang Wannian, and veteran generals Qin Jiwei, Yu Qiuli, Zhang Aiping, Li Desheng, Xiao Ke, and Liao Hansheng. Attendees included people from the Taiwan Affairs Offices of the Central Committee and the State Council, the Ministry of Defense (MOD), various military regions, and strategy research departments and think tanks. In terms of substantive deliberations, the conference was apparently directed toward evaluation of a fairly long-term plan for reunification with Taiwan. Final reunification was to take place between 2009 and 2014. By that time China's level of economic development would have risen substantially, lessening Taiwan's apprehensions that its own economy would be dragged down by massive poverty on the mainland. By persisting in the quest for peaceful unification for another fifteen to twenty years, perhaps even making concessions in the process, China would demonstrate its patience and sincerity. If Taipei then continued to reject peace talks and reunification, the use of force would seem more reasonable.[35] The theme of the conference was patience, symbolized by Liu Huaqing's speech to the assembly. China had waited forty-five years for unification, Liu pointed out, and just as Comrade Deng Xiaoping had said, it could wait a while longer. The general principle of "one China" could not be compromised, however. If Taiwan split from the motherland or if a "foreign invasion" of Taiwan took place, China would be compelled to solve the Taiwan issue by military means. Meanwhile, the PLA would continue to arm and train for the day of reunification.

Following the August 1994 conference, Jiang Zemin decided to put his imprint on Taiwan policy by issuing his Eight Point Proposal. After replacing Yang Shangkun as head of the Leading Group of Taiwan Affairs in 1993, Jiang had not played a particularly important role in setting Taiwan policy. Given the attention paid by previous paramount leaders to Taiwan and given the mounting controversy over Taiwan policy during the previous two years, it seemed appropriate that Jiang now involve himself. His proposal was drafted by the Taiwan Affairs Office of the State Council and promulgated in January 1995 after approval by the Politburo. Military leaders' skepticism of its moderate tone was confirmed, they believed, by Lee Teng-hui's Six Point Proposal issued three months later. China's irresolution was encouraging Lee in his "splittism," PLA leaders charged. They proposed that China express its contempt by having low-ranking ARATS staffers reply to Lee's Six Points. That was opposed and overridden, however, by Wang Zhaoguo's proposal that the response be made by the Taiwan Affairs Office of the State Council in order to maintain goodwill with Taiwan. When Lee's visit to the United States was announced a short while later, the PLA found further confirmation of its criticism of the weak, conciliatory approach to Taiwan.[36]

Even after the announcement of Lee's visit, the conciliationists pushed forward. On 27 May—five days after the announcement that Lee would be issued a U.S. visa—ARATS vice chairman Tang Shubei arrived in Taipei for two days of talks with the SEF. Shortly afterward, ARATS and SEF announced that the second meeting of their respective leaders would be held in Beijing in July.[37] Military leaders were livid at such continuing weakness.[38] They drafted a report calling for more forceful measures against Taiwan, including military measures. Liu Huaqing and Zhang Zhen reportedly lobbied Jiang Zemin in favor of the military proposal. Finally in mid-June a meeting of the Leading Group on Taiwan Affairs, in which Liu and Zhang participated without voting rights, approved the substance of the military view. The meeting decided to postpone the second ARATS-SEF summit, recall the Chinese ambassador to the United States, openly criticize Lee Teng-hui as the chief representative of the Taiwan independence forces, and stage military exercises aimed at Taiwan. The meeting also decided that the U.S. decision to invite Lee was part of the plot to encircle and split China, and must be handled by tough tactics. Military tactics should be used toward Taiwan to deflate the arrogance of Taiwan independence. Both Qian Qichen and Wang Zhaoguo undertook self-criticisms at the meeting, and Wang was replaced as secretary general of the Leading Group on Taiwan by Major General Xiong Guangjie, director of the General Staff Department's Intelligence Department.[39] The type of policy toward Taiwan and the United States preferred by the PLA was implemented beginning in mid-June 1995. Military advice and preferences had finally prevailed.

Did PLA leaders expect that a more confrontational approach to the United States would lead to PRC-U.S. military conflict? If so, how did this square with their appreciation of China's distinctly inferior position in the military balance?

The swift, decisive, and low-casualty U.S. victory over Iraq in 1991 made a deep impression on China's military leaders.[40] Iraq's army was large and battle-hardened by the eight-year war with Iran. Iraq's weaponry was essentially Soviet—similar to the PLA's own armory. Moreover, Iraq's strategy was similar to that which the PLA would perforce follow in war with the United States: deny victory to superior enemy forces, protract the fighting, wear down the enemy's strength, and break its will to persist. The dramatic defeat of this strategy by U.S. high-tech weaponry was a great shock to China's military leaders. How could they have continued to advocate confrontation with the United States? Was not the contradiction between the shock of the recent U.S. victory and the putative PLA prescription of confrontation with the United States so great as to require our discounting the Hong Kong media's "evidence" of PLA lobbying for a tough policy after the 1992 F-16 sale to Taiwan? There are three reasons why I believe not.

First, Chinese strategic thinking has often concluded that periods of weakness require forceful policies precisely because the enemy may be tempted to exploit China's vulnerability.[41] This may be prevented by demonstrating to the superior enemy through forceful actions that China will not be intimidated into passivity and acquiescence. There are many cases of this inverse relationship between vulnerability and assertiveness in Chinese foreign policy: the decision for war with the United States in October 1950; the decision to launch intense political struggle against Khrushchev in 1960 just as China's economy was collapsing; the 1962 decision for war with India when China was experiencing mass famine and its alliance with Moscow had collapsed; and the 1969 decision for military confrontation with the Soviets on the Ussuri River as the PLA was preoccupied with the chaos of the Cultural Revolution. In these and other similar instances China's leaders concluded that foreign adversaries were trying to exploit China's weakness, and that the way to counter this was through firm, confrontational policies that would force the enemy to stop, take stock, and abandon its efforts. As often as not, Chinese leaders have concluded that weakness required firm assertiveness, not passivity.

Second, confrontation does not necessarily lead to war. Indeed, it may deter war. An assertive, confrontational policy of tit-for-tat does not necessarily entail military conflict. China can draw upon forms of sanctions other than war. In the modern Sino-U.S. scenario, it can conspicuously acquire what it needs economically from countries other than the United States. It can refuse to cooperate with Washington on issues of nuclear or ballistic missile proliferation. It can actively oppose U.S. initiatives in the UN. It might, for example, have vetoed rather than abstained when the Bush administration sought Security Council approval in November 1990 "to use all necessary means" to secure "immediate and unconditional" Iraqi withdrawal from Iran. Or it might punish smaller international actors—such as Lee Teng-hui's Taiwan regime—who go along with the nefarious anti-China schemes of U.S. hegemonists. There is a big gap between punitive, confrontational policies and military conflict. Even if distinct undertones to the broader political confrontation emerge, that does not mean that actual military conflict will result. China's leaders retain the initiative in determining escalation to a higher, military level of conflict.

The third reason has to do with what Allen Whiting terms the Chinese calculus of deterrence, in which limited blows against a perceived foreign aggressor are used to force the aggressor to shift course.[42] Such timely blows may deter expanded aggression against China that would otherwise lead to a later but larger war. Whiting refers to limited *military* blows against foreign powers, but the same logic applies to the use of nonmilitary sanctions. Of course, Chinese tit-for-tat retaliation did ultimately become military in the Taiwan Strait, though not aimed directly against the United States.

Viewed from this perspective, China's military coercion of Taiwan between June 1995 and March 1996 was part of an effort to deter continued, expanded U.S. aggression against China. By bringing the United States face to face with the realities of confrontation, albeit only an indirect military confrontation with China, and by demonstrating that the superior military and diplomatic position of the United States would not compel China to acquiesce to unpalatable anti-China actions by the United States, Beijing sought to reign in what it viewed as American aggression against China.

Having reviewed the domestic linkages of the Taiwan issue in PRC politics, we can now return to the question of the applicability to China's case of the hypotheses developed by Edward Mansfield and Jack Snyder. The crux of the Mansfield-Snyder explanation is intensifying elite competition in a situation of low institutionalization. This competition leads to efforts to mobilize mass support via democratization and prestige strategies abroad.[43]

The CCP is deeply and perhaps increasingly divided by processes of marketization. Some portions of the CCP have adapted successfully to market economics, while others have failed miserably. Many of these failed groups (e.g., state-owned heavy industry) were among the most politically influential and prestigious elites in the prereform period. There is also a strong geographic element, with elites in coastal regions adapting more successfully than those in the interior. Different success rates lead to different views on further market-oriented reform.

The interests of the non-market-adaptive state enterprises coincide with those of Marxist-Leninist troglodytes who apparently remain very influential in the ideological apparatus. Some of these people are deeply skeptical about the whole course of Deng's reforms because it deviates from the ideology they mastered and upon the basis of which they have the power to define the standards of political correctness for society as a whole. Although now only occasionally allowed to publicly vent their continuing adulation of the old ideology, they remain at their posts. At the other end of the ideological spectrum are proreform liberals— former followers of Hu Yaobang and Zhao Ziyang. While their former leaders are gone, they too remain at their posts. These conflicting views and interests are held together by fear of a popular revolt like that of 1989 in China or creeping anti-Communist disintegration like that of the USSR in 1990–91. Positively, they are held together by militant nationalism. These deep divisions among the civilian elite give increased weight to the views of the military whose support is sought by disputing civilian interests.

Another key element of the Mansfield-Snyder paradigm is involvement of the masses in politics. All of the transitional polities they discuss in their effort to explain their statistical results achieved mass involvement primarily through semicompetitive elections: France of Napoleon III, mid-Victorian Britain, Wilhelmine Germany, and Taisho Japan. These electoral processes were widely seen as unfair and biased, and therefore did not play a major role in mediating elite conflict. For the same reason, they were not the only form of mass participation. Because ordinary people had little faith in the electoral process, they often resorted to extraparliamentary means to advance their views. Yet the imperfect electoral process did provide a way for various elites to compete with one another in mobilizing popular support.

China in transition is clearly different. It is just beginning to develop competitive elections at the village level, and its electoral process does not provide a way for competitive elites to mobilize and demonstrate popular support—at least not yet at the national level. In other ways, however, one does find competitive elite mobilization of the masses in Chinese politics. In his analysis of the zig-zag course of reform in post-Mao China, Richard Baum stresses the role of conflict between two wings of the reform coalition that displaced Mao's designated successor, Hua Guofeng.[44] Deng Xiaoping balanced between groups of conservative reformers represented by senior veteran Chen Yun and liberal reformers represented by Secretary General Hu Yaobang, first supporting one group and then swinging his support to the other in a zig-zag course of policy. Mass mobilization was an important strategy of the liberal reform periods. In order to create a political climate conducive to policy experimentation and innovation, the liberal reformers, with Deng's support, permitted popular forces to actively criticize conservative policies. The democracy wall movement of 1978–79 was the first and classic example of this. Alienated former Red Guards were allowed to openly vent their grievances through wall posters and samizdat publications. According to Baum, each of the three liberal reform thrusts of the 1980s involved similar mobilizations. These can be seen as a manifestation of inter-elite conflict, as an effort by one elite to mobilize popular support in order to strengthen its position vis-à-vis another elite. As we learn more about the socio-political origins of the militant nationalism emerging in China, we may find that it is linked to inter-elite conflict.[45]

Finally, China fits the Mansfield-Snyder paradigm in that fear of popular rebellion has been a factor motivating elite resort to foreign policies of nationalism and prestige. In a number of the cases explored by Mansfield and Snyder a deep gulf existed between ruling elites and the ordinary people. One major benefit of nationalism (from the elite perspective) was that it obfuscated this cleavage and bound the masses in obedience to the state. Since the 1989 upheaval in China and the collapse of communist regimes in Eastern Europe and the Soviet Union, fear of rebellion has been strong among China's elite. This may be a major factor persuading them of the wisdom of forceful, assertive foreign policies that risk confrontation with other powers—confrontations that bind the masses to the state.

6 / The U.S. Visa Decision
and Beijing's Reaction

On 22 May 1995 a White House spokesman announced that President Lee Teng-hui would be given a visa to visit the United States as a private individual. Lee was permitted to enter the country to deliver an address at the spring commencement ceremony of Cornell University, where he had received his Ph.D. in agricultural economics in 1968. Lee's visit would be the first by a Taiwan president since 1979. The visa decision, part of the process of adjustment in U.S.-Taiwan relations that began in mid-1994, prompted China's leadership to decide on military measures directed at Taiwan.

Like most important decisions, the U.S. decision to issue Lee Teng-hui a visa was complex. It can be analyzed in terms of the sentiments and calculations of the individual who had the ultimate power of decision, President Bill Clinton; the institutional interests of the organizations making up the U.S. government and the political relationships among those institutions, particularly the peculiar institution of separation of powers; and organizational processes and miscommunications.

Bill Clinton had warm feelings for Taiwan. As governor of Arkansas he had visited Taiwan four times promoting trade. He was treated as an honored guest, as is Taipei's wont with visiting influential Americans, and witnessed first hand Taiwan's economic and political progress.[1] Clinton's few interactions with China's top leaders, on the other hand, had been strained. During his first meeting with president Jiang Zemin in Seattle in 1993, Jiang lectured Clinton for half an hour on the evils of U.S. interference in China's internal affairs. Speaking from notes, Jiang turned aside Clinton's efforts to direct the conversation along less hostile lines. Presidents are human beings and one cannot dismiss the possibility that Clinton got a bit of personal satisfaction by saying "no" to Beijing on an issue as close to its heart as Taiwan. He had, after all, little reason to be sympathetic to China and its leaders.

Clinton's political interests were also served by ignoring Beijing's

wishes over Taiwan. His reversal on MFN had been politically costly. By
saying no to Beijing, Clinton strengthened his domestic political position. That was especially important after his party's devastating setback
in the mid-term elections of November 1994, when, for the first time
since 1948, Republicans seized control of both houses of Congress. The
Republican Party was united and invigorated under the leadership of
new House Speaker Newt Gingrich, and determined to use control of
Congress to attack the Clinton White House, preparing the way for a full
Republican takeover of government in November 1996. Clinton's standing in the polls was at a record low and many Democratic members of
Congress welcomed opportunities to disassociate themselves from him.
The Republican Congress attacked Clinton on many issues, including
foreign policy, China policy, and, more particularly, Taiwan.

On 2 May 1995 the House of Representatives voted 396 to 0 in favor of
a resolution urging the administration to issue a visa to Lee Teng-hui,
allowing him to visit the United States as a private individual. During
the debate over the resolution, several members indicated they would
support legislation should the administration ignore the resolution.
Congressional resolutions merely express the sentiment of Congress and
are not legally binding on the president. Legislation, however, has the
force of law. A week after the House vote, the Senate voted 91 to 1 in
favor of a similar resolution.[2] It is important to note that those votes
were completely bipartisan. Republicans may have attacked Clinton on
what they sensed was a popular issue, but Democrats disassociated themselves from an unpopular and ineffectual President. Both parties responded to strong popular sentiments sympathetic to Taiwan and negative toward China's leaders.

Any U.S. president—and especially a weakened one such as Clinton
after November 1994—must carefully pick his fights with Congress. He
will avoid fights he is likely to lose, since a Congressional override of his
veto will tar him as weak. If he chooses to take on a hostile majority in
Congress, one of his few weapons is appeal to public opinion. This,
however, requires taking a stance on a popular issue on which he is sure
to have wide public support. That simply was not the case with denying
Taiwan's president a visa because of Beijing's objections.

Political ineptitude by the administration gave ready ammunition to
Congressional critics of its Taiwan policy. On 9 March 1995, several days
after the State Department announced that President Lee would *not* be

granted a visa, the White House announced that Gerry Adams, leader of the Provisional Wing of the Irish Republican Army, would be granted unlimited visits to the United States over a period of three months, could raise funds, and would be received by Clinton in the White House. The contrast with Lee's treatment in Honolulu a year earlier was striking. The head of a terrorist organization was allowed to enter the United States, over the objections of a close U.S. ally, Britain, yet the head of a functioning democracy was not, because of objections by the unfriendly regime in Beijing.[3]

While not fundamental determinants of the Lee visa decision, miscommunications arising from simple organizational inertia affected the impact of that decision on Beijing. Inept U.S. handling of the visa decision contributed to Beijing's hostile response. The decision was announced after repeated, apparently authoritative, U.S. assurances to PRC representatives that Lee would not be allowed to visit. With the conclusion of the Taiwan Policy Review in September 1994, the State Department indicated that top U.S. leaders would not visit Taiwan, nor would Taiwan's top leaders be allowed to visit the United States.[4] The State Department's position on this issue was virtually identical to that of its Chinese counterpart, the MFA: given Lee's status, a visit by him to the United States would unavoidably be seen as a change in the unofficial nature of U.S. relations with Taiwan, thereby endangering the underpinnings of U.S. relations with the PRC. Such assurances by the State Department to the MFA apparently continued until right before the 22 May announcement. In the words of China's subsequent protest, "The sound of these remarks had barely subsided when the U.S. administration suddenly made a U-turn. Does the U.S. administration have any regard for its international credibility when it goes back on its own word on such a major issue of principle?"[5]

Secretary of State Warren Christopher tried to "telegraph" Foreign Minister Qian Qichen during a meeting in April 1995 that mounting Congressional pressure was "a very serious problem" regarding Taiwan. He had "pressed on the Taiwan situation" several times in Congress, Christopher told Qian, but "failed to persuade anyone that I talked to." Christopher intended those words as a warning to Qian that the State Department's point of view might not prevail in Washington. Qian did not pick up on the subtle implications of Christopher's message. He later told a U.S. visitor, "I was assured a visa would not be issued. Imagine what I thought and what was thought of me when the visa was granted."[6] That was not the last time in 1995 that Washington's lack of clarity contributed to Sino-U.S. misunderstanding.

United States embarrassment of the MFA undercut the latter's position in China. In the debates that ensued after the U.S. announcement, the MFA attributed the move to internal U.S. politics, but this explanation was dismissed by China's hard-liners. One could not believe the words and justifications of the U.S. hegemonists, the hard-liners argued. They lied to deceive and dupe China, and the U-turn on the Lee visa issue was a case in point. The MFA had fallen for U.S. hegemonist lies. A more realistic approach was required.

China's hard-liners' explanation of U.S. policy toward Taiwan was simple: the United States pursued a secret strategy to contain China, which posed a threat to U.S. hegemony. Without Taiwan, China would be weaker, its access to the Pacific Ocean restricted. The shifts in U.S. policy toward Taiwan intended to institutionalize and perpetuate the division of Taiwan from the mainland, to create an independent Taiwan. Policy toward Taiwan was a piece of a larger pattern; all around China's periphery the United States sought to contain China. Therefore, a hard-headed, tough, tit-for-tat policy towards the United States was required.

In the past the United States has in fact pursued a long-term secret strategy toward China quite at variance with its publicly enunciated policies. During the 1950s the U.S. strategic objective vis-à-vis China was to draw it away from the Soviet Union, which was viewed as presenting the gravest threat to the United States. This strategy was pursued, however, by publicly stressing the commonality of all Communists, Soviet and Chinese, while holding Moscow rhetorically responsible for Chinese actions, and by stressing the monolithic nature of the Sino-Soviet bloc.[7] Given the precedent of the 1950s, we must concede that it is possible, or at least it was possible in that era, for the U.S. government to pursue a long-term secret strategy toward China at variance with its public claims. The "containment" paradigm can also account for a lot of the data. Even the frequent declarations by U.S. representatives that the United States was not pursuing a strategy of containment can, from the perspective of that paradigm, be taken as evidence that it, in fact, was!

There are three reasons why a "muddle" explanation of the Lee visa decision seems more solid than a "containment" conspiracy explanation. First, American society of the 1990s is far more open and critical of governmental authority than was the case in the 1950s. The Vietnam

War and the Watergate affair gave rise to a more probing media and an officialdom less respectful of government secrets. I frankly doubt that the U.S. government is today capable of keeping secret a strategy such as that imputed by the "containment" explanation. Second, the actions of the Clinton administration do not suggest a clear vision of strategic threat from any power, let alone from China. They suggest no grand vision, but a groping toward the future. Third, there are several salient facts that do not fit with the containment conspiracy model. The renewal of MFN is especially anomalous. If U.S. leaders and their strategists really wanted to stifle China's development, they would have long ago revoked MFN. Similarly, the relatively relaxed U.S. attitude toward transfer of very sophisticated dual-use technology (at least prior to the 1996 confrontation) does not fit with the "containment" model. Finally and most importantly, the driving force for adjustment of U.S. policy toward Taiwan came not from the strategic policy centers of the executive branch, but from the Congress. Congress is notoriously open. It is inconceivable that it could be the fount of, or even remain mum about, a long-term secret strategy. There is also abundant evidence that congressional actions on Taiwan were driven by the desire to cater to popular sentiment while achieving domestic political objectives.

Not all influential people on the Chinese side shared the "containment" misperception of U.S. policy. Analysts in the MFA and the Chinese Academy of Social Sciences, among others, had a more sophisticated understanding of the U.S. policy process. In the heated atmosphere that ensued after Washington's 22 May announcement, however, it was difficult for them to make their case. The strident voices of the hardliners often dominated discussions about how China should respond, and established a criteria of political correctness in which suggestions that the United States was not trying to contain China, or that China should not strike back firmly, were seen as unpatriotic. Confronted by such a militant attitude, more sophisticated voices sometimes remained quiet. At least one research center prepared a paper urging a low-key response to the U.S. visa decision, but spiked it as the political atmosphere heated up.[8]

The day after the U.S. announcement, China's MFA issued a "strong protest" expressing the "utmost indignation" of the Chinese government against the "extremely serious move of openly creating 'two Chinas, or 'one China, one Taiwan.' " The U.S. action "totally contravened the fundamental principles" of the three joint communiqués, the MFA said. Given the fact that Lee Teng-hui was "president of the Republic of

China," a visit by him "under whatever name or in whatever way" would inevitably "cause" the creation of "two Chinas, or one China, one Taiwan." Moreover, the U.S. action was not isolated, but part of an upgrading process of U.S. relations with Taiwan. Recently "the U.S. administration has gone further and further on the question of Taiwan. It has taken one measure after another to upgrade U.S.-Taiwan relations." With the issuance of a visa to Taiwan's "president," the MFA protest said, "we cannot but ask, 'Does the U.S. administration have any intention at all of honoring [the three joint communiqués]?' What course does it want to put Sino-U.S. relations onto?"[9]

A series of sanctions followed. The first move, on 23 May, was the abrupt termination of a visit to the United States by a seven-member delegation led by PLA air force commander Yu Zhengwu. The group promptly returned to China. On 26 May Beijing announced that a scheduled visit to the United States by Defense Minister Chi Haotian, intended to reciprocate a visit by U.S. Defense Secretary William Perry to China in October 1994, was being "postponed." In effect, Beijing was canceling links between the U.S. and PRC militaries. On 28 May it announced the suspension of a number of talks with the United States and canceled visits by U.S. Arms Control and Disarmament Agency director John Holum, who was to discuss nuclear energy cooperation; Deputy Assistant Secretary of State for Political Military Affairs Thomas McNamara; and Deputy Assistant Secretary of State Robert Einhorn, who was to discuss U.S. intelligence reports of Chinese sales of missile technology and components to Pakistan and Iran. During the next several months Beijing also rejected U.S. offers to send a high-ranking U.S. official, such as Deputy Secretary of State Peter Tarnoff, to Beijing to explain the U.S. decision to issue Lee a visa.

The State Department struggled to keep Lee's June visit to the United States unofficial and low key. No administration officials met with Lee. Three senior Republican senators saw him during his stop in Syracuse, New York, but that was beyond the administration's control. State Department pressure apparently forced the cancellation of a press conference scheduled for the day of Lee's Cornell speech. Throughout the visit, State Department spokesmen stressed its private, nonofficial character, and that U.S. policy toward the Taiwan-China issue remained unchanged. Those moves did little to assuage Beijing's anger.

The PLA felt that a far stronger reaction was required. Deng Xiaoping, who in 1992 had overruled the PLA's wish for a strong U.S. F-16 sale, was no longer able to do that in 1995. The F-16 incident now clearly seemed to be part of a shift in U.S. policy toward Taiwan that had escalated, many PLA leaders concluded, because of China's weak response in 1992 and again following Lee Teng-hui's Southeast Asia "vacation diplomacy" in 1994.

On 16 June, nearly a month after the U.S. visa decision and shortly after the lobbying by Liu Huaqing and Zhang Zhen at the meeting of the Leading Group on Taiwan Affairs, the MFA announced the recall of Ambassador to the United States Li Daoyu to China "to report on his work." Simultaneously, U.S. Ambassador Stapleton Roy completed his scheduled four-year tour of duty in Beijing and departed for a new diplomatic post. For some time the Clinton administration had sought Chinese approval (a normal diplomatic courtesy) for the appointment of former U.S. senator James Sasser as Roy's replacement. Beijing was reluctant to agree to Sasser's appointment, probably because he had been associated with various moves to sanction or censure China in Congress. Soon after the announcement of Lee's visa, however, it became known that agreement to Sasser's appointment was "further complicated" and was unlikely in the near future. For the first time since 1979, Washington and Beijing were without ambassadors in one another's capitals. Beijing also stepped up pressure on Taiwan. On 16 June Beijing's ARATS notified Taipei's SEF of cancellation of a second meeting between Koo Chen-fu and Wang Daohan scheduled for late July in Beijing.[10] A series of vitriolic polemics against Lee Teng-hui followed. The stridency of those polemics had not been seen since China adopted the policy of "peaceful reunification" in 1979.

Washington downplayed China's response to the Lee visa and minimized Beijing's de facto downgrading of relations from the ambassadorial level, urging China to reconsider. "We continue to seek a constructive relationship with a strong, stable, open and prosperous China which is integrated as a responsible member of the international community," the State Department said. President Clinton's decision to issue Lee a visa "did not change [U.S.] policy towards China." The United States hoped the Chinese government would "reconsider its action and return Ambassador Li [Daoyu] to his post very soon."

7 / Beijing's Probing
of U.S. Intentions

B etween 21 and 28 July 1995 the PLA conducted missile and live-fire tests in a circular area of ten nautical miles radius eighty miles northeast of Taiwan, conspicuously near the air and sea lines of communication between Taiwan and Japan. When announcing the "tests," Beijing warned foreign vessels and aircraft to avoid the area. Foreigners complied. Over a period of a week the PLA fired four M-9 missiles with a range of six hundred kilometers and two DF-21 missiles with a range of more than one thousand miles into the test area. Those tests were part of larger, longer military exercises that began in late June and were code-named Blue Whale 5. An aqua-colored whale in the shape of Taiwan was the symbol of Taiwan's pro-independence Democratic Progressive Party. Blue Whale 5 also involved firing by coastal artillery batteries and simulated air and naval strikes. The location of those and other PLA demonstrations are shown in Map 1.

At the end of July, Defense Minister Chi Haotian delivered a eulogy on the occasion of the PLA's sixty-eighth anniversary. He warned that China "will not undertake to give up the use of force, and will not sit idle if foreign forces interfere in China's reunification and get involved in Taiwan independence," or if the Taiwan authorities insist on splitting China.[1] A second round of tests underlined those words. Between 15 and 25 August the PLA conducted live-fire exercises in a much larger area in the seas ninety miles north of Taiwan, firing six missiles into the test area. Again warning was given to foreign planes and vessels, which rerouted traffic to avoid the test area.

These missile tests were a significant threshold. For the first time China fired its ballistic missiles far out into a sea zone conspicuously adjacent to Taiwan. The purpose was clear: to demonstrate that the PLA could use its missiles to disrupt Taiwan's sea and air traffic. Yet the United States did not respond by warning Beijing. Not until six months later, with the mid-December passage of the aircraft carrier *Nimitz*

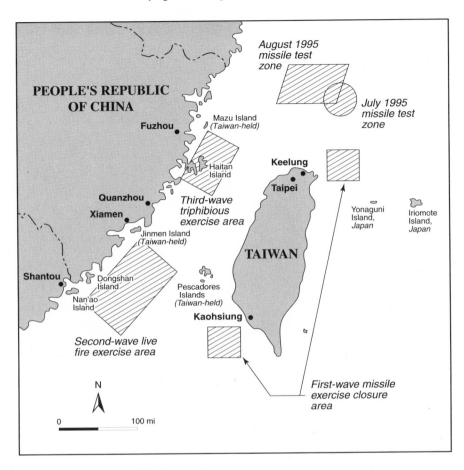

Map 1. PLA military activities in the Taiwan Strait area, 1995–96

through the Strait, was a countervailing military signal sent. Meanwhile U.S. diplomatic presentations to China continued to downplay the Taiwan issue in hopes of "putting that issue behind us." Whether or not the mid-1995 rocket demonstrations were intended as a test of U.S. resolve, they served that purpose. The virtual nonreaction of the United States provided strong evidence for those inside the Chinese policy process who argued for military coercion of Taiwan partly on the grounds that the United States was not likely to intervene.

Against that background of forceful Chinese probing of U.S. intentions, U.S. policy toward cross-Strait relations sought subtlety. Since 1971 U.S. policy had minimized public demonstrations of the U.S. commitment to defend Taiwan.[2] It was feared that such demonstrations would embarrass and anger Beijing, while encouraging proindependence elements within Taiwan to believe that they could proceed with provocative actions (e.g., changing the name or the flag of the country or formally declaring "independence") because they could be assured of U.S. support in extremis. To avoid encouraging hotheads on either the mainland or Taiwan, it was deemed best to say little or nothing about the U.S. commitment to the defense of Taiwan. After all, that had been clearly stated in 1972, 1979, and again in 1982.

In the 1972 communiqué, the United States had "reaffirmed" its "interest in a peaceful settlement of the Taiwan question by the Chinese themselves."[3] "With this prospect in mind," the United States was to withdraw its military forces from Taiwan. The 1979 normalization communiqué did not contain a U.S. statement about its continuing interest in Taiwan's security. A unilateral U.S. statement issued at the same time did, however, state: "The United States is confident that the people of Taiwan face a peaceful and prosperous future. The United States continues to have an interest in the peaceful resolution of the Taiwan issue and expects that the Taiwan issue will be settled peacefully by the Chinese themselves." Those words were carefully negotiated by U.S. and Chinese representatives. They were not contradicted by China's leaders at the time they were spoken—a condition that also was negotiated. By insisting that only the communiqués themselves contained the "principles" governing U.S.-PRC relations, Beijing tried to obviate the unpleasant concessions it was compelled to make in the normalization negotiations in 1978. Finally, the 1982 communiqué said that the United States "understands and appreciates" China's "policy of striving for a peaceful resolution of the Taiwan question." "The new situation which emerged with regard to the Taiwan question also provided favorable conditions for the settlement of United States–China differences over the question of United States arms sales to Taiwan," the 1982 communiqué said. In his statement at the time of the 1982 communiqué, President Ronald Reagan explained, "We attach great significance to the Chinese statement in the communiqué regarding China's 'fundamental' policy of peaceful unification, and it is clear from our statements that our future actions will be conducted with this peaceful policy fully in mind. . . . We have an abiding interest and concern that any resolution be peaceful."

The Taiwan Relations Act had further strengthened the U.S. commitment to Taiwan's security. Section 2(b)6 provided that the United States would maintain the capacity "to resist any resort to force or *other forms of coercion* that would jeopardize the security, the social or economic system, of the people of Taiwan" (emphasis added). Section 2(b)4 specified such nonbloody methods as "boycotts and embargoes" as among the "other than peaceful means" that may be taken as constituting a "threat to the peace" of the region.[4] From Beijing's perspective, the TRA is purely unilateral U.S. legislation that violates superior bilateral agreements reached by Washington and Beijing during the normalization negotiations of 1978–79.[5] In the agreements and understandings reached bilaterally by the United States and China in 1971–72, 1978–79, and again in 1982, China agreed, *implicitly,* to respect Washington's interest in a peaceful settlement of the Taiwan question. It was Washington, acting unilaterally in the TRA, that expanded "peaceful" to exclude various sorts of nonbloody coercion. In Beijing's view, China cannot be expected to abide by principles to which it did not agree, and which are a unilateral U.S. construction. China's actions in 1995–96 were not "nonpeaceful," in that they were not violent, harmful, or destructive. They did not, therefore, transgress U.S. interests recognized by Beijing.

Given the longstanding policy of U.S. concern for Taiwan's security from unprovoked PRC attack, U.S. foreign policy makers concluded that China's leaders understood the U.S. position well enough, that further reiteration would have been unnecessary and provocative, and that it was best left implicit and unsaid in the tense atmosphere of mid-1995. That caution was reasonable and understandable. In retrospect, however, U.S. policy appears to have been too subtle. The first U.S. military move in response to China's series of threats against Taiwan came on 16

December 1995 when the aircraft carrier *Nimitz* passed through the Taiwan Strait. By then it was too late. China's leaders had already decided on expanded military coercion of Taiwan.

Throughout the summer and fall of 1995 Beijing pressured the United States to give "firm commitments" that Lee Teng-hui and other top Taiwan leaders would not again be allowed to visit the United States. Beijing urged that a "fourth communiqué" be signed clarifying the U.S. stance on the Taiwan issue. Since the actions of the United States had injured and damaged the very basis of Sino-U.S. relations, Beijing said, it was necessary for the United States to take "concrete action" to repair that damage. Ideally that fourth communiqué should issue from a full, formal, state-level meeting between Presidents Jiang Zemin and Bill Clinton. At a minimum the United States should give "firm assurance" that Lee Teng-hui and other senior Taiwanese officials would not be permitted to visit the United States again. Beijing suggested that if the United States agreed to such measures, Sino-U.S. relations could be rapidly repaired. Ambassadorial relations could be restored, military links resumed, and talks and cooperation restarted on a range of issues. The United States replied by seeking Chinese assurances on human rights, transfer of technology used in nuclear missiles and weapons of mass destruction, market opening and access, and intellectual property rights, and expressed its concern with peaceful settlement of the South China Seas and Taiwan issues. The United States said it had no plans to issue visas to Taiwan leaders in the "near future," but refused to formally commit itself; it declined discussion of a fourth communiqué.[6]

The first high-level U.S.-PRC contact after the visa announcement was a meeting on 1 August between Secretary of State Warren Christopher and Foreign Minister Qian Qichen at Brunei during the annual ASEAN conference. Two weeks before a "senior MFA official" had outlined for a *New York Times* reporter China's maximal and minimal aims for the upcoming meeting. Cordial relations between China and the United States could be restored, the official said, only when President Clinton affirmed that there was but one China and that *Taiwan is a part of China*. At a minimum, before other high-level meetings could take place, the president would have to declare that Taiwan's president would not be allowed to make any more visits to the United States. Unless agreement was reached over Taiwan, the official warned, the voices in China's leadership who argued that the United States should be treated as a hostile power would become increasingly prominent.[7] Shortly before the meeting Qian told the press, "What we are going to do is to make the U.S. realize the importance of Sino-U.S. relations to prompt them to take the right track."[8]

The United States refused to concede even Beijing's minimal demand. It did, however, offer a few concessions. In a speech to the National Press Club shortly before his departure for Brunei, Christopher announced that the United States had decided not to impose economic sanctions on China in retaliation for the sale of missile technology to Iran and Pakistan. He also indicated that when he met Qian in Brunei he would deliver a letter from President Clinton to President Jiang stressing the U.S. desire for a cooperative relationship with China and proposing a summit meeting during Jiang's upcoming visit to New York for the celebration of the UN's fiftieth anniversary. Regarding Beijing's demand for a U.S. guarantee against future visits by Taiwan's president, Christopher said flatly that no such guarantee would be forthcoming. He softened this, however, by adding that Lee's recent private visit had been a "special situation and a courtesy."[9]

Additional U.S. concessions came in Clinton's letter to Jiang delivered by Christopher during a one-and-a-half-hour meeting in Brunei. Clinton's letter has not yet been made public in the United States.[10] According to a version of it published in the CCP-controlled Hong Kong newspaper *Dagong bao* (Impartial Daily) Clinton used some new verbiage to formulate the U.S. position on the ultrasensitive Taiwan issue:

> The United States recognizes the PRC as the sole legitimate government of China. The United States *respects* China's position that there is only one China in the world and that Taiwan is part of China. *The U.S. government will handle the Taiwan question on the basis of the one China policy. The U.S. government is against Taiwan independence and does not support Taiwan's admission to the United Nations* [emphasis added].[11]

The italicized portions above indicate new U.S. concessions to Beijing on the Taiwan issue. The formulation that the U.S. "respects" China's position that Taiwan is a part of China had not previously been used by the U.S. government in formal communications with the Chinese government. In the Shanghai communiqué of 1972 the U.S. government had "acknowledged" the position of "all Chinese on either side of the Taiwan Strait" that Taiwan is a part of China. The United States "did not challenge" that position. In the 1979 normalization communiqué and again in the 1982 arms sales communiqué the United States had "acknowledged the Chinese position" that Taiwan was part of China. For more than twenty years the United States had strictly and carefully hewed to those words. The use of the word "respect" conceded an additional increment to Beijing. "Not challenging" merely meant not rejecting. "Respect" implied intent to do nothing at cross purposes. The words "is against" in regard to the U.S. position toward Taiwan independence embodied a similar concession. Beginning with Henry Kissinger's first, secret trip to Beijing in July 1971, the U.S. position had been that it "would not support" Taiwan independence. That formulation was reiterated over the years, but was not embodied in the various communiqués or unilateral declarations associated with those communiqués. "Would not support" is negative and passive; "is against" is positive and active. Such nuances may seem like quibbles, but regarding the ultrasensitive Taiwan issue they represented valuable, if small, concessions. State Department wordsmiths certainly considered implications carefully and chose those words as modest moves designed to assuage Chinese anger. Clinton's statement to Jiang that the United States "does not support Taiwan's admission to the United Nations" was also a concession. Since the UN debates of 1971, when the United States argued in favor of Taiwan's representation in the General Assembly, the question of the U.S. position on that matter had remained open. Now Clinton and Christopher had shut it. Viewed objectively, those three concessions must be seen as gains from Beijing's decision to respond harshly to the U.S. decision to issue a visa to Lee Teng-hui.

What Clinton did not say in his letter, however, was more important than what he said. He apparently said nothing about the U.S. interest in the peaceful solution of the Taiwan issue by the Chinese themselves, which had been at the core of both the Shanghai communiqué and the 1982 arms sales communiqué, as well as President Carter's 1978 statement on normalization. Reiterating it in the context of mid-1995 would certainly have been appropriate, but coming after a series of the most provocative military exercises conducted by China since the 1950s and during a period in which Beijing plunged Sino-U.S. relations into deep freeze because of Taiwan, the Clinton administration felt it wise to avoid that touchy topic. Instead, when Christopher conveyed Clinton's letter to Qian at Brunei, he stressed that the United States wanted constructive relations with a powerful, open, and prosperous China.

China's sanctions of mid-1995 did not succeed in achieving its minimal demands. Qian expressed regret that the United States was unwilling to give the requisite assurances about future visits by Lee, but said that "China attaches importance" to the new U.S. statement on its "one China" policy. "At the same time," however, Qian quoted "an ancient Chinese proverb" to the effect that "promises must be kept, and actions must be resolute. A commitment can be valuable only when it is realized by practical action." Following his meeting with Christopher, Qian told the press, "The development of Sino-U.S. relations is based on principles determined by the three communiqués, which have the Taiwan issue as the core." Facts had proven, Qian said, that Lee Teng-hui's "private visit" was absolutely a political action aimed at creating "two Chinas, or one China, one Taiwan." The adverse consequences of that visit could not be denied and the United States bore full responsibility for them. In spite of such rhetoric, Qian's "body language"—the apparent absence of personal rancor in his delivery of "tough words"—suggested to the U.S. side that the worst was over and that U.S.-PRC relations might start to improve.[12] That expectation was to prove valid, at least over the next four months.

While not feeling it necessary to call to Beijing's attention the U.S. interest in a peaceful resolution of the Taiwan question, the State Department hastened to assure the U.S. Congress that it had that interest very much in mind. Several days after the Brunei meeting, Deputy Assistant Secretary of State for East Asia and Pacific Affairs Kent Wiedemann touched on Taiwan's security when he briefed the House International Relations Committee on the administration's new policy on Taiwan and the UN. While the United States could support any arrangement regarding the UN that was agreed to by both Beijing and Taipei, it would not support Taiwan membership in the UN over and against Beijing's opposition, since to do so would "put at risk the economic and political progress achieved by the people of Taiwan"—in straight talk, it might provoke a PLA attack on Taiwan. The sole and abiding concern of the United States, according to Wiedemann, was that the resolution of the Taiwan issue be peaceful. Although Clinton had not, apparently, made this extremely important point in his letter to Jiang, Wiedemann delivered a powerful warning that U.S. "adherence to the three communiqués depends on peaceful resolution of the Taiwan issue." Regarding the PLA missile demonstrations off Taiwan, Wiedemann found them to be "not helpful," but proceeded to add, "But we do not believe China poses an imminent military threat to Taiwan. In fact, we believe Taiwan has never been more secure."[13] Apparently, the State Department's clarity and firmness was for the benefit of Congress, not Beijing.

Qian and Christopher agreed at Brunei that their deputies would continue talks. That laid the basis for a visit by Deputy Secretary of State Peter Tarnoff to Beijing at the end of August. Tarnoff's discussions with Vice Foreign Minister Li Zhaoxing did not bridge differences on any substantive issues, but Tarnoff was encouraged by the "tone" of the meetings. Tarnoff told reporters that he had placed great stress on reiterating that "far from seeking to isolate China, we desire to engage the People's Republic in a wide-ranging and constructive relationship with us and with the international community." Tarnoff also said he did not encounter any "demands or threats" regarding Taiwan.[14] Chinese commentary on Tarnoff's visit termed it "useful," observing that "recently the U.S. side has time and again indicated that it has fully realized the importance and sensitivity of the Taiwan issue in Sino-U.S. relations" and "that it has no intention of diverting itself from the 'one China' policy that it has pursued for a long time."[15]

Shortly after Tarnoff's visit, Beijing announced that Ambassador Li Daoyu would return to his post in Washington, D.C., and that General Li Xilin would represent Defense Minister Chi Haotian at ceremonies in September at Pearl Harbor commemorating the end of World War II.[16] In late September Beijing gave its approval for the posting of Jim Sasser as the new U.S. Ambassador to China.[17] These ambassadorial relations, military links, high-level exchanges, and official talks in August and September 1995 were restored in spite of the fact that Washington had not met Beijing's minimal demand.

Underscoring Washington's disregard for Beijing's "Taiwan principles," shortly after the Brunei meeting Wiedemann briefed the head of the Taipei Economic and Cultural Affairs Office in the United States, Benjamin Lu, while Lynn Pascoe, head of the American Institute in Taiwan, simultaneously briefed ROC Vice Foreign Minister Stephen Chen on the substance of the recent Qian-Christopher talks. Those meetings were an expression of the more direct high-level contacts possible as a result of the Taiwan Policy Review of 1994. In the briefings, the U.S. side explained that Washington had not acceded to Beijing's demands for a ban on subsequent travel by Taiwan's president to the United States, had not discussed a rumored "fourth communiqué" dealing with Taiwan, and had not recognized or implied that Taiwan was a province of the

PRC.[18] Again the important point is that the United States openly, if very quietly, disregarded Beijing's "principles," even while Beijing moved to repair the damage inflicted after May 1995.

Washington had in effect called Beijing's hand and the question now was whether China would back down or raise the bid further. In spite of China's sanctions during the months following the imbroglio over Lee Teng-hui's visit, Washington still rejected Beijing's "principles." Should China back down before U.S. obstinance, or should it use military instruments to wage a tit-for-tat struggle with the hegemonists? Should it further escalate the pressure on Washington, or on Taiwan, or on both? Beijing answered those questions by adopting different tactics toward Washington and Taipei. Since May 1995 Beijing had sought to punish both Washington and Taipei, but by the end of September 1995, it was working on improving relations with the United States while continuing and indeed increasing pressure on Taiwan. That improvement in Sino-U.S. relations occurred in spite of U.S. refusal to give the assurances sought by Beijing suggests that tactical considerations underlay the shift. Very probably the repair of relations was part of Beijing's diplomatic preparation for intensified pressure on Taiwan. Improved Sino-U.S. relations would encourage the United States to stay out of the upcoming, anticipated confrontation across the Taiwan Strait. During the summer of 1995 Beijing taught the United States the lesson that ignoring Beijing's principles on the Taiwan issue would lead to severe retrogression of relations. In the fall it moved to repair relations while making future improvements contingent on U.S. respect for those principles.

The U.S. government was relieved that Beijing had shifted course. In mid-October shortly after Tarnoff's visit, Assistant Secretary of State for East Asia and the Pacific Winston Lord reported to the Senate Foreign Relations Committee on the "Security and Military Considerations" of U.S. policy toward China.[19] Coming a month or so after the end of Beijing's second round of missile tests off Taiwan, this Congressional appearance would have been an excellent time and place to give warning to Beijing, yet no clear signals were forthcoming. Lord mentioned a number of Chinese actions that "concerned its neighbors" (i.e., not the United States): its "opaque" defense budget, ambitious military modernization program, sales of missile technology, actions and claims in the South China Sea, and nuclear testing. Last on the list was Taiwan, where Beijing's "two recent military exercises—including missile firings in the vicinity of Taiwan—surely did not contribute to the region's sense of peace and stability." Immediately after listing these concerns of the region, however, Lord asked, "Does all this mean that China is an aggressive power bent on dominating or threatening its neighbors?" and then answered, "In a word, no. China has pursued a policy aimed at developing friendly relations with its neighbors . . . including Taiwan with which it has extensive trade and investments." Although Lord said that the United States was not willing to "acquiesce" in what it saw as "inappropriate behaviors by China," he did not indicate that actions such as the recent missile tests were "inappropriate."

The next—and possibly most critical—U.S.-PRC interaction during the fall of 1995 was the meeting of Jiang Zemin and Bill Clinton on 24 October. The meeting came after China's decision to restore ambassadorial and military ties with the United States, but apparently before the decision to go ahead with the coercive exercises scheduled for early 1996. The Clinton-Jiang summit seems to have been an important influence on China's decision to proceed with the exercises.

Public declarations shortly before the summit suggested the Taiwan issue would dominate the meeting. The day before the meeting, Jiang made clear in a public speech that Taiwan was at the top of China's agenda. Taiwan was a "major issue of principle, at the heart of the three joint communiqués which formed the foundation" of Sino-U.S. relations. The United States had "explicitly acknowledged," Jiang said, that Taiwan was part of China, and China valued the U.S. "pledge" that it would "pursue a one China policy" and maintain only unofficial relations with Taiwan. Jiang noted that when the Taiwan issue was handled properly, Sino-U.S. relations had developed smoothly, but when handled improperly bilateral relations had suffered setbacks.[20] An editorial in *People's Daily* on the day of the summit titled "Realizing the Reunification of the Motherland Is the Lofty Mission of the Chinese People" set the same tone, claiming that Taiwan authorities had not responded positively to Jiang's Eight Points, but continued to advocate "Taiwan independence with a new tactic."[21] Taiwan independence elements would certainly "be put on trial and punished by the people" for their "perverse acts." That harsh public rhetoric, probably intended for public audiences in both China and the United States, seemed to be at variance with the content of the Jiang-Clinton meeting.

The atmosphere of the meeting was apparently cordial.[22] Jiang raised the Taiwan issue, but the U.S. side was glad to see that it did not "dominate the agenda" as it had during the summer of 1995. Clinton apparently reiterated the contents of his 1 August letter to Jiang, including his promise to "respect" Beijing's position that Taiwan is part of China. Discussions covered a wide range of issues including intellectual property rights, China's entry into the World Trade Organization, and nuclear proliferation. Both leaders agreed on the need for Sino-U.S. cooperation. As an MFA spokesman said after the meeting, the two countries "bear great responsibilities for the world's peace and development" and "share broad and important interests. We hope that healthy and steady Sino-U.S. relations can be established on the basis of the three . . . joint communiqués. This is in the fundamental interests of the two countries, and is conducive to safeguarding peace and stability in the Asia-Pacific region and in the world at large."[23] Both sides downplayed the Taiwan issue during the summit talks; although they apparently stated their respective positions on Taiwan, they did not dwell on it, and were happy to spend most of their time discussing other, less emotional issues. Most important perhaps, Clinton apparently did not call to Jiang Zemin's attention the U.S. interest in the peaceful resolution of the Taiwan issue, nor to its "grave concern" under the Taiwan Relations Act with "any threat to the security or the social or economic system of the people on Taiwan."[24] The basic decision to move forward with the early 1996 coercive exercises was apparently made shortly after Jiang's return from his summit with Clinton.[25]

The final high-level U.S.-PRC interaction before Beijing launched its coercive campaign against Taiwan was a mid-November visit by Assistant Secretary of Defense for International Security Affairs Joseph Nye, the first high-level exchange of military officials since May 1995. Nye hoped to reassure PLA leaders that the United States was not attempting to contain China, and desired dialogue and cooperation rather than confrontation.[26] Instead, Taiwan dominated talks. By signaling their intention to resort to military coercion, Chinese leaders tried to probe the probability of U.S. intervention in the upcoming confrontation. Every Chinese who met with Nye's group stressed the Taiwan issue. Their rhetoric was often "trenchant"; there "was no give whatever." They made it clear that the PLA was reviving military plans and operational contingencies toward Taiwan that hadn't been thought about since the 1950s. In extensive closed-door meetings, PLA leaders "subtly explored" how the United States would respond in the event of a military crisis over Taiwan. Nye and his group refused to discuss "contingency planning," saying only, "We stand for peaceful resolution of disputes across the Strait." Any use of force against Taiwan, Nye announced at a press conference in Beijing, "would be a serious mistake."[27] The United States maintained its "long-standing position that the Taiwan issue must not be resolved by force," he told the Chinese leaders. "I also reminded Chinese officials that U.S. domestic law and national security strategy state that instability in the Taiwan Straits could be a threat to U.S. national security interests and that actions that undercut stability hurt long-term prospects for our relations."[28]

Those words constituted the strongest warning delivered before the onset of the PLA's Taiwan campaign. They came too late, for the decision to implement the PLA's Taiwan plans had already been made. It would have taken a very powerful Chinese leader to cancel them and turn back at that point on the basis of Nye's warnings. Moreover, it was not at all clear that U.S. leaders were resolute enough to act quickly and decisively in the event of a cross-Strait confrontation. The words and nonactions of U.S. leaders throughout the latter half of 1995 suggested otherwise.

The State Department's parochial interests helped produce the low-key U.S. response of mid-1995. It perceived that its advice on the visa question had been overridden, and the consequences were much as it had predicted—a sharp deterioration in Sino-American relations. Then it was expected to come in and clean up the mess. This had come about through a Taiwan end-run around the State Department to Congress. Taiwan was well connected with Republican members of Congress and used this to foil the State Department's professional advice. Taiwan, from the State Department's perspective, manipulated U.S. politics. It tried to set U.S. foreign policy and take control out of the hands of those entrusted with it—the State Department itself. Taiwan's actions touched on old institutional memories still alive in the corridors of Foggy Bottom. During the late 1940s the pro-KMT China Lobby and its friends in Congress excoriated the State Department for the "loss of China." Then in the 1950s Chiang Kai-shek tried to entrap the United States in war with China. Now Taiwan's well-heeled representatives in the United States had tried to do something very similar! The United States should let them stew in their own hot water. Perhaps the shock of facing the PLA alone for a while would puncture Taipei's arrogance and make it more manageable. The "Taiwan problem" was to a substantial extent one of keeping an assertive and popular Taiwan from running away with U.S. China policy. It was only as the stakes grew with vastly expanded PLA military pressure against Taiwan in early 1996 that those parochial State

Department views were set aside and a colder, more dispassionate view of U.S. interests taken.

The U.S. failure during mid-1995 to give clear and direct warnings to Beijing over the U.S. interest in a peaceful settlement of the Taiwan problem was also based on a belief that such warnings were unnecessary and would handicap moderate Chinese leaders while further antagonizing more anti-U.S. ones. The U.S. executive branch was confident that China would not endanger its economic development by reckless military action. United States leaders hoped to minimize the impact of the recent shifts in U.S. Taiwan policy, putting the Taiwan issue behind them as quickly as possible. The modifications in Taiwan policy were over and done with. The best course now was believed to be minimization of offense to Beijing, to cause it the least loss of face, to get on with issues on which prospects for cooperation were better. That approach was reasonable, but in retrospect seems to have been flawed. By failing to send clear and firm warnings following the PLA missile demonstrations and hot rhetoric of mid-1995, Washington inadvertently signaled Beijing that the United States would not intervene in a cross-Strait confrontation, at least as long as it did not escalate to a direct attack on Taiwan.

The Pentagon seemed to have favored clearer, less ambiguous signaling to Beijing during the last quarter of 1995. Divergent perspectives of the State and Defense Departments surfaced during September 1995 when two U.S. Air Force officers from the U.S. embassy in Beijing were detained by Chinese authorities in the vicinity of Xiamen, Fujian, and then expelled from China. The PLA was then in the process of redeploying to that region the units that would conduct the 1996 exercises, and U.S. military authorities apparently had dispatched the officers to collect information. The State Department, however, was aghast. Secretary Christopher demanded a probe of the incident, suggesting that those who had authorized the officers' mission were engaged in activities running counter to U.S. policy.[29] In November it was Assistant Secretary of Defense Nye who delivered the clearest warnings to Beijing. Then the *Nimitz* passage in December was made on the authority of CINCPAC—if we believe official statements regarding that transit. While the State Department was preoccupied with the task of soothing China's hurt feelings so that U.S.-PRC relations could get back to normal, the Defense Department remained responsible for preparing for military conflict with foreign powers, for which it needed to collect information. From the Pentagon's perspective, clear signaling would be useful if it led to greater mutual understanding that might make Beijing take stock, thereby reducing the likelihood of military conflict. Anger and bitterness on the Chinese side was an acceptable cost for deterring military conflict. The Pentagon's job was not to minimize tensions in bilateral relations. As the old adage says, "Where you stand depends on where you sit."

Underlying the miscommunication between Washington and Beijing regarding the use of force was another, more basic, U.S. failure, one linked to Taiwan's epocal transition to democracy. Although the U.S. administration made "enlargement" of the area of democracy the centerpiece of its post–Cold War strategy, it gave no warning to Beijing that a military campaign to destabilize Taiwan's new democratic political institutions would be antithetical to U.S. interests. Beijing was left to believe that the only major U.S. interest was "peace" itself, and that as long as Taiwan's new democratic polity was coerced and destabilized by nonbloody means, U.S. interests would not be trampled on.

8 / The December Legislative Yuan Elections

A major object of Beijing's coercive policies was Taiwan's political process, key to which were the elections to Taiwan's Legislative Yuan scheduled for December 1995. These were only the second fully direct, popular election for the Legislative Yuan, the first having been in 1992. They were widely seen in Taiwan as a prelude to Taiwan's first direct election of its president in March 1996. The December 1995 elections thus marked an important step forward in the institutionalization of Taiwan's new democratic processes. The December elections took place in the shadow of Beijing's July–August missile demonstrations and subsequent continuing PLA maneuvers. Beijing's moves influenced the political process, and the election's outcome—the erosion of Lee Teng-hui's position, combined with dramatic gains for the New Party—confirmed to CCP leaders the ability of military coercion to affect Taiwan's electoral process.[1]

Lee Teng-hui's modification of Taipei's traditional "one China" policy and his pragmatic diplomacy of 1993–94 were unpopular among a significant section of the KMT, which viewed Lee's actions as abandoning the principles of Sun Yat-sen, Chiang Kai-shek, and Chiang Ching-kuo and as tantamount to declaring Taiwan's independence. Disagreements over these issues commingled with disputes over power and domestic policy. Lee was moving Taiwan in the direction of a more presidential and less ministerial government. He was also consolidating his political base, edging out people traditionally influential within the Party. Many of these "new outsiders," or members of the "nonmainstream" faction, were first- or second-generation mainlanders. Some in the Party also felt that Lee was autocratic and close-minded—unwilling to alter direction or to heed those beyond his base of loyalists. Others felt there was a pressing need for reform in such areas as corruption and the undue influence of money and criminal elements in politics. In short, the KMT was increasingly fractious.

Even before the May 1995 announcement of Lee's obtaining a visa to visit the United States, there had been a deepening split in the KMT. In April Chiang Kai-shek's son Chiang Wei-kuo addressed a rally commemorating the twentieth anniversary of his father's death. Chiang treated the crowd to a biting denunciation of Lee Teng-hui, accusing him of "stealing Chinese territory by creating a new country on Taiwan." Several days later a member of the KMT Central Committee called on "real KMT members" to join a new anti-Lee caucus to "save and reform" the Party. Lee Teng-hui was a "traitor," he said. The man was expelled from the KMT but refused to depart, saying that he had been elected by the Party rank and file. Efforts to patch over the growing differences between Lee's mainstream and the nonmainstream factions failed.

Many in the nonmainstream group criticized Lee's upcoming visit to the United States. Some noted that the trip was being handled by the Presidential Office rather than the Ministry of Foreign Affairs, and charged this was another example of Lee's ignoring his own top advisors and making decisions in a dictatorial fashion. Others felt that the trip was unnecessarily provocative. Rather than risk confrontation with Beijing, Taiwan's president should attend to pressing domestic problems or, for that matter, facilitate the growing cross-Strait relationship upon which Taiwan's economy increasingly depended. Many feared that Lee's U.S. visit might precipitate a clash with the mainland. A poll taken in June indicated that 38 percent of respondents opposed the trip if it risked military confrontation in the Strait. Only 36 percent supported the visit if it risked confrontation.[2]

Beijing did what it could to exacerbate these fears. On 1 July it accused President Lee of "wrongdoing"—he had "seriously damaged" cross-Strait relations by making his U.S. trip. Xinhua News Agency was even more explicit, saying that China would "use fresh blood and lives" to prevent Taiwan from rejecting unification. The beginning of PLA missile demonstrations and military maneuvers in mid-July gave substance to these threats.

Political divisions deepened in August as the KMT prepared to convene a plenary meeting of the 14th Party Congress. Shortly before that meeting Chen Li-an announced he would seek the presidency as an alternative to Lee Teng-hui. Son of Chen Cheng (one of the KMT's top leaders in the 1950s and 1960s), Chen Li-an had been a member of the KMT for forty-two years, had served as secretary general of the KMT Central Committee for four years, minister of defense for three years, and president of the Control Yuan for two years. Needless to say, his challenge represented deep dissatisfaction with the course of policy under Lee. Chen's open revolt against Lee and his subsequent departure from the KMT was a shock to the Party. It also drew attention to the problems of money politics and corruption—issues upon which Chen focused and which, he charged, the KMT under Lee had neglected.

Party vice chairman Lin Yang-kang, another long time KMT functionary, announced that he too would run for president. Lin had served as president of the Judicial Yuan, mayor of Taipei, governor of Taiwan, minister of interior, and vice premier. The increasingly crowded field of presidential contenders forced Lee to make his own declaration of candidacy. Many in the nonmainstream faction of the KMT immediately opposed Lee's bid. This opposition was given voice by Hau Pei-tsun. Hau had become a hero during his command of the defense of Jinmen in 1958. From 1987 to 1989 he served as chief of the general staff—a position in which he reportedly played an important role in securing military acceptance of Lee Teng-hui's succession to Chiang Ching-kuo after the latter's death in 1987—and from 1990 to 1993 he was premier.[3] Hau symbolized the cohort of mainlander leaders who had dominated military-security affairs during the Chiang years but who had lost influence under the tutelage of Lee. He was deeply opposed to Lee's tinkering with Taiwan's traditional "one China" policy and had repeatedly clashed with him over this issue.[4]

Hau's open rebellion against Lee threatened the mainstream faction's support base among the large and politically coherent military community, which has traditionally been important to the KMT. Retired soldiers and their families number 580,000 out of a total population of 21 million, and this substantial group has often voted as a bloc in support of KMT candidates. Continued loyalty of this critical constituency was threatened both by its skepticism about what many deemed Lee Teng-hui's toying with Taiwan independence and by a steady erosion of the living standards of retired military personnel. Legislators predicted that failure of a KMT effort in late October to pass a bill increasing funding for housing for retired military personnel would halve KMT supporters in districts in which these people lived. As a respected military professional and hero, Hau Pei-tsun was in an excellent position to focus this discontent and co-opt Lee's mainstream support from this important constituency.

Fear of war with Beijing resulting from Lee's policy innovations was an important ingredient in the psychological complex behind the disintegration of the KMT. Beijing did what it could to deepen this fear. Shortly after Lee formally announced his candidacy for president in August, *Renmin ribao* (People's daily) denounced him as a "schemer and double-dealer" who was entirely responsible for the recent deterioration of cross-Strait relations. He was following in the steps of his father, who had proven himself to be a "100 percent traitor" by serving in the Japanese colonial administration of Taiwan.[5] Xinhua added that "to sweep Lee Teng-hui into the trash bin of history is the common historical responsibility of Chinese on both sides of the Taiwan Strait."[6] Beijing's threats were taken quite seriously by many people in Taiwan. *Lianhe bao* (United daily news), one of Taiwan's major newspapers and a strong critic of Lee Teng-hui, declared that Lee's policies had caused "serious public anxiety." "Unless the threat of war is dispelled," the paper said, "economic anxieties will lead to political chaos. By then, Taiwan will have to face an internal crisis whether war breaks out or not."[7]

The hemorrhaging of the KMT continued as the Legislative Yuan campaign unfolded. In September a number of second-generation mainlanders left the KMT to join the New Party. Dozens of KMT members of the Legislative Yuan refused to sign a petition supporting Lee. Legislative candidates began trying to distance themselves from the KMT by avoiding the display of party insignia, avoiding references to Lee, stressing local issues, and so on. Lin Yang-kang and Hau Pei-tsun began openly campaigning for New Party candidates. When criticized by KMT loyalists for this breach of party unity, they responded with a statement declaring that it was Lee Teng-hui who had "betrayed the nation and destroyed the party." Eventually Lin and Hau were expelled from the KMT. Midway through the legislative campaign Chen Li-an registered as a candidate for president, formalizing his opposition to Lee Teng-hui.[8]

In mid-October demonstrations of PLA capabilities vis-à-vis Taiwan resumed with large naval operations along China's Yellow Sea coast north of Taiwan. The exercises involved an amphibious landing against a hostile shore. While PLA aircraft engaged simulated enemy aircraft overhead and while ship-born artillery and missiles bombarded enemy shore defenses, amphibious craft were lowered into the water to carry troops and tanks ashore. Amphibious tanks swam ashore under their own power, while submarine and antisubmarine forces blocked the landing area from enemy naval attack. The exercises were observed by Jiang Zemin and Liu Huaqing together with six other CMC members. To ensure that the message got out, shortly after the exercises Chinese authorities took the unusual move of releasing photographs of the maneuvers to Japanese newspapers.[9]

On 15 November, eight days before the beginning of the formal two-week campaign period prior to the 2 December Legislative Yuan elections, the PLA began a new round of exercises. These were the largest and most complex amphibious maneuvers yet attempted by the PLA. They continued for ten days and involved a simulated invasion of Dongshan Island off the coast of southern Fujian. Unlike the maneuvers the previous month, these were joint service operations planned, commanded, and executed by ground, naval, and air units operating in close support. Two air force divisions of F-7 and F-8 fighters provided air cover. Naval and air forces cleared water obstacles while screening the beachhead area from enemy naval forces. While fire from warships and aircraft pounded enemy shore defenses, amphibious forces landed and established a beachhead. The invasion forces then regrouped and used helicopters and tanks to expand the beachhead, creating conditions for landing a second wave. Enemy counterattacks were beaten off and the enemy-held island was swiftly subdued. Between sixteen thousand and eighteen thousand military personnel participated in the exercise, for which the South China Fleet mobilized two hundred landing craft and one hundred other naval vessels. The exercises had been planned directly by the CMC, with operational planning involving staff officers from all of China's Military Regions.[10]

The November Dongshan exercises were suggestive of an invasion of Taiwan. In a Chinese television report on the exercises underway along the Fujian coast the commentator said the purpose was to "safeguard the nation's sovereignty and territorial integrity." Two days after the conclusion of the exercises, Hong Kong's *Wenhui bao* quoted a research fellow of the Taiwan Research Council in Beijing to the effect that the recent exercises demonstrated the Chinese government's determination to "firmly oppose and contain" Taiwan independence. The exercises were a "most serious warning" to political forces that believed they could "break Taiwan away from China through so-called 'democratic procedures' with the support of foreign forces." If the "Taiwan authorities" tried to achieve Taiwan independence by "placing sovereignty in the hands of the people," then "non-peaceful means [could] be said to be necessary to settle China's reunification issue."[11] Almost everyone in

Taiwan saw the November exercises as a threat directed at Taiwan, warning it against electing proindependence candidates.

The day before the polls opened on 2 December, Beijing announced that it would hold further, even longer military exercises before the March 1996 presidential election. These would include simulated large-scale attacks and bombing runs. The PLA had discovered many blind spots in Taiwan's radar coverage during earlier drills, Beijing's announcement said. These warnings caused the Taipei stock market to fall 120 points—about 2.6 percent of its total value—within a little over a week. The value of the Taiwan dollar also fell as people fearful of war rushed to purchase foreign currencies.[12] Many people recalled the scenario of a best-selling 1994 book depicting an all-out PLA seizure of Taiwan via a swift high-tech assault. The author of that book had warned:

> To avoid having to deal with an elected new government in Taiwan, which will make it more difficult to govern Taiwan after reunification by force, the Chinese Communists should schedule their invasion countdown with the Presidential election day as day zero. On that day the Chinese Communists will announce that, at the request of the compatriots on Taiwan and because of the eruption of internal upheavals on Taiwan and [because] the direct Presidential election are signs of Taiwan independence, troops are being sent to Taiwan to quell the social unrest and to complete the historic reunification of China.[13]

When the results of the 2 December election were tabulated, it was clear that the KMT had suffered significant setbacks, while the New Party emerged as the clear winner. The KMT lost seven Legislative Yuan seats, retaining just eighty-five, or 51.5 percent of all seats, a bare majority. In terms of popular vote, the KMT received only 46 percent. This was the first time it had failed to win a popular majority in a major election, and represented a sharp fall from the 53 percent received in 1993. The New Party, on the other hand, tripled its legislative seats, jumping from seven to twenty-one. This gave the New Party 12 percent of the Legislative Yuan, won with 13 percent of the popular vote—this for a party merely two years old, with little money or organization. As important as the bare statistical tabulation were the broader political implications of the election. The New Party did quite well outside of Taipei, its traditional bastion, and proved it was more than a regional party. It did well in several southern urban areas. It demonstrated a broad appeal to Taiwan's educated and middle classes, proving that it was more than a party representing the 15 percent mainlander population. The KMT emerged from the election demoralized and fragmented.

The DPP drive to become Taiwan's ruling party also suffered a modest setback in the December election. While its representation increased by four seats to a total of fifty-four, or 32.9 percent of the legislature, this was far less than its leaders had hoped for. Party leaders had long predicted that they would win a majority if all of the Legislative Yuan were democratically elected (rather than appointed by the president, as was the case before Taiwan's democratic transition in the earlier 1990s). Moreover, the Party had made impressive gains in the 1992 legislative elections and some of its leaders predicted it would gain power in several years. Juxtaposed to these grand expectations, the DPP's gains in December 1995 were quite modest. The DPP also suffered through the dramatic emergence of the New Party. Taiwan's party system had been transformed from a two- to a three-party system. The DPP could no longer claim that it was the only viable opposition party. To many, the New Party increasingly looked like the most viable opposition.[14]

The basic appeal of the New Party was its stance on the economic, social, and political problems plaguing Taiwan, and the basic problems of the KMT were those associated with its forty-five-year grasp on political power. Ruling parties in democratic countries around the world were voted out of office in the early 1990s because of a series of epochal political and economic transitions, and many of the same forces were at work in Taiwan. Yet one must also recognize that fear of war with the mainland was an important element of the political atmosphere, and that fear was deliberately stimulated by Beijing's actions.

From Beijing's standpoint, the results of the December elections proved most promising. American political scientist John Copper concluded that Beijing's coercive maneuvers probably can be judged to have succeeded, hurting the KMT and the DPP while helping the New Party.[15] There had been little negative reaction from other countries. Even the United States had responded only in a tardy and ambiguous fashion.

9 / The Confrontation

Cina's probing of U.S. intentions during Assistant Secretary of Defense Nye's visit in November 1995 and the increasingly apparent link between PLA pressure and Taiwan's electoral process led to a rethinking in some quarters of Washington. On 12 December, shortly after his return to the United States, Nye addressed the Asia Society in Seattle. He stressed the U.S. interest in peace and stability in the Taiwan Strait, saying that this had been one of two main areas of disagreement during his recent discussions with Chinese leaders. Pressed during the question-and-answer session about the U.S. response to Chinese probing on the issue of possible use of force against Taiwan, Nye stressed the imponderable nature and dangers of escalation inherent in such a situation. "Nobody knows" how the United States would respond to cross-Strait conflict, Nye said. "Therefore actions which escalate risks in the Taiwan Strait, are actions which pose an enormous risk of some larger thing, of which we don't know the answer." The dangers of escalation on such an issue "which is taken very seriously by both sides, could be catastrophic."[1] As ambiguous as his words were, they constituted the first high-level and public warning to Beijing during the mounting crisis that the U.S. might intervene in a cross-Strait war.

Nye's words were underlined on 19 December when the nuclear-powered aircraft carrier USS *Nimitz* transited the Taiwan Strait on its way from Japan to the Persian Gulf area. This was the first time in seventeen years that a U.S. carrier had passed through the Strait. The circumstances of the *Nimitz*'s passage left open to question, however, whether the highest level of U.S. leadership had endorsed, or indeed even knew about, the *Nimitz*'s passage. When the transit was announced six weeks later, it was reported to have been authorized by CINCPAC headquarters in Honolulu.[2] If the U.S. president didn't authorize the *Nimitz*'s passage, if those in charge at CINCPAC or the Pentagon didn't want to let him know what they were doing—and certainly CINCPAC and the Pentagon understood the significance of such an action—would that president be likely to approve similar deployments in more risky situations? And if the president knew about the *Nimitz*'s planned route but didn't want to publicly associate himself with it, would he be bold enough to order far more risky action in the near future? If an action such as the *Nimitz*'s passage had taken place in late August, shortly after the conclusion of the PLA's second round of exercises, and been accompanied by demonstrations of presidential support and authoritative statements reiterating the interest of the United States in the peaceful resolution of the Taiwan issue by the Chinese themselves, the United States would have sent a much clearer signal to Beijing. The confrontation of 1996 might have been avoided. On the other hand, it might still have occurred but escalated to an even higher level of confrontation.

The *Nimitz*'s passage through the Strait was almost certainly observed by PLA intelligence, and the CMC understood the threat implicit in this movement. Rather than back down before U.S. threats, China upped the ante. Former assistant secretary of defense Chas W. Freeman, in China for talks with senior Chinese officials at the end of 1995, was told that China was planning a missile attack against Taiwan during the week following the presidential election there. One missile per day would be launched for thirty days. Chinese officials also subtly raised the question of possible Chinese use of nuclear weapons against the United States in a war over Taiwan. Freeman returned to the United States and reported to Clinton's National Security Advisor Anthony Lake on 4 January.[3]

A meeting of China specialists from inside and outside the government was convened under Lake's auspices in mid-January. The meeting focused on Beijing's increasingly belligerent rhetoric and the multiple reports of planned military action against Taiwan appearing in the Hong Kong and foreign press. The mid-January meeting substantially increased government awareness of and concern over the possibility of Chinese military action against Taiwan. At the end of January the White House announced the *Nimitz*'s passage six weeks earlier.

Mounting congressional pressure began pushing administration policy in the direction of greater firmness. The PLA exercises during the last quarter of 1995 prompted requests that the president report to Congress on Taiwan's security pursuant to his obligations under the Taiwan Relations Act. Clinton replied that since the purpose of the Chinese exercises was to "send a political message to Taiwan and the United States, and not to prepare for imminent military action against Taiwan," he was not required to report to Congress.[4] In spite of such reassurances, congressional criticism continued to mount. A Sense of the Congress resolution was introduced on 31 January calling on the president to condemn China's military intimidation of Taiwan and to report to Congress on how the United States could defend Taiwan against a Chinese ballistic missile attack. The Republican Policy Committee in the House of Representatives produced a paper highly critical of the administration's ambiguous policy, charging that the administration had given China "a green light to bully Taiwan." Finally, the East Asian and Pacific Affairs Subcommittee of the Senate Foreign Relations Committee under its chairman, Republican senator Craig Thomas from Wyoming, scheduled hearings on Taiwan's security to begin 7 February.[5]

Congressional pressure also greatly increased the costs to Clinton of any miscalculation. The administration had bet that China would not actually attack Taiwan and would not shed blood in its military actions. If this calculation turned out to be wrong, the fact that congressional critics had long been calling for a clearer and firmer policy would create an instant chorus of "We told you so." Moreover, the track record of warnings by Clinton's congressional critics would create a persuasive "proof" of congressional farsightedness. If the administration's calculation was wrong and Beijing attacked Taiwan-held territories, ships, or airplanes, Clinton would be in a lose-lose situation. If he then ordered U.S. military intervention, regardless of its ultimate success, its proximate cause would be seen as the prior passivity and ambiguity of the administration. If the situation escalated to a U.S.-Chinese military clash, administration passivity might be deemed equivalent to the Truman administration's famous miscue of January 1950 when Secretary of State Dean Acheson signaled Kim Il-sung, Stalin, and Mao Zedong that the United States would not intervene to block an attack on South Korea. If, on the other hand, the Clinton administration chose not to intervene after a PLA attack on Taiwan, the consequence would be a dramatic diminution of Taiwan's security. In this case, administration ineptness might be compared to Jimmy Carter's bungled attempt to rescue hostages from the Tehran embassy in the spring of 1980. Whether the United States intervened or remained passive following a PLA attack against Taiwan's possessions, the cost of prior ambiguity would be high. The Taiwan issue could become a major issue during the 1996 U.S. presidential campaign. A major defeat over Taiwan might even revitalize Clinton's now-frayed Republican opposition, possibly costing him reelection. Calculations having to do with both domestic politics and the increasingly ominous signals coming out of Beijing dictated greater clarity and firmness.

Congress and the executive branch also differed regarding the importance of Taiwan's democratization in defining U.S. interests regarding Taiwan. The State Department's avoidance of comment on Taiwan's democratic transition was studied. An April 1995 report by Assistant Secretary of State for Democracy, Human Rights, and Labor John Shattuck on "Democracy in Asia" conspicuously avoided even a mention of Taiwan. While discussing positive and negative developments in virtually all the countries of Asia (Mongolia, Burma, North and South Korea, Pakistan, India, China, Indonesia, Cambodia, Vietnam, Malaysia, Afghanistan, Sri Lanka, Japan, and the Philippines) and at least two regions (East Timor and Hong Kong), the report did not mention Taiwan.[6] This was in spite of the rapid and substantial democratization of Taiwan during the 1990s, and in spite of Shattuck's professing that "support for democracy and human rights in this dynamic region is a key element of U.S. policy for the region." The most likely explanation of this omission is that State Department officials felt that raising the Taiwan issue would anger Beijing. Many in Congress felt that the State Department's self-censorship contributed to Beijing's misperception of U.S. policy.

Just prior to the Senate's 7 February hearings on Taiwan's security, administration spokesmen began to find opportunities to express their concern with that issue. Asked by reporters on 6 February how the United States would respond if Taiwan were attacked, Secretary of Defense Perry referred to the TRA's statement that such an eventuality would be of "grave concern" to the United States. He did not see an "imminent danger," Perry said, but he was "concerned" about Chinese military maneuvers aimed "in not so subtle ways to threaten Taiwan, to try to influence their election."[7]

On 4 February PLA deployments for the 1996 exercises began. Troops and air forces from across China began redeploying to the Nanjing War Zone, which had been set up in fall 1995. Elements from all three of the PLA-Navy fleets were activated under the new Nanjing command. This was the first time a PLA-Navy exercise had involved elements of all three fleets. Air defense units equipped with SA-10B missiles were also moved to the exercise area.[8] According to Japan's defense agency, by the beginning of March 150,000 troops had been concentrated for the upcoming exercises. About three hundred aircraft, including the PLA's recently acquired Russian Su-27 air superiority fighters, were moved to airfields within striking range of Taiwan.[9] The force composition of the two PLA concentrations—on the Dongshan-Nan'ao Islands area at the southern end of the Strait and Haitan Island at the northern end—reflected their assigned missions dealing with achievement of air and sea superiority and amphibious assault. Aircraft included fighters for air-to-air combat and bombers and attack aircraft for air-to-surface attack in support of fleet operations. Naval ships included destroyers, frigates, patrol craft, and nuclear and diesel submarines. A putative invasion force was concentrated in the north. Elements of eight infantry divisions were assembled along with troop transports, landing craft, mine sweepers, and the necessary air and naval escorts.[10]

Insight into the concept underlying the exercises was provided by the well-connected Hong Kong journal *Guang jiao jing* (Wide angle) in December 1995. For a long time Taiwan's defense strategy had concentrated on ground forces, neglecting air forces and especially naval forces, the magazine reported. Belated efforts to strengthen air and naval forces were underway, but probably would not achieve much success before the end of the century. The PLA objective was therefore to seize control over the air and sea approaches to Taiwan while using missiles to paralyze ports, nuclear power plants, transportation hubs, command-control-and-communication centers, airports, and radar stations. Multiple waves of swift attacks would then be launched at enemy-held shores. Helicopters, parachutes, and fast small boats would deliver crack troops in swift three-dimensional attacks. Heavy air and naval bombardment would open the way for assault forces in modern hover craft and landing craft. Once a beachhead had been secured, a second wave of troops would be ferried over using civilian vessels. Extensive air, artillery, and armor support would then be used for a three-dimensional, in-depth assault to pacify the enemy-held area.[11] The exercises were nothing less than a simulation of an all-out invasion of Taiwan. According to Hong Kong's *Ming bao,* air and sea approaches to Keelung were the hypothetical targets of the northern PLA force, while Kaohsiung was the southern target. The PLA reportedly anticipated sacrifice of five of its aircraft to every enemy aircraft downed. It would prevail over Taiwan's forces through attrition.[12]

On 5 March Xinhua announced the first wave of exercises—a series of missile exercises to run from 8 to 15 March, beginning just after the start of the three-week campaign period preceeding Taiwan's 23 March presidential election. The two designated target areas, relatively small squares thirty-two miles from Taiwan's southwest coast and only twenty-two miles from the northeast coast, were more than fifty miles closer to

Taiwan than those used in the July–August 1995 tests. As illustrated by Map 1, the major commercial harbor of Kaohsiung and naval base of Tsuoying lay just east of one test, while the harbor of Keelung and naval base at Su'ao lay just west of the other. Chinese commentary pointed out that these were "exercises"; the mid-1995 firings had been "tests." Exercises involved training in operational usage, whereas tests merely proved the capability of a particular weapon system. The Xinhua announcement of the new exercises noted that it came on the seventeenth anniversary of the PLA's victorious withdrawal from Vietnam after "teaching it a lesson" in 1979.[13] The day Xinhua announced the upcoming first wave of exercises, the MFA warned that if outside powers intervened, "The Chinese government will not sit by watching with folded arms."[14] On 8 March three M-9 short-range ballistic missiles (SRBM) were fired from the mountainous region of western Fujian into the southern and northern closure areas. Another was fired into the southern area on 13 March.[15]

The 8–15 March first-wave exercises crossed the threshold precipitating U.S. intervention. There could be no mistake regarding their purpose: intimidation of Taiwan's electorate as they went about electing their president. From the U.S. administration's perspective, the key question was, Where will the PLA stop? A campaign of media leaks via the Hong Kong and foreign press over the preceding several months suggested that China was preparing to actually strike against Taiwan or its outlying possessions. The frequency and detail of these reports implied a degree of high-level authorization. Were the leaks merely part of Beijing's psychological war against Taipei? Or were they also trial balloons testing U.S. resolve and willingness to intervene? What was the best way to halt an escalation of pressure against Taiwan that might, finally, culminate in the direct application of military force? Would not clear and substantial U.S. military intervention serve that purpose? Over the previous eight months the United States, with the significant exception of the mid-December *Nimitz* passage, had followed a policy of nonintervention while downplaying the Taiwan issue and minimizing the threat to Taiwan. Did Beijing still misread this policy? In any case, would not continued nonintervention in the face of Beijing's new provocation merely encourage even greater Chinese boldness?

On the evening of 7 March Anthony Lake, Warren Christopher, and William Perry hosted a dinner for visiting Chinese dignitaries. Over their meal Perry communicated "very clearly and very unequivocally" the U.S. belief that the announced missile firings were "reckless." If any of the missiles malfunctioned they could fall in populated areas. Moreover, with target areas so close to Taiwan, the firings "could only be viewed as an act of coercion." The next day Perry told the press that a battle group based upon the aircraft carrier USS *Independence* had been deployed to within "a few hundred miles" of Taiwan.[16] A few days later the Pentagon said that the battle group included the destroyers *Hewitt* and *O'Brien*, the cruiser *Bunker Hill*, and the frigate *McClusky*. The main body of the battle group remained in international waters northeast of Taiwan, while the *Bunker Hill* took up a position south of Taiwan.[17] The *Bunker Hill* had the capability to track and collect information on the M-9 flights. United States Air Force RC-135 reconnaissance aircraft also apparently monitored the technical data transmissions from the M-9s to Chinese ground stations tracking the flights.[18]

Beijing was not deterred by Perry's warnings and U.S. military movements. On 9 March, the day after the disclosure of the *Independence* deployment, Xinhua announced a second wave of PLA exercises off Taiwan. These were to be live-fire exercises by air, land, and naval forces over nine days between 12 and 20 March in a large diamond-shaped area of seventeen thousand square kilometers off the coast of southern Fujian. As the CCP-controlled Hong Kong newspaper *Wenhui bao* pointed out, the exercise area was roughly the shape and about half the size of Taiwan. It came close to the midline of the Taiwan Strait, a line that was psychologically important for people on Taiwan. The same newspaper carried a speech by CMC vice chair and defense minister Chi Haotian delivered on 8 March, the day the first wave of exercises began, stressing the need to reunify Taiwan and China. "Without any doubt" such reunification would be realized, Chi said. "Lee Teng-hui and his gang" were "facing a grim situation" because of their attempts to "split China." While peaceful reunification was "of course" the best choice, China would "never tolerate any attempts to split our country using all kinds of schemes." Chi quoted CCP army founder Zhu De to that effect: "As long as Taiwan is not *liberated,* the Chinese people's historical humiliation is not washed away; as long as the motherland is not reunited, our people's armed forces responsibility is not fulfilled."[19] This was the first time in many years that a top Chinese leader had spoken openly of the "liberation" of Taiwan.

After the announcement of the PLA's second wave of exercises but before maneuvers had actually begun, the United States issued a further warning. Speaking on the television program *Meet the Press* the morning of 10 March, Secretary of State Christopher explained that "part" of the U.S. "one-China policy" was Beijing's "commitment" to "deal peacefully with the issue of Taiwan, not to solve that issue by force." What China had done in "the last several weeks," Christopher said, had "caused some questions about whether or not they intend to do that." China's actions were "reckless," "risky," and "smacked of intimidation and coercion." The situation was "of great concern" to the United States. "We've made it quite clear to the Chinese that if they try to resolve this problem through force rather than through peace, that will be a grave matter with us. We've made it as clear as we possibly can to them, because we don't want any miscalculation on their part." There would be "grave consequences" if China tried to resolve the Taiwan issue by force. "We have real interests in Taiwan, and I don't want the Chinese to misunderstand about that."[20]

The day after Christopher's statement the Pentagon announced that a second aircraft-carrier battle group, headed by the USS *Nimitz*, had been ordered east from the Arabian Sea to join the *Independence* off Taiwan.[21] This battle group included the cruiser *Port Royal*, the destroyers *Callaghan* and *Olendorf*, the frigate *Ford*, the submarine *Portsmouth*, and two replenishment ships underway, the *Willamette* and the *Shasta*. According to the Pentagon, the purpose of those deployments was to "make sure there is no miscalculation on the part of the Chinese as to our interest in that area" and to "reassure our friends in the region that we will maintain an interest in both the peace and the stability in that region." The Pentagon spokesman declined to go into particulars of how the United States would respond to a Chinese attack on Taiwan other than to say that such a move would be of "grave concern" to the United States.[22]

Deployment of a second battle group was in some ways more important than deployment of the first. One aircraft carrier could be seen as a symbol, a demonstration, or political theater. Two represented a more real capability. The decision on the second deployment was apparently related to U.S. uncertainty regarding PRC intentions.

Top advisors of U.S. leaders prepared a list of escalating moves the PLA might take before the threshold of violent bloodshed was crossed. Beijing could move its missile closure areas even closer to Taiwan, effectively shutting several ports to commercial traffic. Even if the chance of a vessel's being hit by an M-9 warhead was extremely small, foreign shipping companies would not want to take the risk. Beijing also had a number of ways in which to interfere with commercial air traffic in and out of Taiwan. Washington did not know how far Beijing intended to go with such additional moves. If the United States waited until Beijing crossed, or at least came closer to, the threshold of violence, this might allow nonbloody coercion to substantially disrupt Taiwan's electoral process. Passivity on the part of the United States would have an adverse impact on its allies, especially Japan, and could adversely affect public opinion in a U.S. presidential election year.

In Beijing some people believed there was no reason for the United States to be uncertain of what China intended to do. Through its limited force deployments to the Strait region, China had signaled that it did not intend to actually attack Taiwan. While fire-breathing propaganda might issue from the CCP's Hong Kong media, China had not deployed the material means to effect an actual invasion. An invasion would require far more troops, aircraft, and, especially, civilian vessels to ferry troops than were mobilized for the March 1996 exercises. Chinese analysts believed that U.S. leaders should know from intelligence gathered by U.S. satellite reconnaissance that Chinese intentions were limited to influencing Taiwan's leaders psychologically. Distinction between China's propaganda and real capabilities should show that the PLA did not intend to actually attack Taiwan. When, in spite of this knowledge, the United States intervened, a second layer was added to the Chinese feeling of betrayal. As a result of high-level interactions in mid-1995, Chinese leaders had concluded that the United States would probably stay out of a Chinese effort to discipline Taipei. Yet Washington had now chosen to intervene.

Beijing's MFA strongly condemned the U.S. decision to deploy carrier battle groups as "unwise" and warned the United States to "be careful not to send a wrong message" to Taiwan. If the Taiwan authorities interpreted the U.S. carrier deployments as "instigation and support" for Taiwan independence, the situation would become "very dangerous" (*hen weixian de*).[23] Those words were quite moderate in tone and substance. Substantively, they implied that the U.S. deployments were not, in and of themselves, "instigation and support" for Taiwan independence, which the Chinese for some time had asserted was precisely the true purpose of U.S. policy. Were that found to be the U.S. objective in sending aircraft carriers, the only proper response would be further escalation in a tit-for-tat struggle against the United States. Moreover, implicit in the MFA's words was a request for U.S. cooperation in dealing with the Taiwan issue. In effect the MFA was trying to defuse the escalating confrontation. More bellicose statements issued from sources under the control of the CCP's ideological apparatus. New China News Agency charged that the U.S. carrier deployments "openly provoked China." The United States was "playing with fire." These actions demonstrated that the United States was the "biggest supporter and behind-the-scenes boss of Lee Teng-hui's line" of "hidden Taiwan independence."[24]

The second wave of PLA exercises began on 12 March as planned. This was the day after Washington had announced deployment of the second carrier battle group. Over seven days between 12 and 20 March fifty warships, including the cream of all three PLA-Navy fleets, practiced the seizure of air and sea superiority in the southern end of the Strait.[25] China's newly acquired Su-27 air superiority fighters exercised in the vicinity of Dongshan and Nan'ao Islands. Guided missile destroyers, escort ships, patrol combatants, patrol craft, support ships, and nuclear attack and diesel submarines, as well as fighters and bombers, practiced antisurface, antisubmarine, air defense, and naval gunfire support operations.[26] Among the vessels deployed was the PLA's new 039 Song–class attack submarine first launched in May 1994, and two Kilo-class attack submarines recently purchased from Russia. Scientific survey ships were pressed into duty to conduct electronic reconnaissance tasks—a practice not common in previous PLA-Navy exercises. The exercises emphasized close coordination among sea, air, and submarine forces amid electronic warfare. Chinese military sources believed that in numbers of service arms and weapon types employed, the degree of difficulty and complexity of coordination, and the intensity and realism of the operations, the second wave of exercises set a new standard for the PLA.[27]

On 15 March, four days after the United States announced deployment of a second carrier battle group and three days into the second wave of exercises, Xinhua announced a third wave to begin on 18 March and end on 25 March, two days after Taiwan's presidential election. The exercise area, six thousand square kilometers around Haitan Island off Fujian's coast at the northern end of the Strait,[28] reportedly was selected because of the similarity of its topography to that of Taiwan.[29] The scenario would involve seizure of a large hostile-held island by forces inserted by surface amphibious craft, helicopter, and parachute. Once the exercises were underway it was reported that they involved large-scale and complex coordination of land, air, and naval forces operating in close support. "More than thirty thousand" troops practiced swift seizure of air and sea approaches to designated landing beaches, loading and transport of forces to assigned assault zones, and landing of the first wave with combined amphibious, helicopter, and parachute assault. Once ashore, assault units broke through and penetrated enemy defensive positions. Meanwhile, PLA ships and warplanes screened the assault zones, engaging enemy planes and ships that broke through the protective screen. Destroyers, frigates, and escort vessels engaged in "electronic confrontation" with enemy ships and planes, while providing supportive fire for the assaulting ground force. Mine sweepers and antisubmarine vessels cleared mines and other underwater obstacles. When solid obstacles were encountered they were fired upon by antisubmarine warfare (ASW) vessels with five-tube antisubmarine rocket launchers. This was the first time this tactic was publicly revealed. Overhead PLA fighters engaged enemy fighters trying to disrupt the landing, while other aircraft provided close air support for the assault force.[30]

The PLA employed in the third-wave exercises many of the modern-style amphibious craft it had acquired during the 1980s. These transported the main assault force and reequipped the beachheads. PLA Marine Corps assault units moved ashore in sophisticated hover craft and type-73 tracked amphibious assault vehicles. The PLA also used the exercises to test its capacity for emergency wartime mobilization of civilian vessels. These vessels were charged with ferrying in reserve and militia units, allowing the main force of crack troops to continue their rapid drive forward. Conscripted civilian vessels were employed in a number of innovative fashions. Several cargo ships were fitted with rocket-firing vehicles and used as temporary artillery platforms.[31]

United States sources conclude that inclement weather forced the cancellation of most of the planned third-wave exercises.[32] Sources close to the PLA acknowledge interference by "powerful winds and huge waves, and poor visibility in the air," but assert that most of the operations were nonetheless carried out. These sources compare the situation to "exercises being conducted during a typhoon"—a feat difficult to imagine.[33] It is thus unclear what portion of the maneuvers, scheduled over eight days, were actually carried out. At a minimum, the PLA learned the dependency of amphibious operations upon the weather, while Taiwan learned that the PLA was thinking seriously about its amphibious capabilities.

The initiation of a second and then a third wave of exercises in the face of deployment of two U.S. battle groups demonstrated that China would not be intimidated by Washington. The day before the third wave of exercises was scheduled to begin, Premier Li Peng delivered a warning to the United States. The U.S. show of force in the Taiwan Strait was not only futile, but would further complicate the situation, Li said. "If someone threatened the use of force against China, the outcome has already been proven by past experience. This will not bring about any beneficial result."[34] Li did not, however, reiterate China's refusal to renounce the use of force against Taiwan. While planning for the third wave had been underway for months, it is certain that those plans were reviewed after Washington's 11 March announcement of carrier deployment. The decision was made to continue implementation of the plans as scheduled. China would not be cowed by U.S. gunboat diplomacy. As a *Wenhui bao* editorial said on 20 March:

> By dispatching an aircraft carrier . . . the United States is just trying to test the will and nerves of the Chinese people. If China gives the impression of weakness, the United States and the Taiwan independence forces will be insatiable. China's prompt announcement [of a third wave] shows that it did not hesitate just because the USS *Nimitz* announced it would sail into the Taiwan Strait.[35]

The day after the deployment of the second U.S. battle group was announced, an editorial in *Dagong bao* warned:

> Here it is necessary to remind certain Americans: Do not forget the lessons you learned from the battlefields in Korea and Vietnam. Do not put the interests and even lives of American people at stake. . . . Whoever dares to meddle in, or even invade, Taiwan, the Chinese people will fight them to the end until their final victory.[36]

The next day reporters from the same paper interviewed PLA generals attending the National People's Congress (NPC) session in Beijing, who stated that they did not "expect a war," but "if someone interferes and invades our territory they will certainly repent."[37] A team of staff reporters for *Wenhui bao* interviewed generals who had attended a People's Political Consultative Conference meeting in Beijing and conveyed their views. The generals announced that the PLA was "fully able to handle modern high-tech warfare" and "there is no question about its ability to cope with all possible situations in the Taiwan Strait."[38] The article quoted the former deputy commander of the Chengdu Military Region to the effect that U.S. actions indicated that the United States intended to interfere in China's internal affairs, and that when this occurred the PLA would "definitely not sit idly by and remain indifferent." The political commissar of the Chengdu Military Region warned, "China has dealt with the United States on more than one or two occasions. What was the outcome? The United States was defeated on every occasion." A "special article" in the same issue of *Wenhui bao* raised the possibility of a general war between China and the United States:

> [Have] U.S. politicians made preparations for a showdown with the 1.2 billion Chinese people in terms of global strategy? Do they really want to see a war break out in East Asia? Do they really want something like the situation in the early 1950s in which China and other countries joined hands to resist the United States? Do the American people really want to let their children shed their blood for the sake of the dream of a handful of Taiwan independence elements to "found a country"?[39]

An editorial in the same issue suggested that China would win a protracted war with the United States. Despite the fact that the United States was "fierce in appearance," it did not dare "to confront China with toughness." In Somalia, Bosnia, and Chechnya, the United States "hesitated to advance for fear of losing the lives of U.S. servicemen. Former president Jimmy Carter took military action to rescue the hostages in Iran," met failure, and "eventually lost his presidency." Another *Wenhui bao* article discussed how the PLA might go about "dealing a head-on blow" to U.S. carriers. While U.S. aircraft might be superior, the PLA had thousands of aircraft, including "hundreds" of advanced aircraft such as the Su-27. Moreover, it had many missiles, torpedoes, and cannons fired from the shore; and ships and submarines. Aircraft carriers were, after all, big targets creating large magnetic and hydraulic pressure signals, and strong radar and acoustic signatures. The PLA was fully prepared to sink these vulnerable ships if they "rashly create trouble in the Taiwan Strait."[40]

The fact that this belligerent rhetoric came from the Hong Kong Communist press made it unofficial and less authoritative, and put some distance between those fighting words and the PRC government. Official government statements avoided such strident rhetoric; statements that came from the MFA were even more restrained. China's Hong Kong papers functioned under the supervision of the CCP's ideological apparatus, whose functionaries tended towards hard-line positions. We should not, however, dismiss entirely those rhetorical blasts from Hong Kong. Even greater distance could have been created by leaking relevant material to Hong Kong's non-China press, as had been done with the reports of planned military actions against Taiwan during late 1995 and early 1996. *Wenhui bao* and *Dagong bao* have long been recognized as quasi-official PRC mouthpieces. Special articles and editorials threatening military action against the United States under the tense conditions that existed in mid-March certainly were approved by higher-level Party authorities. The emphasis of those newspapers on military matters and the issue of threats must generally have been approved at the highest level in Beijing. Moreover, this rhetoric dovetailed with Li Peng's stern warning of 17 March. Beijing was sending different sets of signals with differently nuanced messages. The message of the signals emanating from Hong Kong was that China would not shrink from war with the United States.

In contrast to this fire-breathing rhetoric, China's military movements during the confrontation were carefully nonprovocative. The PLA did not fill the Strait with air superiority fighters. It did not simulate massed strikes by large numbers of precision attack aircraft. Overall, air participation in the March exercises was moderate. The PLA did not mass the large armada of warships and civilian vessels necessary for a genuine assault on Taiwan. Its ships and planes did not cover the approaches to Taiwan or approach U.S. ships in the area.[41] Nor did PLA radar lock on to U.S. warships and planes in a fashion suggesting possible target acquisition.

A contrast with the October 1994 Sino-U.S. naval confrontation in the Yellow Sea is illustrative. In that instance the PLA dispatched a nuclear attack submarine to intercept a U.S. battle group centered around the carrier *Kitty Hawk* and including a nuclear-powered cruiser and destroyer, an ASW destroyer, a frigate, and an escort vessel. After the PLA sub encountered the U.S. fleet in the seas between the Korean and Shandong Peninsulas, it surveilled the flotilla for several days in spite of continual monitoring by ASW aircraft from the *Kitty Hawk*. Two days into the stand-off the PLA dispatched two F-7 fighters to support its sub. Because of the distance from air bases the F-7s remained at the scene for only a brief period. The lone PLA sub then continued to dog the U.S. battle group until it left the area.[42] The CMC would easily have ordered moves such as these had it wished to convey an increased level of threat to American forces during the March 1996 confrontation. That it did not do so indicated a decision not to escalate the confrontation.

The United States also acted in a way that minimized escalation. Its ships kept out of the Strait, both because of limited maneuverability and to avoid provoking Beijing. The U.S. battle groups kept a good distance from the entrances to the Strait and from Taiwan itself.

While both sides acted with caution, it would be wrong to conclude that the 1996 confrontation was not genuinely dangerous. China and the United States were locked into an escalating spiral, with each viewing the actions of the other as threatening and believing that failure to respond firmly would only further embolden the other. For both sides the perceived stakes were high. Both were intensely aware of possible loss of credibility if they appeared to back down before the assertive moves of the other. Major domestic considerations limited flexibility and mandated toughness for both. This situation could have led to a war that neither side initially wanted or intended.

10 / Were China's Leaders
Surprised by U.S. Intervention?

The question of whether China's leaders were surprised by the U.S. decision to deploy two battle groups off Taiwan is important, as it touches directly on the question of whether China miscalculated. That in turn tells us about the nature of Chinese elite perceptions of the world and about China's decision-making processes. Most important of all, it tells us about the risks inherent in confrontations such as that of 1996, which threaten to become a permanent fixture of post–Cold War Sino-U.S. relations. If China's leaders were surprised by U.S. actions, we must estimate much more highly the dangers of gross miscalculation that might have led to war.

Let me begin by reviewing the answer to this problem developed in several preceding chapters. China's leaders had concluded by November 1995 that the United States probably would not intervene and approved the exercises of early 1996 on the basis of that assumption. United States signaling in December then prompted a reappraisal of that assumption in January 1996. Intervention by the United States was judged more likely, perhaps even probable, but the exercises continued as scheduled. The U.S. reaction was expected to be largely symbolic and minimal. When that turned out not to be the case, China's leaders, or at least many of them, were indeed surprised. Powerful cognitive and political forces probably prevented full recognition of the implication of this miscalculation in China.

Chinese leaders were probably divided over whether the United States would intervene in the upcoming campaign to intimidate Taiwan through military means, and over whether that intervention would be quick and forceful enough to make a significant difference. Their surprise when the United States finally did intervene suggests that the mainstream Chinese point of view held that the United States would stay out or, at least, would not intervene decisively. A minority point of view was that the United States would probably intervene in a decisive and effective fashion. Some who stressed the likelihood of U.S. intervention were also those who had emphasized the domestic dynamics (and not a grand anti-China strategy) driving U.S. policy on Taiwan. This set of arguments, easily characterized as unpatriotic and weak, was politically difficult to make in the context of 1995 and 1996 Beijing. Some hard-liners also believed that the United States would probably intervene. Since they thought that the United States was in fact following a covert containment policy and that U.S. professions to the contrary were insincere, it followed that once the PLA took decisive action against Taiwan, U.S. intervention would follow. From that perspective, adopting a tough policy toward Taiwan while Washington professed to desire a strong China and to "respect" China's sovereignty over Taiwan was a good way to test U.S. intentions. Forcing the United States to act would expose the true containment essence of U.S. policy.

The proponents of military action against Taiwan pointed to the fact that during the high-level Sino-U.S. interactions during 1995, the U.S. side gave only very weak and ambiguous warnings against Chinese use of military force against Taiwan. This was in spite of China's provocative missile tests of July and August 1995, and its militant rhetoric about the need to speed up the reunification of Taiwan with the PRC. It seemed that any action short of outright war would be tolerated by Washington.

During the summer of 1995, an extensive discussion of the probability of U.S. intervention was underway in Beijing. A number of China's America watchers, in China and in the United States, were asked to write papers or participate in workshops addressing that issue.[1] A variety of views were presented in those discussions. The dominant opinion seemed to be that the U.S. was not likely to intervene, at least not in a prompt and effective fashion. An article by Wang Fei-ling represented this point of view. Appearing first as an invited piece in Hong Kong's *Mingbao Monthly,* it was republished in the "internal" (*neibu,* restricted circulation) Chinese journal *Gang tai ao wenxian* (Documents from Hong Kong, Taiwan, and Macau), which is distributed nationwide to some nine million cadre above the county level. Such wide circulation would have been unlikely without high-level party authorities' condonement of the general message of the piece. Wang Fei-ling had lived in the United States for many years and taught for a year at the U.S. Military Academy at West Point. His views were thus probably deemed especially well informed in Chinese policy circles.[2]

Wang's piece marshaled dozens of arguments to demonstrate that the

United States would not intervene directly in a cross-Strait war. Wang quoted U.S. military officers as feeling that such a war was "unlikely, unnecessary, not worthwhile, and most unfortunate," and as believing that Taiwan had adequate strength to defend itself. "One can infer from this," he concluded, "that if war in the Taiwan Strait appears likely, the United States will undertake diplomatic activity . . . to prevent the outbreak of war in order to avoid putting itself in a very difficult situation." If war actually broke out in spite of U.S. efforts to prevent it, Washington would probably use "indirect military intervention" to assist Taiwan. It might supply advanced weapons and electronic intelligence to Taiwan, perhaps even going so far as to send technical advisors to help in operating those systems. The United States would also use political and economic measures to help Taiwan. It might issue declarations and increase its military presence in the Western Pacific. It would, however, "abstain from any military intervention." If the United States tried to take Taiwan under the protection of its air and naval strength, perhaps by reflagging Taiwan's commercial vessels with the U.S. flag, as it had done for Kuwait during the Iraq-Iran war, it would encounter difficulties. Domestic opinion in the United States would make such an approach unsustainable for a long period. The PLA's abundant missiles would pose a real threat to U.S. carriers, the sinking of one of which "would be a very big blow to U.S. resolve." The United States might be tempted to protect its carriers by striking against the mainland missile bases, but that was unlikely since Chinese nuclear rockets now covered "half the United States." Wang also offered practical advice about ways to further reduce the likelihood of U.S. intervention. A large-scale conventional attack resulting in heavy civilian casualties would increase the likelihood of U.S. intervention. But if Beijing used "civilized" means to put increasing pressure on Taiwan's sea lines of communication, "then the probability of U.S. military intervention [would not be] great."

Other bits of evidence pointed in the same direction. Several fairly high-level Chinese civilian and military officials interviewed by this author in the weeks after the March confrontation confessed to being surprised by U.S. military deployments; only one PLA officer insisted otherwise. Similarly, a Chinese-born American with many years of residence in the United States—who is a high-level executive in a major U.S. corporation and who is heavily involved in Sino-U.S. business transactions with frequent travel to China—was also convinced that the United States would not intervene militarily on Taiwan's behalf. The threat to

extensive U.S. economic interests in China if the United States intervened militarily in the Taiwan question was too great and too obvious,
he explained. United States firms interested in China had been mobilized by the regular struggles over MFN and were now quite potent politically. Besides, Clinton had made export promotion and job creation his
top priorities, and those would not be served by confrontation with
China. No, my acquaintance told me with confidence, the United States
would not come to Taiwan's rescue. This man was the sort of person
whose views were valued by China's leaders and their intelligence services. Similar opinions no doubt were widespread among well-informed
Chinese.

The experience of other China watchers was similar. Paul Godwin of
the U.S. National Defense University was told during 1995 by PLA military academics that the experience of the United States in Somalia,
Bosnia, and Haiti showed that it would not intervene in a cross-Strait
confrontation.[3] Senior military officials in the U.S. Embassy in Beijing
recounted similar experiences, along with their efforts to explain that
the abrupt U.S. withdrawals from Somalia and Haiti should not be taken
as indicative of how the United States would act in other situations in
which its major interests were at stake. One such official felt that such
warnings often fell on deaf ears. The Chinese had been misled by the
low-key U.S. reaction to the July–August missile tests, he believed.

According to one Hong Kong report, toward the end of 1995 an assessment by CCP leaders of the previous several months of military pressure
on Taiwan determined that the United States had been forced by
China's firmness to stay out of the Taiwan issue. Japan, too, had as-
sumed an ambiguous attitude. That success gave China greater freedom
of movement in dealing with the Taiwan issue. Beijing hoped that if it
used force against Taiwan, the United States would not become substantively involved in the conflict.[4]

Part of this attitude can be attributed to the tendency to hear and see
what one wants to hear and see. There is a rich literature analyzing the
powerful human tendency to filter information through preestablished
belief systems and to structure perceived data in ways that accord with
deeply held values.[5] If Chinese nationalist values dictated that Taiwan's
early unification with the mainland was a good thing, people embracing
those values would make observed facts harmonious with them. A person ardently desiring Taiwan's unification with the mainland would

want to believe that the people of Taiwan shared that desire, that its realization could be achieved at modest cost and would benefit all but a few people, or, to return to the issue at hand, that reasonable U.S. leaders would not intervene militarily to block coerced unification. There would also be a strong tendency for naysayers bearing bad news to be viewed as transgressors of the specified core values. A person who pointed out facts indicating that the people of Taiwan might not want unification with the PRC, that the costs of attempting to achieve that unification might be very high, or that the United States would probably intervene militarily if the PRC attacked Taiwan, would be seen as unpatriotic. Thus, contrary evidence would be ignored, discounted, or interpreted in a fashion harmonious with the underlying core nationalist belief. Chinese acquaintances who participated in closed discussion of these issues during the summer of 1995 indicated that the atmosphere of those meetings was often quite tense, with strident superpatriots cowing more cool-eyed analysts who seemed to dwell on the difficulties likely to be encountered by the proposed coercive operations.

Signals from the United States—Assistant Secretary Nye's comments before the Asia Society on 12 December and the *Nimitz*'s transit of the Strait a week later—apparently led to a reappraisal of the likelihood of U.S. intervention. A new, warier line toward the United States that resulted from the reevaluation was promulgated at an early March session of the National People's Congress. Previously a "sixteen-character guideline" regarding Sino-U.S. relations had been promulgated by Jiang Zemin following his November 1993 meeting with Clinton at the APEC summit in Seattle: "Increase trust, reduce trouble, develop cooperation, and refrain from confrontation" (*Zengjia xinren, jianshao mafan, fazhan hezuo, bu gao duikang*). The new sixteen-character guideline announced by Premier Li Peng after the early March 1996 NPC session was, "Seek common ground while reserving differences, increase common understanding, reduce trouble, and refrain from confrontation" (*Qiu tong cun yi, zengjia liaojie, jianshao mafan, bu gan duikang*). The difference between the two was subtle but significant. "Trust" and "cooperation" were replaced by "understanding" and "seeking common ground while reserving differences." Li Peng's revision clearly implied a more contentious relationship with the United States. Significantly, however, both included the injunction "refrain from confrontation." Hawkish elements reportedly proposed the formulation "Heighten vigilance, fear no trouble, accept cooperation, prepare for confrontation" (*Tigao jingjue, bu pa mafan, keyi hezuo, zhunbei duikang*). Li Peng's version was a partial concession to this hard-line perspective but rejected readiness for "confrontation."[6]

This modification of policy toward Taiwan did not lead to a change in the scheduled coercive exercises. It did, however, lead to greater psychological preparedness for confrontation with the United States. According to Hong Kong's *Xin bao* (New daily), CMC vice-chairman and Politburo Standing Committee member Liu Huaqing delivered an important speech in early March shortly before China commenced the first wave of exercises. That speech was subsequently distributed by the CMC's General Office. According to Liu, because the United States did not want to see China become powerful, there could be a stage of confrontation with the United States extending for five or ten years or even longer. In that context the possibility of local military conflict would not be ruled out. Referring to the December *Nimitz* transit, Liu Huaqing said:

> Recently, the United States has intentionally displayed its naval strength in the Taiwan Strait. . . . Although the United States has the right to carry out activities on the high seas, we will fight back if the U.S. military forces carry out military provocation of our Navy and Air Force on the high seas. There was a military confrontation between China and the United States on the high seas of the Yellow Sea in the autumn of 1994. We clearly stated our position at that time. If the United States carries out military provocation first, we will resolutely fight back and we are sure of winning the battle. If the United States intrudes into our territorial airspace or waters, we will have no choice but to deal a devastating blow at the intruders. If the United States occupies Taiwan or stations troops in Taiwan, it will be tantamount to a U.S. declaration of war against China, and we will then declare a state of war and wage a war to fight aggressors and defend the motherland. The United States will then have to pay a more painful price than it did in the Vietnam War.[7]

Having decided to continue with the planned exercises in spite of the U.S. warnings of December and January, Chinese leaders warned the PLA to prepare for the contingency of a clash with the United States. Liu's speech was also a pep talk to the PLA at the beginning of a course that might result in conflict with the United States. It is important to note, however, that this was internal rhetoric, not publicly and officially directed toward the United States.

The reevaluation of January–February 1996 led to a modification rather than basic rejection of the analysis of October 1994. The United States might intervene directly and militarily in a cross-Strait confrontation, it was now decided, but it would not do so quickly or decisively. Its intervention would be essentially symbolic. When the United States quickly deployed—even before the first wave of exercises had begun—first one carrier battle group and then a second, Beijing was shocked.[8] Two U.S. carrier battle groups had the ability to destroy virtually the entire Chinese navy swiftly and with virtual impunity. People's Liberation Army leaders knew that.

11 / PRC Strategy

If we assume that in the Taiwan Strait crisis military instruments were used to achieve political objectives, we must ask what objectives Beijing sought through its campaign of military coercion against Taiwan. Very probably that campaign had minimal and maximal objectives toward both Taiwan and the United States. Those can be outlined in table 1.

The proximate target of Beijing's coercive exercises was the psychology of the people of Taiwan. Beijing hoped to create a sense of apprehension and fear in the minds of those people. War and all its suffering was imminent! The Chinese Communists were determined and prepared to attack regardless of costs! Perhaps they were not entirely rational! War had to be avoided by whatever means necessary! If that was not possible, then people should fend for their own families! Those were the sentiments Beijing hoped to cultivate.

These mass fears would be both stimulated and focused by Taiwan's March 1996 electoral process. A great deal of excitement surrounded the elections, which people in Taiwan saw as a turning point for Taiwan and its relations with the United States, mainland China, and the world generally. There was a sense that history was being made. Beijing planned to convert this state of roused emotion and interest to fear through the exercise of military coercion. At a minimum, the electorate might swing away from Lee Teng-hui's war-threatening "Taiwan independence" and vote for more acceptable (to the CCP) New Party candidates. Taiwan's much-vaunted presidential elections might also be disrupted by pressure-induced instability. The atmosphere during the campaign period was certain to be tense even without Beijing's moves, as the stakes were high and partisan suspicions deep. Riots and politically inspired brawls were not an unusual part of Taiwanese politics even in the calmest times. Under heavy pressure, who knew what might happen? With luck there might be widespread panic and rioting, perhaps even leading to reimposed martial law or suspension of the scheduled presidential elections.

Table 1
Minimal and Maximal PRC Objectives
toward Taiwan and the United States

	TOWARD TAIWAN	TOWARD THE U.S.
Minimal Objective	Compel to suspend "pragmatic diplomacy"	Convince that transgressions of PRC "principles" on Taiwan would be costly
Maximal Objective	Compel to accept "one country, two systems" formula	Persuade to recognize that Taiwan is part of the PRC

Mass fear would have two positive consequences for PRC strategy. The first, socioeconomic instability, would manifest itself in heavy selling of Taiwan currency, stocks, and property; capital flight; hoarding of essential goods; purchasing of gold bullion; dispatching of families overseas; mass exodus from airports and harbors; riots; runs on banks; and other forms of panic. The second, political consequence would be action against Lee Teng-hui and the DPP, who were taking Taiwan into war. Such action could take many forms, such as votes for the New Party, which Beijing viewed as more reliably Chinese nationalist and more willing to repair relations with Beijing on the latter's terms.

The threat of war might also politically activate Taiwan's military officer corps, who would have to bear the brunt of fighting against an overwhelmingly superior enemy and who did not, in many cases, care for Lee Teng-hui's departure from the "one China," anti-PRC principles of Chiang Kai-shek and Chiang Ching-kuo. Under Chiang Kai-shek virtually all military officers, especially high-ranking ones, were mainlanders, not native Taiwanese. Blatant discrimination against native Taiwanese declined under Chiang Ching-kuo, but for various cultural reasons military careers continued to be far more attractive to young people from mainlander families. Young Taiwanese were far more likely to choose industry, commerce, law, or education. Especially at the higher ranks of the officer corps, which were reached only after decades of service, individuals of mainlander background continued to predominate in the mid-1990s. Many of them—that is to say, a large part of Taiwan's officer corps—were unhappy with Lee Teng-hui's departure from the orthodoxies of the Chiang family. Beijing's strategists probably hoped that these political tendencies would lead to divided loyalties and equivocation among Taiwan's military leadership.

Analysts in the PRC with whom I talked in Beijing in mid-1995 stressed that Taiwan did not have a sense of nationhood that would allow it to persevere in spite of adversity. Taiwan's society seemed highly vulnerable to destabilization. Nearly half of Taiwan's population had foreign passports, foreign property, or relatives abroad, which would enable them to flee overseas in an emergency. A large but undisclosed number of Taiwan government officials had foreign passports—a fact that has been a source of concern and scandal in Taiwan. During periods of high tension, emigration increased. During the fall of 1994, for example, it was up 30 to 40 percent over the previous year, influenced by larger than usual PLA exercises along the Fujian coast.[1] Beijing was probably misled by its wishes and its own propaganda, which maintained that Lee Teng-hui's policies were very unpopular. An early 1993 article in *Guang jiao jing*, for example, asserted that

> KMT veterans, the non-core [non-mainstream] party faction, and a considerable number of the military are not willing to surrender in this way [to Lee's policies] . . . not only the non-core faction and Hau Pei-tsun oppose Taiwan independence, but a majority of local Taiwan people are also against independence and against the division of the motherland . . . Lee Teng-hui's willful acts . . . will create instability and turbulence in Taiwan's political and social situation.[2]

Beijing's immediate political objective was to use fear of war to create economic, social, and political crisis—or better yet, panic—in Taiwan. That crisis would then be defused by opening talks with Beijing under either a clear "one China" formula or, if things went far enough, the "one country, two systems" rubric. If Taipei could be induced to accept the latter formula, Beijing was prepared to be very generous. Taiwan could retain its own socioeconomic system and its own armed forces; Beijing would not dispatch its military to Taiwan. Taiwan would retain its own autonomous legislative and judicial powers; Beijing would not send administrative personnel. Beijing would not impose taxes or other financial levies on Taiwan. The island would retain complete tariff autonomy, and would be able to enter into economic and commercial agreements with foreign countries. Beijing required only a few symbolic changes associated with recognition that Taiwan was, after all, a part of the PRC. Nothing really substantive would have to change. The few possible symbolic changes might include the ROC's becoming a Special Administrative Region of the PRC, with its president as that region's chief administrator. Perhaps it might adopt a new flag. That was all. Beijing's maximal hope was that when such reasonable, moderate demands were juxtaposed with the alternative of war and destruction, Taiwan would act reasonably and accept Beijing's offer. Short of this, Taipei might simply agree to suspend its objectionable pragmatic diplomacy and return to the "one China" position of, say, Chiang Ching-kuo.

During the first stage of its campaign against Taiwan independence, Beijing planned to use "nonbloody" tactics.[3] It would actively use its instruments of military power, but not for killing or destruction. Strictly speaking, these tactics were "peaceful," as are those of an armed man who demands money from a bank. The man may leave the bank with the money, without having fired his gun, yet his methods are clearly coercive.

The use of nonbloody tactics reduced the likelihood of American intervention in two ways. First, it allowed Beijing to insist its actions were peaceful and did not, therefore, violate the U.S. interest in a peaceful resolution of the Taiwan problem. The United States had repeatedly said that its only abiding interest in the Taiwan problem was in its peaceful resolution. By refraining from killing and destruction, Beijing could plausibly assert that its actions did not violate U.S. principles. Even if that sophistry was not persuasive to the more clear-eyed men and women who make U.S. foreign policy, it would be persuasive to much of the U.S. public. At a minimum Chinese use only of nonbloody tactics would divide American public opinion. Maximally, should U.S. decision makers choose to stay out of the emerging cross-Strait exchange it would provide a basis for their doing so. Chinese reliance on nonbloody tactics would save American face.

Second, these tactics kept the focus on factors internal to Taiwan. Violence grabs public attention. Bloodshed and destruction would focus international media attention on PLA actions in a way that nonbloody tactics would not. Chinese strategists understood that the more developments seemed to be a function of Taiwan's own internal weaknesses and divisions, the less likely Washington would be to involve itself in a quagmire. As Wang Fei-ling explained in his August 1995 *Mingbao Monthly* article, chaos or division within Taiwan would reduce the likelihood of U.S. intervention. The United States was, because of past experience, extremely reluctant to become involved in another country's internal politics. Thus, if there were internal disorder within Taiwan, or even more if one party or group openly appealed for mainland use of force against Taiwan independence, the probability of U.S. intervention would be greatly reduced.[4] By adhering to nonbloody tactics while doing what it could to foster instability, Beijing hoped to focus attention on the weaknesses of Taiwan's polity.

An even more fundamental reason for Beijing's eschewal of bloodshed in 1996 was that violent military conflict could have escalated into a war that China might have lost. Chinese military modernization efforts had closed much of the qualitative gap between the PLA and Taiwan's armed forces. Yet the PLA relied primarily on modernization of tactics and force structures combined with obsolete weapons and individual bravery to defeat better-armed enemies. A substantial gap still existed, especially in critical areas such as avionics and electronic warfare capabilities.[5] The PLA air force's close-support capabilities were also very limited.[6] These were especially serious shortcomings for a military considering an amphibious assault on Taiwan. Such an assault against an objective as large and well-defended as Taiwan would be so difficult that former U.S. Navy admiral Eric McVadon compared it to World War II's Normandy invasion and the planned U.S. invasion of the Japanese Home Islands.[7] While the PLA clearly had begun to take large-scale amphibious operations seriously, it was a long way from possessing capabilities that would have permitted an assault against Taiwan with a high probability of success. Regarding maritime transport capabilities, for example, even if China had been able to mobilize the thousands of civilian vessels necessary to ferry across the Strait the half-million or so soldiers required to subdue Taiwan, coordination of such an effort would have been extremely difficult. If bad weather had intervened, it would have been virtually impossible. Even under conditions maximally favorable to the PLA, Taiwan's forces would have found a "target-rich environment" with Chinese assault vessels easy pickings. Could the PLA have put adequate forces ashore in spite of a heavy casualty rate? Even without U.S. intervention this would have been highly problematic and risky. The aftermath of a Chinese defeat would almost certainly have included a formal Taiwan declaration of independence from China and a much-intensified Taiwan national defense effort. Defeat could also have induced an uprising against the CCP regime à la the Argentine model after the Falkland-

Malvinis war. High risks and uncertainties meant that Beijing had to move carefully. By relying on nonbloody tactics, Beijing was able to maintain a politically acceptable situation while awaiting a correlation of forces favorable to decisive PLA solution of the Taiwan question.

Does this mean that Beijing was not prepared to go beyond bloodless tactics in 1996? Before answering that we must note that there remained several levels of escalation before the threshold of bloodshed. Beijing might, for example, have had its submarines periodically surface off several of Taiwan's ports. It might have detained Taiwan-flagged ships at some distance from Taiwan's shores. It might have proclaimed a quarantine zone off Kaohsiung and then begun interfering with third-country traffic in and out of that port. Had such moves not sufficed, was Beijing prepared for bloodshed? It will be many years before we can answer this question with any degree of confidence. My own hunch is that—under certain circumstances—it was. In fact, it would have been foolish not to have been.

The critical variables had to do with the U.S. reaction and with the level of disorder generated within Taiwan. Military instruments are always blunt, imprecise means of achieving political objectives. No one could know whether the impact of the planned campaign of bloodless coercion on Taiwan's polity would be minimal (as turned out to be the case) or quite substantial. There might have been mass capital flight, social chaos, exodus, and so on. There could have been riots and clashes between demonstrators and the police. What if there had been extensive disorder, in the midst of which some group appealed for mainland intervention? This would not have been too difficult for the PRC Ministry of State Security (MSS) or the CCP's United Front Department to arrange.

China's reaction would almost certainly have depended on the U.S. reaction. No one, including top U.S. leaders, knew how the United States would react under such circumstances. What if it had remained passive or adopted only ineffectual measures? Would U.S. leaders and the public have wanted to invest national prestige in a Taiwan wracked by internal division and disorder? It seems likely that had Taiwan descended into chaos and the United States remained passive or ineffectual, it would have been foolish for the PLA not to move swiftly. Resolution of the Taiwan problem through bold action would have been tremendously beneficial to Jiang Zemin, the PLA, and the CCP itself.

Taiwan sources indicate that Beijing sought to multiply the effect of its bloodless coercion through use of its clandestine agents within Taiwan. Most of the evidence in this regard comes from Taiwan's internal security organs, whose veracity in earlier decades was proven unreliable. Moreover, disinformation about the CCP's subversive activities within Taiwan would have won U.S. sympathy during the 1996 crisis. In spite of this, there are several reasons for not dismissing this evidence.

The first reason has to do with what organizational theory teaches us about governmental decision making. Once top leaders have decided it is necessary to "do something," they will ask bureaucratic agencies for proposals. Leaders will then pick and choose from a menu presented by the bureaucracy. Securing a piece of the policy action then becomes a political game in which influential agencies tend to be successful. In China's case it probably worked something like this: In late October the CCP Politburo Standing Committee and the CMC decided to adopt further forceful measures against Taiwan. They set broad parameters and asked the major agencies of government for proposals. At the head of the queue was, of course, the PLA. Not too far back in line would have been the MSS and the United Front Department of the Central Committee. Both have agents in Taiwan and the former is politically influential in Beijing. Those agencies would have wanted a piece of the policy action—especially on such an important mission as the liberation of Taiwan. Thus, they would have laid before China's top leaders their own proposals. According to an authoritative Chinese source, the MSS is represented on the Taiwan Affairs Leading Small Group.

Another reason for not dismissing information about CCP activities within Taiwan concerns China's strategic tradition, which from Sun Zi to Mao Zedong has stressed the psychological aspect of strategy—the use of deception, demoralization, fomenting division in the enemy camp, and so on. The best strategy is one that defeats the enemy without fighting. Even Mao's strategy of protracted people's war predicated ultimate victory on breaking the will of the enemy. Alongside this tradition is the operational history of the PLA, in which careful attention to subverting the enemy frequently paid an important role in victory.

The final reason for giving some credibility to Taiwan reports is that use of subversion within Taiwan makes sense—at least if our reconstruction of Chinese strategy is substantially correct. If the proximate target of the PLA's bloodless coercion was indeed the psychology of the people of Taiwan, it would have made excellent sense to leverage the impact of that coercion through active measures there.

According to reports by Taiwan's security agencies, from late 1995 through the presidential election in March there were at least seven cases of CCP activities designed to sow unrest.[8] China was reported to have several thousand agents in Taiwan, among them people illegally smuggled in, along with Taiwan business leaders, scholars, and tourists who had visited the mainland and had been won over to the patriotic cause. Spreading rumors was one major activity of this clandestine infrastructure. Rumors designed to increase the fear of Communist attack or to intensify hatred among various social groups (Taiwanese versus mainlanders, DPP versus KMT, etc.) were disseminated. Often the media or the campaign headquarters of political parties were the targets of rumors. There were reports that the United States was preparing to evacuate its citizens from Taiwan, that Thailand was preparing to do the same for its laborers working in Taiwan's factories, or that the rice supply in some cities had already been exhausted by panicked buyers. Security agencies warned the media and partisan campaign organizations about passing on unverified reports.

Another technique reportedly used by the CCP was exacerbation of economic panic. China reportedly went through the overseas Chinese business community in Hong Kong to dump large amounts of Taiwan dollars on the market timed to drive down the value of that currency, increasing the sense of panic. Chinese business leaders with operations on the mainland who needed the cooperation of authorities there reportedly went along with those schemes for a combination of pecuniary and patriotic motives. The Chinese underground also tried to influence Taiwan's military. In the year preceding February 1996, Taiwan's military counterintelligence reported thirty instances of military personnel being approached by mainland agents.

Finally, Beijing's clandestine services reportedly hired overseas Chinese criminal organizations to assassinate various presidential and vice presidential candidates. Taiwan's National Security Agency reported that fifty people associated with overseas criminal gangs had returned to Taiwan at the time of the election and frequently appeared at campaign activities. Shortly before the election, heavy police security was provided to all candidates. The candidates themselves were advised to wear bullet-proof vests.

Beijing's announcement of the first wave of exercises on 5 March 1996 did indeed precipitate a modest panic. People in some cities rushed to stores to purchase and hoard cooking oil, rice, toilet paper, and other essentials. Many people exchanged Taiwan dollars for U.S. dollars. Over a ten-day period in early March, $370 million was withdrawn from local banks. So heavy was the demand for U.S. dollars that some banks placed a limit of $3,000 per transaction. Emergency plane-loads of U.S. dollars were flown in to meet local demand. Simultaneously there was a massive outflow of capital from Taiwan. During the first half of March U.S. $5 billion left Taiwan, establishing a new record. Capital outflow for that period was 27 percent above the same period the previous year. Heavy selling of stock had begun in January 1996 and intensified as the crisis escalated. By March the government dipped deeply into emergency funds to stabilize currency and stock prices. Within two weeks Taiwan's foreign currency reserves fell from U.S. $90 to $85 billion.[9] Meeting such emergencies is one reason why Taiwan maintains such large foreign currency reserves. The situation finally was stabilized around 18 March.

The U.S. dispatch of two carrier battle groups helped quell fear and apprehension. Beijing's strategy to target Taiwan's mass psychology was vulnerable to countermeasures designed to reassure citizens. The speed and forcefulness of U.S. action was crucial. Had action been delayed by several weeks, or been less forceful, it might have been too late or too little.

12 / Nuclear Coercion
with Chinese Characteristics

One of the most important yet murkiest aspects of the Taiwan Strait crisis is China's possible use of nuclear coercion. Did China employ its nuclear arsenal during the crisis to deter U.S. intervention on behalf of Taiwan? Our conclusions here must be tentative, for the evidence is ambiguous and circumstantial. Yet I believe we can conduct a preliminary investigation and make a tentative conclusion. I believe that the evidence suggests that Beijing did indeed undertake nuclear coercion of the United States.

American scholar Paul H. B. Godwin studied the role of China's nuclear weapons in its military strategy. In 1985, according to Godwin, the CMC redefined China's basic military strategy. No longer would China's military prepare primarily for a large-scale, protracted war with an invading superpower. The likelihood of such a "people's war" was now held to be very low. More likely were "partial wars" (*chubu zhanzheng*) in which China would engage an adversary in regions around its periphery. Partial wars differed fundamentally from the old "people's war." They would not be won through a strategy of protracted attrition. Partial wars were short, intense, and fought for limited objectives. Belligerents would not have time to mobilize latent human and industrial resources, but would fight with forces in existence at the onset of fighting. To win such wars, the PLA needed smaller, more highly trained and better-armed units with greater mobility and firepower. Those forces would seek to inflict decisive defeats on China's enemies in the opening stages of a partial war.[1] Such was the type of war against Taiwan that the PLA rehearsed in 1995 and 1996.

Godwin concluded that one key role of China's nuclear forces in the event of a partial war was to deter hostile intervention by a nuclear power on behalf of China's immediate adversary. Several of China's potential adversaries in partial war were smaller, nonnuclear powers, but which were aligned with a nuclear superpower. Vietnam and India were aligned with the USSR, while Taiwan was aligned with the United States. In the event of partial war between China and one of those lesser powers, China would use its strategic nuclear forces to counter Soviet or American intervention on behalf of their local clients. If Washington or Moscow attempted to use their nuclear superiority to sway Beijing from a course of action on which it had decided vis-à-vis a third power along its periphery, China's own nuclear forces would counter superpower nuclear weaponry. This would assure that China would not be prevented by superpower "nuclear blackmail" from pursuing a course of action that China's leaders deemed essential to national interests. Thus, Godwin noted that with PLA maneuvers designed primarily to test conventional capabilities, there was usually a nuclear component in which China's strategic forces prepared for "nuclear counterattack operations." Similarly, another prominent analyst of China's strategic doctrines and forces suggested that the purpose of China's strategic nuclear forces was to cause a superpower to hesitate long enough so that its eventual intervention on behalf of a local client might come too late.[2]

China's nuclear forces, as well as all China's rocket forces both nuclear and conventionally armed, are operated by the PLA Second Artillery Corps. Second Artillery units were involved in most of the exercises against Taiwan in 1995 and 1996.[3] While some of the Second Artillery operations were distinctly nonnuclear (e.g., the firing of conventionally armed missiles off Taiwan), others were probably in line with standard operating procedures for possible use of nuclear weapons: preparation of "nuclear counterattack operations" to deter intervention by a nuclear superpower. Even the firing of missiles into the seas off Taiwan may have involved nuclear contingencies. According to Hong Kong press reports, the mid-1995 tests were part of preparations for using tactical nuclear weapons against hostile fleets. China had made great strides in miniaturization of tactical warheads, these reports said, and such warheads would have far greater defensive power against an aggressor fleet than would either conventional artillery or antiship rockets. Enemy fleets of up to one hundred warships could be destroyed in an instant by several tactical warheads.[4] Although use of nuclear weapons to interdict a U.S. fleet moving toward Taiwan from Japan or South Korea would from a U.S. perspective constitute "war fighting" rather than deterrence, Chinese planners may have felt it useful during the 1995 exercises to suggest—and prepare—a range of possibilities regarding possible nuclearization of a war over Taiwan. By suggesting that China was prepared to use whatever weapons it had in response to U.S. intervention, Beijing would increase U.S. apprehension.

At the end of 1995 and early in 1996, Chinese officials subtly raised with U.S. leaders the possibility that a nuclear exchange between China and the United States could grow out of confrontation over Taiwan. An important such probe was directed toward former assistant secretary of defense Chas W. Freeman during talks in Beijing late in 1995, after China's decision to execute the March exercises and following Joe Nye's warnings of mid-November. A "Chinese official" told Freeman that China could act militarily against Taiwan without fear of U.S. intervention because U.S. leaders "care more about Los Angeles than they do about Taiwan." A "senior Chinese official" told Freeman that China was prepared to "sacrifice millions of men" and "entire cities" to ensure the unity of China. Freeman concluded that "some in Beijing may be prepared to engage in nuclear blackmail against the U.S. to insure that Americans do not obstruct" PLA efforts vis-à-vis Taiwan.[5]

Did Chinese officials tell Freeman this with higher authorization? I believe they must have had such approval. Chinese officials speaking to a former high-ranking U.S. official who remained well connected with U.S. policy circles, and in circumstances of spiraling U.S.-PRC tension, would not have dared to speak about so portentous an issue as a possible Chinese nuclear attack on the United States without higher approval. Almost certainly those comments were approved through the General Staff level. Quite probably they were approved by the CMC.

Politburo approval cannot be ruled out. Politburo Standing Committee member Qiao Shi raised the issue of a U.S.-PRC nuclear exchange during a discussion with a visiting American professor in January 1996. Qiao did not expect the United States to "dispatch troops" (*chu bing*) to help Taiwan. But even if it did, the United States no longer would play a decisive role. Even in the "worst-case scenario" China would not be without means of retaliation. If Beijing were subject to nuclear attack, China would retaliate against New York City, Qiao told his American visitor.[6] Qiao's words conformed to Beijing's policy of "no first use" of nuclear weapons, and were therefore less provocative than those of the anonymous officials who talked with Freeman. The point, however, was essentially the same—that U.S. intervention in a cross-Strait confrontation could lead to a U.S.-PRC nuclear exchange.

A series of nuclear-weapon and strategic-rocket tests was another element of Beijing's nuclear signaling. During the summer of 1995 China conducted two underground nuclear tests in western Xinjiang. The first was on 15 May, a week before the United States announced that Lee Teng-hui would be issued a visa to visit the United States. The second was on 17 August, two days into the second round of missile tests north of Taiwan and, coincidentally perhaps, one week after the fiftieth anniversary of the atomic bombing of Nagasaki. Both the May and the August tests were reportedly part of a multiyear program to improve the weight-to-yield ratio and accuracy of PLA nuclear warheads. When announcing the explosions, Chinese officials reiterated China's pledge not to be the first to use or threaten to use nuclear weapons against any nonnuclear country or region.

Along with those nuclear explosions was the test of a new, solid-fuel, mobile intercontinental ballistic missile (ICBM) on 29 May 1995. The missile, designated the Dongfeng (DF)-31, could deliver a warhead of two hundred to three hundred kilotons at a range of eight thousand kilometers (4,960 miles). That was adequate to reach the west coast of the United States—although the May 1995 test covered a range of only 1,240 miles. The significance of the DF-31 was its improved accuracy and survivability. Thanks in part to technical help by expatriate Russian scientists in improving guidance systems, the DF-31 was far more accurate than China's existing ICBMs. Because it could be moved about by truck, the DF-31 was far less vulnerable than China's silo-based ICBMs to preemption by U.S. or Russian forces. A nuclear warhead for the DF-31 was said to be under development and was expected to be ready by 1996.[7]

Chinese nuclear testing continued after the declension of the Strait crisis. On 8 June and 29 July 1996 China tested two more nuclear devices as part of its effort at warhead miniaturization. Two days after the last test, China announced a moratorium on further tests and declared its willingness to participate in efforts at Geneva to negotiate a comprehensive test ban treaty.[8]

These tests of nuclear bombs and the missiles to deliver them were not intended primarily as signals to the United States over Taiwan. They were clearly part of an effort at strategic force modernization that reached the testing stage several years before the Taiwan issue erupted and that continued after the declination of the crisis. Beijing pushed to complete a nuclear weapons development program before the conclusion of a comprehensive test ban treaty at the end of 1996. The tests, did, however, have several important linkages to the mounting crisis over Taiwan. First, given strong Western and Japanese opposition to China's continued nuclear testing, China's continuation with such tests demonstrated that it would do what it felt its national interests required regardless of protests by foreign nations—that China would not be swayed by foreign opinion and sanctions. That underlined China's prickly nature and suggested to foreign powers that they should not challenge Beijing. The nuclear tests of mid-1995 also underlined China's ever more powerful nuclear arsenal. Finally and most importantly, the nuclear and missile tests of 1995 gave substance to vague but repeated nuclear insinuations that issued from Beijing beginning in late 1995.

It is possible that China's leaders did not consider or were unaware of what sort of signals the tests would send to the United States as the PLA moved forward with its coercion of Taiwan. It is more likely, however, that they understood that the tests would underline China's strength and determination, raising additional concerns in the United States about the wisdom of confronting China. Besides, why would China have delayed testing so as not to scare the Americans?

Evidence for Chinese nuclear coercion is not clear cut. There is a big gap between actions and intentions, and most of the evidence about Chinese intentions is circumstantial. My tentative conclusion is that China's leaders did indeed use the country's nuclear capabilities to deter or hinder U.S. intervention. During the long years of cold war with the USSR, the United States became accustomed to Soviet nuclear threats, which were often crude and direct, sometimes delivered with table-pounding, fire-breathing rhetoric and unmistakable purpose. Chinese nuclear diplomacy is more subtle and indirect, yet the purpose is the same: to make the United States hesitant to pursue a course of action antithetical to its opponent's interests.

United States leaders noted and publicly dismissed China's nuclear signaling. On a C-SPAN television program on 17 March, near the height of the crisis, reporters asked Assistant Secretary of State Winston Lord about reported Chinese threats to use nuclear weapons against Los Angeles if the United States defended Taiwan against a PLA attack. Lord conceded that "some Chinese lower-level officials told some visiting American officials that we wouldn't dare defend Taiwan because they'd rain nuclear bombs on Los Angeles." Lord dismissed this as "a little disinformation," "some psychological warfare," and "not official."[9] Lord's characterization of Chinese signaling is essentially the same as the analysis presented here: it was an "unofficial" attempt to influence U.S. psychology. Of course, Lord's words minimizing Chinese signaling should also be seen as an effort to prevent sensationalistic U.S. media from inflaming popular anti-China sentiment.

The strongest objection to a hypothesis of Chinese effort at nuclear coercion of the United States during 1995–96 is the seeming irrationality of such an effort. Given the vast nuclear and technological superiority of the United States, it would be insane for any Chinese leader to even toy with the use of nuclear weapons against the United States or against U.S. forces in the western Pacific. But while actual initiation of nuclear combat may be irrational, cultivation of a belief that China was quite prepared to wage nuclear war may make sense. During the late 1950s and 1960s Chinese spokesmen railed about how China could survive and even win a nuclear war. Nuclear weapons were U.S. "paper tigers" in the jargon of the day. Even if U.S. nuclear bombs devastated China's cities, its vast rural populace would survive to carry the war to final victory. While this fire-breathing rhetoric seemed irrational to many at that time, in retrospect it can be seen as a way of telling U.S. leaders that China would not be intimidated by U.S. nuclear superiority. It also lessened the likelihood that the United States would attack China expecting that nuclear weapons would deliver a relatively cheap and swift victory. China's nuclear bluster of the 1960s was a way of telling U.S. (and later Soviet) leaders to expect a large, protracted, costly and unwinnable war if they dared to clash with China. The far more subtle nuclear signaling of 1995–96 may have served a similar purpose.

The logic of nuclear deterrence of the United States is suggested by a popular book on the 1996 confrontation published in Beijing in August of that year.[10] After reviewing political developments up to early 1996, it discusses China's military superiority. It reviews PLA ground, air, and naval forces. The section on strategic rocket forces begins with the observation that China was the only world power to engage in military conflict with the nuclear-armed USSR. This was done on the basis of China's "nuclear triad" of bombers, land-based missiles, and submarine-launched nuclear missiles, which the book reviews in detail. From the book's standpoint, the 1996 confrontation was a great success for China. The strength of China's reaction to Clinton's approval of Lee Teng-hui's visit far exceeded anything anticipated by the U.S. government or people. Beijing recalled its ambassador, launched a "new Cold War style" propaganda campaign against the United States, began military pressure against Taiwan, and "finally conducted a series of nuclear tests to develop the mainland's second generation of tactical nuclear weapons." The result of this was that the anti-China chorus in the United States "shut up and stopped their noisy show." On the basis of this experience it can be concluded, the book said, that the United States would remain passive in the event of a war to reunify Taiwan and China. The United States and Japan might issue a few protests and complaints, but these would amount to nothing compared to the roar of the guns.[11] Although this book is, of course, propaganda designed to foster patriotic fervor, it may reflect to some extent the calculations of China's elite.

Although no rational Chinese leader would countenance the first use of nuclear weapons against the United States, some could, and apparently did, conclude that China's interests would be served by rousing apprehension among U.S. leadership of possible nuclear war. China's nuclear signaling during 1995–96 was designed to tell Washington and the American populace that China was determined to proceed with its coercion of Taiwan and that U.S. intervention would result in a Sino-U.S. war that would be open-ended, very costly, and difficult to conclude.

13 / The International Effect
of the Crisis

B eijing's attempt to coerce Taiwan had an impact across Asia and even in Europe. When the smoke cleared, the crisis had increased both apprehension regarding China's willingness to use military force and concern about the steady growth of Chinese military power, and had weakened the belief that China's growing economic interdependence would make it less reliant on military power. It was difficult, after all, to find a better example of economic interdependence than the Taiwan-mainland relationship. Yet that did not stop Beijing from threatening Taiwan with war.

The Strait crisis also caused allies of the United States around the world to consider the implications of their alliance in the event of military conflict between China and the United States. Previously, the possibility of Sino-U.S. conflict had seemed so remote that it was not worth pondering. The Strait crisis forced the issue to the foreground. From Tokyo to Berlin, U.S. allies began thinking through, probably for the first time, how their obligations as an ally of the United States could bring them into conflict with China, and whether the gains of continued alliance with Washington were worth the costs of deteriorating relations with Beijing. That sort of recalculation of national interests may prove to be an insignificant epiphenomenon. Or it might ultimately prove to be the beginning of a new pattern of global polarization that will characterize the post–Cold War world.

Because of Japan's relatively great national power, the impact of the Strait crisis on Tokyo was most important. The crisis came at a time when Japan and the United States were in the final stages of rethinking their alliance. Over the previous year, leaders in both Washington and Tokyo had expressed concern that commercial conflicts had dangerously eroded their security relationship. Moreover, an alliance originally founded to counter the USSR had lost its rationale and needed to be rethought. The issuing of the Nye Report by the Pentagon in February 1995 marked the start of this process of reevaluation.[1] The U.S.-Japan

Joint Declaration on Security Alliance for the Twenty-first Century signed by President Clinton and Prime Minister Ryutaro Hashimoto on 17 April 1996 was, perhaps, its conclusion. The escalating cross-Strait confrontation, which came in-between, did not change the direction or outcome of the U.S.-Japan review, but it did accelerate and strengthen the process leading to reaffirmation of the alliance. Beijing's attempt to coerce Taiwan made very clear the sort of instability and threat to peace that U.S. and Japanese leaders hoped their renewed alliance would address.

The basis for Tokyo's approach to the Strait crisis was the Sino-Japanese communiqué of 1972, in which Tokyo had gone substantially further in meeting Beijing's demands than had the United States in the Shanghai communiqué. Beijing had, of course, reiterated its position that Taiwan was an inalienable part of the territory of the PRC. Tokyo stated that it "fully understands and respects" Beijing's stand, and had "absolutely no intention of supporting a two-China policy."

As Beijing moved toward a round of missile demonstrations near Taiwan in March 1996, Tokyo expressed its "concern." Prime Ministers Li Peng and Ryutaro Hashimoto met in Bangkok shortly before Beijing's 5 March formal announcement of the first wave of exercises. Hashimoto conveyed Japan's view that heightening tensions in the Taiwan Strait were not desirable for peace and stability in East Asia. Traffic on the high seas near the test area could also be affected. Therefore, Japan was watching the situation closely. The Japanese government wanted all problems concerning Taiwan and China to be solved peacefully, Hashimoto said. Both sides of the Taiwan Strait should act on the basis of the principle of peaceful settlement. Li conceded that tension had increased, but said that it was because Lee Teng-hui was seeking independence. Li said that China's "fundamental policy" of peaceful unification and "one country, two systems" would not change. He also asked for assurances that Lee Teng-hui would not be allowed to visit Japan.[2]

After Beijing announced the first and second waves of missile demonstrations, the director general of the Asian bureau of Japan's Ministry of Foreign Affairs (MOFA), Ryozo Kato, called PRC embassy counselor Zheng Xianglin to his office to convey Japan's request that China exercise "self restraint" in its policy toward Taiwan and seek a resolution of the current dispute in a peaceful fashion. Heightened tension in the Taiwan Strait would not be favorable to peace and stability in the Asia-Pacific region, Kato said. Japan understood that China had the right under international law to carry out military exercises on the high seas. Yet it felt that, politically speaking, China's current exercises heightened tension. Zheng defended China's exercises as "normal" efforts to defend a country, traced increased tensions to Lee Teng-hui's declaration of independence, and said Japan should not be too concerned about China's exercises. Kato replied that Japan was worried and reiterated the call for self-restraint.[3] Apparently these Japanese protests were merely oral.[4] Presentation in written form would have indicated a slightly higher level of seriousness.

Japan's embassy in Beijing also conveyed Tokyo's concern about the safety of civil aircraft and ships near the Chinese missile test areas. China replied that their safety would be ensured as long as they kept away from the designated exercise areas. The Japanese island of Yonaguni was only sixty kilometers away from the missile target area and Tokyo was concerned that a missile might accidentally fall there. It conveyed several messages to Beijing regarding the concern of the people on Yonaguni. Japan Asia Airways, the Japan Airlines subsidiary that serviced Taiwan with daily flights between Naha and Taipei, rerouted its flights to the east, lengthening flight time by five or ten minutes, a minor disruption. No change in the routes between Japan and Southeast Asia was required.[5] The navigation routes of vessels bound to and from Japan were not affected.[6]

Pressure quickly mounted within Japan's Liberal Democratic Party (LDP) for a stronger expression of concern over Beijing's actions. Press commentary overwhelmingly supported that point of view and targeted Japan's generous aid program to China, which had been suspended in August 1995 after Beijing persisted in conducting nuclear tests in spite of Japan's protests. The Social Democratic Party, then heading the ruling coalition, had left untouched the far more important yen loans to China. Grant aid had totaled approximately ¥95.7 billion, only about one-sixteenth of much larger loans. Three rounds of loans extended between 1979 and 1995 were worth a total of ¥1.6 trillion. Those had a ten-year grace period, after which they were to be repaid over a period of twenty years. They carried an interest rate of 2.3 percent per annum.[7] These were very generous terms, making their suspension a tempting way to express displeasure with China.

Shortly after Beijing launched its first and second waves of exercises over Japanese protests in March, the head of the LDP Research Commission on Foreign Affairs convened a meeting at Party headquarters to discuss relations with China. Some participants called for freezing yen loans and others for bringing the issue of China's exercises before the UN Security Council. Even though Beijing would exercise its veto, such an action would underline the seriousness of Japan's concern. In response to this and other similar pressure, on 13 March the Japanese government clarified its protest against Beijing's coercive exercises by postponing negotiations on a fourth round of yen loans. Those working-level negotiations had been scheduled to begin in late March. A rough framework for a yen loan totaling approximately ¥580 billion for three years between FY 1996 and 1998 had been agreed upon. The funds were to go for forty projects including improvement of airports and water supply in inland areas. The Japanese government decided on postponement of negotiations over implementation of, rather than outright suspension of yen loans so as not to "seriously affect future relations between the two countries" and lead to retaliatory measures against Japanese firms and investors active in China.[8]

Another aspect of increased Japanese firmness was a new-found willingness to comment on Taiwan's democratization. At a news conference on 13 March Chief Cabinet Secretary Seiroku Kajiyama harshly criticized the Chinese military exercises, saying that they "constitute a threat to democratic election processes and politics."[9] Ten days later, on the evening of Taiwan's presidential election day, Foreign Minister Yukihiko Ikeda told the press, "It is of deep significance that the leader was elected by the people. I hope that the election results will become a turning point for solving the Taiwan issue peacefully."[10] Three days later that formulation was repeated by a MOFA spokesman.[11] Those words were highly significant. Japan had discovered it had an interest in seeing that democratic political institutions in Taiwan were not destroyed by armed coercion by Beijing.

The Japanese government conveyed its displeasure to Qian Qichen when he visited Tokyo in early April. During a three-hour discussion with Qian, Foreign Minister Ikeda conveyed a subtle but powerful threat. Ikeda said that public opinion survey data indicated that "many Japanese people" saw China's recent exercises as an attempt to settle the Taiwan issue by applying military pressure. "Japanese people reacted strongly against China's actions, and I cannot help having doubts about what China did," Ikeda was reported as saying. There was also, Ikeda told Qian, the view within the LDP and other parties in the ruling coalition that the fourth round of Japanese yen loans to China should be shelved or frozen to lodge a more serious protest against China's actions. "We hope China will try to resolve the issue [with Taiwan] through dialogue in line with its peaceful reunification policy," Ikeda told Qian. According to a MOFA spokesman, although the exercises did not pose a problem regarding international law, "heightening tensions across the Taiwan Strait is not desirable and we hope that self-restraint will be exercised." Japan hoped for a renewal of cross-Strait talks and other measures to reduce tension. Contained in these carefully crafted words was the implicit threat to shelve yen loans if China continued actions such as the early 1996 military coercion of Taiwan and nuclear testing.[12]

The significance of those criticisms must be measured against Japan's post-1952 tradition of extreme sensitivity to China. Because of Japan's prior aggression against China, combined with the growing economic importance of China to Japan throughout the post–World War II period, Japanese leaders have typically refused to criticize Chinese actions even when they disagreed with them. Tokyo finally broke with this long tradition of reticence in mid-1995 in response to China's continued nuclear testing. Ikeda's comments to Qian Qichen in April 1996 were a marked continuation of that new policy of open criticism.

Qian acknowledged the strength of Japan's reaction. "Aside from the United States," he said, "another nation that reacted strongly to our military drills was Japan. Other nations did not react so strongly."[13] In response to Japan's criticism, Qian stressed that the Taiwan issue was entirely an internal Chinese affair in which foreign nations should not interfere. He also expressed Beijing's fears that the Taiwan issue might be drawn into the purview of the U.S.-Japan security treaty. Regarding the U.S.-Japan summit scheduled for 17 April and the announced intention to sign a communiqué on joint security during that summit, Qian said China hoped that the U.S.-Japan security treaty would not become "inconsistent" with the sound development of PRC-Japan relations.[14] China hoped, Qian told Prime Minister Hashimoto, that the upcoming U.S.-Japan summit would not bring any "new problems" to China.[15] Japan's representatives replied that the U.S.-Japan security treaty was not directed against China or any particular country. Its purpose was the defense of Japan and the United States and "for peace and stability in the Asia-Pacific region."[16] It is noteworthy that coverage of the Qian-Ikeda talks by Chinese and Japanese media differed starkly. Apparently as a result of censorship under central directions, China's papers and Xinhua News Agency carried no reference to Japan's criticisms of the Strait exercises.

In spite of Beijing's wishes that its Strait exercises not affect the U.S.-Japanese security relationship, that was not the case. The Strait crisis prompted hard thinking in Japan about choices regarding relations with Beijing and Washington. At a press conference on 13 March as the PLA exercises were in full swing and after Washington had ordered both carrier battle groups to the area, a reporter pressed a MOFA spokesman about Japan's course in the event of a Sino-U.S. clash in the Strait. After the spokesman stressed that such a clash was unlikely, that Japan needed good relations with China, and that it was in a more vulnerable position than the United States, a reporter asked if that meant that Japan would "take a neutral line under a worst-case scenario." The MOFA spokesman replied:

> What I am saying is not about neutrality. Because when we express our concern to the Chinese side, we say, "look, if [the] Taiwan [issue] rises, it will not be good for peace and stability in this region." At the same time, we fully understand that the United States is playing a very important role in peace and stability in this region. Although we have some vulnerability, I do not think that the Japanese position is neutral. It cannot be neutral.[17]

United States leaders were aware of the high stakes for U.S.-Japanese relations in the Strait crisis. If the United States failed to assist Taiwan and acquiesced to PLA coercion of Taiwan, many Japanese would conclude that Japan would have to take responsibility for its own defense. The United States could no longer be counted on. If the United States went to Taiwan's assistance, thereby forcing Tokyo to choose between China and the United States, Tokyo would probably side with the United States, but the result would be immense resentment in Japan. Future Japanese governments would not want to put Japan in that situation again, and would arm to assume responsibility for national defense. Either way the crucial Japan-U.S. alliance could unravel.[18] The best way to avoid such an outcome, U.S. leaders decided, was for Japan and America to stand more closely together, demonstrating to Beijing that it could not minimize the costs of a breakdown in Sino-U.S. relations over Taiwan by exploiting Japan-U.S. contradictions. A closer Japan-U.S. united front was the best way to restrain Chinese adventurism.

Japan's leaders apparently reached similar conclusions. As tension in the Strait escalated in March, Prime Minister Hashimoto used the opportunity to encourage a rethinking of U.S.-Japan defense cooperation in East Asian emergency situations. Hashimoto and other LDP leaders knew they could not go too far in this direction without provoking strong opposition from the Social Democrats, yet they wanted to use the opportunity to stimulate discussion of Japan's use of its collective self-defense rights in emergencies. That desire for national debate was driven by recognition that situations such as that in the Taiwan Strait could affect Japan's security.[19]

One manifestation of the closer U.S.-Japan alliance that emerged from the Strait crisis was the U.S.-Japan Joint Declaration on Security Alliance for the Twenty-first Century, signed aboard the aircraft carrier *Independence* in Yokosuka Bay on 17 April. The Clinton-Hashimoto summit had been agreed to on 17 March at the height of the Strait crisis, and had strained cross-Strait relations as a main topic. According to a MOFA source, the leaders of both countries agreed that "they need to demonstrate to China that they continue to have a great interest in cross-Strait relations" in light of the fact that Beijing refused to rule out the use of force against Taiwan.[20] The Joint Declaration carefully avoided mention of Taiwan. It spoke of a "commitment to the profound common values that guide our national policies: the maintenance of freedom, the pursuit of democracy, and respect for human rights." Taiwan's democratic transition was implicit in those words. Turning to "regional cooperation," the Joint Declaration used very circumspect terms, but the meaning was clear:

> The President and the Prime Minister agreed that the two governments will jointly and individually strive to achieve a more peaceful and stable security environment in the Asia-Pacific region. . . . The two leaders stressed the importance of peaceful resolution of problems in the region. They emphasized that it is extremely important for the stability and prosperity of the region that China play a positive and constructive role, and, in this context, stressed the interest of both countries in furthering cooperation with China.[21]

Stripped of diplomatic ambiguity, those words meant that Japan and the United States jointly opposed efforts by Beijing to coerce Taiwan into submission, but that if Beijing cleaved to peaceful resolution of the

Taiwan issue, they welcomed China fully into the council of world powers. In effect Beijing's actions precipitated what it had long sought to avoid—a Japanese-American understanding to cooperate in defense of Taiwan against unprovoked Chinese attack. In his words to Japanese and U.S. military and civilian personnel assembled aboard the *Independence* for the signing ceremony, President Clinton was less circumspect. Deploying the *Independence* off Taiwan the previous month "helped calm a rising storm." Without firing a shot, that action "reassured nations all around the Pacific." The presence of U.S. forces in the Western Pacific helped "prevent war's return" and preserve stability.[22] The television camera that broadcast Clinton's speech to the world showed in the background a Japanese warship flying the Rising Sun naval flag. That sent a potent and complex message to Beijing.

Two other Asian allies of the United States, South Korea and the Philippines, also were forced to sort out where their interests lay. For South Korea the stakes were extremely high, perhaps as high as war or peace with North Korea and eventual national reunification. As South Korean foreign minister Gong Ro Myung explained as the March crisis escalated, China alone maintained close relations with North Korea, had a great deal of influence there, and was, therefore, in a position to play a role in its opening and restructuring. Such a process might lead to North Korea's joining the international community, to the beginning of direct inner-Korean talks, and eventually to peaceful reunification.[23] On the other hand, if war or intense confrontation occurred in the Taiwan Strait, North Korea might get the "wrong message" and adopt a confrontational approach to South Korea that could lead to renewed war on the Korean peninsula.[24] To deter war, Seoul needed a solid security alliance with the United States. Such a relationship could antagonize Beijing or undermine Seoul-Beijing amity if there were a Sino-U.S. conflict over Taiwan.

From Seoul's perspective, the best solution was to avoid conflict in the Strait. That was the message conveyed by President Kim Young Sam to Premier Li Peng when the two leaders met in Bangkok on 1 March for the Asian-European summit. Rising tension across the Strait was not desirable for peace and stability in Northeast Asia, and the parties concerned should seek a peaceful solution through dialogue.[25] The sensitivity of Seoul's petition to Beijing on the Strait issue was demonstrated by Kim's simultaneous request for Chinese support for improving of relations between North and South Korea.[26] Li Peng told Kim that China wanted stability on the Korean peninsula and that Korean problems should be settled by Koreans. Pointedly, Li then called for Chinese problems to be settled exclusively by China.

As cross-Strait tensions escalated after the beginning of China's missile exercises and America's deployment of aircraft carriers, Seoul reiterated its call for peaceful resolution of the issue and its hope that China would forego further missile exercises. That view was conveyed by Foreign Minister Gong Ro Myung to a visiting high-ranking Chinese official shortly after the beginning of Beijing's missile exercises.[27] On 20 March Gong arrived in Beijing for a five-day official visit. Tension in the Taiwan Strait was one of the top issues on his agenda. Another was North Korea. In talks with Li Peng and Qian Qichen, Gong emphasized his government's view that tension in the Strait could spread to Northeast Asia, affecting the stability of the Korean peninsula. To prevent this, the matter should be settled by peaceful means.[28]

In subtle ways the South Korean government made known its view that further deterioration of relations between China and Taiwan could lead the United States to involve itself more deeply in the Taiwan issue, thereby putting U.S.-PRC ties into grave jeopardy.[29] It also indirectly approved the U.S. deployment of carriers by noting that it clearly demonstrated the important "balancing" or "equalizing" role of the United States in Asia.[30]

The Philippine situation was nearly as delicate as South Korea's. The Philippine discovery in February 1995 on Mischief Reef (claimed by the Philippines and located only some two hundred kilometers west of Palawan Island) of a newly constructed Chinese military facility, and subsequent miniconfrontations between Philippine and Chinese personnel and ships following that discovery, generated apprehension about a possible military clash with China. The Philippines was grossly unprepared for such a contingency and would need U.S. support if it was to have even a remote chance of success. On the other hand, when Philippine-PRC relations were normalized in June 1975, Manila said it "fully understands and respects the position of the Chinese government that there is but one China and that Taiwan is an integral part of Chinese territory."[31] Underlying that, of course, was the Philippine interest in cordial relations with China. The fifty thousand Philippine nationals working in Taiwan during the 1996 crisis were endangered by war. Furthermore, the northernmost Philippine territory, the Batan Islands, lying between the Luzon and Taiwan islands, were only 118 miles (190 kilometers) south of Taiwan, and thus would be vulnerable to misfired Chinese missiles.

As China's missile exercises began in March, Philippine presidential executive secretary Ruben Torres told reporters that the government was watching the Strait situation "very closely" and hoped there would be "no serious consequences." It also hoped the situation "will be solved diplomatically." The main concern of the government, Torres said, was the safety of Philippine workers in Taiwan.[32] As tension spiraled, President Fidel Ramos issued a formal statement calling for "the utmost self restraint" from all parties. Ramos first justified Philippine concern as "a subject of legitimate Philippine interest" on the basis of trade and geographic proximity. From Beijing's perspective, any expression of concern about cross-Strait affairs was tantamount to interference in China's internal affairs. Ramos's statement then "urged" that "the situation in the Taiwan Straits be allowed to return to normal as soon as possible." The Philippines "fully respects the principles of noninterference in the internal affairs of other nations, and supports the peaceful unification of China. At the same time, the Philippines sincerely hopes that the situation in the Taiwan Strait will not be allowed to lead to any unintended erosion of longer-term regional security and regional cooperation which are of enduring and vital importance to the future progress and prosperity of all East Asian nations."[33]

Acting Philippine Foreign Affairs Secretary Rodolfo Severino summoned the Chinese ambassador to Manila to convey the Philippines' call for all parties to exercise restraint in the Strait to safeguard the peace and stability of the Asia-Pacific region. Severino also conveyed those concerns to PRC vice foreign minister Deng Jiaxuan during a visit by the latter to Manila on 13 and 14 March.[34]

President Ramos declared Philippine neutrality and noninvolvement in the event of China-Taiwan conflict. Philippine leaders were acutely aware, however, that their country's alliance with the United States could involve it in war in the event of a U.S.-China clash. The chairmen of the foreign affairs committees of both the upper and lower houses of the Philippine Congress expressed that concern.[35] Government leaders responded by stressing the low probability of such a clash, and events did not compel them to choose sides. The Philippines did, however, allow several of the U.S. warships deployed from the Arabian Sea to the Taiwan area (the tanker *Niagara Falls,* the submarine *Bremerton,* and the destroyers *O'Brien* and *McClussky*) to refuel at Subic Bay. They also proceeded with joint U.S.-Philippine military exercises scheduled for April, while carefully denying that those exercises were in any way connected with the Taiwan Strait crisis.[36] Conduct of the exercises was, however, testament to the value Philippine leaders placed on the security relationship with the United States in a situation of increasing uncertainty.

Elsewhere in Southeast Asia, the reaction to the cross-Strait confrontation varied from country to country. Indonesia, Vietnam, and Malaysia said virtually nothing. Thailand took a distinctly pro-Chinese stance, minimizing cross-Strait tensions and dismissing the issue as "solely China's internal affair." Tension would ease, according to a Thai Foreign Ministry spokesman at the peak of the crisis, if Taiwan stopped pursuing a "two Chinas" policy.[37] Thai prime minister Banhan Sinlapaach was the first ASEAN leader to visit Beijing after the crisis peaked, arriving there on 24 March. He apparently did not express any disagreement with Beijing's recent coercive exercises.[38] Bangkok did not, however, help Beijing deepen the crisis. It could have done this very effectively, by ordering the evacuation in early March of its 150,000 nationals working in Taiwan. Such a move would have contributed to the sense of panic on the island. Of course it also would have cost Thailand substantial foreign currency earnings and divided ASEAN by putting Thailand very clearly in Beijing's camp. Myanmar (Burma) and North Korea also sided rhetorically with Beijing.

In Singapore the reaction was more negative. Early in the crisis Senior Minister Lee Kwan Yew made clear the potentially high stakes involved. Shortly before he entered a hospital for heart surgery and before Beijing announced its first wave of missile exercises, Lee warned that if "miscalculation" got the United States involved, "the costs will be very high for China and the U.S., but highest for Taiwan as its industries and population centers are on the western plain facing China." "Any Chinese attack on Taiwan," Lee frankly warned, "will force the U.S. to react and at least impose an economic embargo on China. Then China's hopes of becoming an industrial nation in 25 years will suffer a major setback." In a war between China and the United States, U.S. forces would prevail "in the short run, at some cost, but the long-term consequences will be enormous." Such a war would be a blow to the growing economic prosperity of the region.[39] That blunt talk about war and its consequences was not what Beijing wanted to hear. Beijing's game plan called for the rest of the world to go about business as normal while China coerced Taiwan into submission. Lee also hinted at Singapore's orientation in the unhappy event of war. "China's leaders have referred to me as an old friend. I am an older friend of Taiwan." Ten days later, at the peak of the crisis, Singapore deputy prime minister and defense minister Tony Tan subtly reiterated that message. Addressing the Parliament as defense minister for the first time since assuming that post seven months earlier, Tan responded to calls for Singapore neutrality in the event of a cross-Strait war by noting Singapore's commitment to the Five Power Defense Arrangement and its "good defense relations" with its ASEAN partners and the United States. Regional stability required strong bilateral relationships interwoven with multilateral arrangements, Tan said.[40] The only bilateral link mentioned was that between Singapore and the United States. The Five Power agreement linked Singapore to Malaysia, Great Britain, Australia, and New Zealand.

Among reactions of the Western powers, those of Russia and Germany were especially important. As tensions mounted in March 1996, Moscow took a clearly pro-PRC stance, reiterating early and unequivocally its longstanding position that Taiwan is an inalienable part of the PRC and that the Taiwan issue is an internal matter for that country.[41] President Boris Yeltsen traveled to Beijing in April, just after the Strait crisis, to sign a series of important agreements. Large-scale Russian assistance to China's military modernization efforts continued apace.

Germany's reaction was also swift and clear, but in the opposite direction, coming down squarely on the side of the United States. This response was important for a couple of reasons. One was the large volume of Sino-German trade. Another was Beijing's strategy of turning to Germany as an alternative to the United States when Sino-U.S. relations soured. Germany, with its high technology and export-oriented economy, had long been one of China's major trading partners. In 1993 it ranked fifth, after (in rank order) Japan, Hong Kong, the United States, and Taiwan.[42] As Sino-U.S. relations deteriorated in mid-1995 after Lee Teng-hui's visit to the United States, China's conspicuous turn toward Germany as an alternative economic partner was in line with a long tradition of seeing Western Europe as a counterweight to the United States and the USSR.[43] In mid-July, shortly after Washington issued a visa to Lee Teng-hui, Jiang Zemin traveled to Germany with a large entourage. During his four-day visit, several Chinese firms concluded an agreement with Mercedes-Benz providing for cooperation in producing vans, engines, buses, and bus chassis in several cities in China. The deal was worth more than $1 billion and gave Benz the leading position in China's huge, largely untapped automobile market. Chrysler and Ford Motor Corporation had been Benz's major competitors for the contract.[44]

While in Bonn, Jiang delivered a long speech to the German Society for Foreign Affairs. One of its key thrusts was China's opposition to big-power politics and hegemonism of all sorts. Another was the common interests of China and Western Europe in world peace, stability, and development. A third was the importance of the principle of noninterference in a country's internal affairs. Jiang did not mention Taiwan in this context—indeed, he did not mention Taiwan at all—but his sophisticated listeners would have understood that Taiwan, along with human rights, was what he had in mind. His final emphasis was on the complementary nature of the German and Chinese economies. There were broad prospects for mutually beneficial economic cooperation if the two sides sought common ground while putting aside differences. In short, if Sino-U.S. relations deteriorated because of United States interference in the Taiwan question, Sino-German cooperation would prosper.

As the March crisis unfolded, several prominent members of Helmut Kohl's government staked out unprecedently firm positions. On 19 March Defense Minister Volker Rühe told an interviewer that Germany should make it clear to China that political problems between the two sides of the Strait should be solved only by political means. The military tension created by China in the Taiwan Strait had the potential to influence the peace of the Asia-Pacific region and even the world, Rühe said. European leaders should make China understand that this was unacceptable. Germany should squarely confront China's provocative military actions and join the United States in assisting the defense of Taiwan. He called on European leaders not to tacitly accept China's actions, but to demonstrate their firm opposition to them. Within the European Union, he said, Germany should play an active role to see that Europe helped the United States assist Taiwan's defense and that the United States did not alone pay the bill for such action. About the same time, Germany's minister of economic cooperation told reporters that China's maneuvers were a threat to world peace, and that such action definitely was not the purpose for which European nations had given economic assistance to China. The U.S. position in support of Taiwan was entirely correct, he said. The German government should make its position clear, and should develop methods to help the United States assist in the defense of Taiwan. Germany should let the Chinese government know the limits of its policies of military coercion.[45]

These statements did not represent the official position of the German government. Moreover, had the government begun moving to adopt an official position in line with those forceful comments, business interests would certainly have mobilized to defend Germany's traditional policy of separating economics from politics. Yet those comments cast doubts on Beijing's expectation that deterioration of Sino-U.S. relations could be insulated from Sino-German and Sino-European relations.

The international reaction to China's military coercion surprised Beijing, which had hoped that most countries would close their eyes to its effort to punish Taiwan. Beijing had reasoned that costs to other countries of challenging China on the Taiwan issue were simply too great and the probable gains too small to make such challenge worthwhile. Most countries, Beijing hoped, would carry on normal economic and political relations with China, taking little account of what was going on across the Taiwan Strait. If Beijing expected the United States to refrain from involvement, it must also have expected that less powerful nations would avert their eyes and stay silent while Beijing bludgeoned Taipei.

In fact, Beijing's actions quickly internationalized the Taiwan issue in a way that had not occurred since 1971. Capital after capital was forced to reconsider long sacrosanct positions on Taiwan and conclude that those positions did not condone the use of military force—even non-bloody military force—to coerce Taiwan. In effect, a new international consensus began to emerge. Countries that had previously not felt compelled to speak out on the hypersensitive Taiwan issue now found their voices. In doing so, they found that they did not stand alone in condemning China's use of military coercion. By going too far, Beijing catalyzed international opinion against itself.

14 / Appraising the Gains and Costs
of Beijing's Coercive Exercises

W as Beijing's exercise of coercion successful? Did it achieve its objectives? If so, did the costs of those achievements justify the gains? In answering those questions we must be acutely aware of preestablished beliefs and values. Both the conclusions of China's leaders and their advisors and of American analysts are likely to be deeply colored by cognitive structures derived from emotions and beliefs associated with Taiwan. Yet it is important to attempt to sort out successes and failures, for this may determine Beijing's future management of the Taiwan question.

Beijing clearly did not achieve its maximal objectives vis-à-vis either the United States or Taiwan. It did not persuade the United States to recognize that Taiwan is a part of the PRC. Nor did it persuade Taipei to accept the "one country, two systems" doctrine. Just as clearly, Beijing did achieve its minimal objective vis-à-vis the United States: convincing U.S. leaders that transgression of PRC "principles" on Taiwan would be costly. Many U.S. leaders and analysts had believed that Beijing would not risk "upsetting the apple cart" of economic benefits associated with proper Sino-U.S. relations by forcing the Taiwan issue. Economic development was China's top priority, according to that view, and U.S. support for that goal was too important for Beijing to risk by forcing the Taiwan issue. As long as Washington or Taipei did not confront Beijing with some egregious loss of face, it was widely believed in the United States, China would not resort to military means to settle the Taiwan issue. After March 1996 such illusions were far less common. Most Americans were more willing to accept Beijing's oft-repeated assertion that no cost was too great to protect "sovereignty," meaning the PRC's claim to Taiwan. By bringing the United States face to face with the real possibility of military conflict with China, Beijing gave credibility to its warnings. In the future such warnings are less likely to be dismissed as rhetorical ripostes issued largely for reasons of Chinese internal politics. As Zhou Enlai said after Chinese forces intervened in Korea against the United

States, in the future the United States would know that China meant what it said. Beijing also secured significant modifications of U.S. policy in Beijing's favor. The United States explicitly promised not to support either independence for Taiwan or its membership in the UN. While there was no U.S. promise regarding future visits by Taiwan's president to the United States, such visits are likely to be extremely infrequent.

More broadly, China gained increased status as a major power, as a major rival of the United States. It successfully confronted the United States militarily. From a position of material inferiority it stood its ground and achieved important political objectives. This success will strengthen arguments of future militants who press for tough, confrontational tactics toward the United States and other countries.

It is less clear whether Beijing achieved its minimal objective vis-à-vis Taiwan of compelling it to suspend "pragmatic diplomacy." Taipei is likely to be cautious in its post-crisis search for broader international recognition of Taiwan's status as a state. In Taiwan, too, illusions about the constraining effects of economic interdependence were fairly common before the crisis. Taiwan investment and trade were so clearly major factors fueling China's economic boom that many people believed Beijing would not risk war with Taiwan. Especially among proindependence supporters of the DPP, it was widely thought that Beijing's threats to attack Taiwan were bluffs. Many DPP supporters believed that this bogus "threat" was used by the KMT to scare voters, thereby keeping itself in power and the DPP out. Since the Taiwan Strait crisis, the credibility of Beijing's threats has increased and may well reduce the popular appeal of bold moves to secure enhanced international recognition. Kuomintang politicians will have less electoral incentive to court votes through such moves.

Against these gains for Beijing must be weighed the costs of achieving them, which were many and heavy. Regarding Sino-U.S. relations, the crisis led to a major modification in the U.S. policy of calculated ambiguity toward cross-Strait relations. From 1971 on, Washington had refused to say how it would react in the event of conflict between the two sides of the Strait. That policy was designed to deter without antagonizing Beijing, while simultaneously reassuring Taiwan and discouraging it from reckless actions that might precipitate a cross-Strait war. The 1996 crisis represented the failure of that policy. The consequent U.S. intervention answered several critical questions about U.S. policy and its underlying intentions. The crisis clarified a threshold well short of bloodshed and demonstrated the overwhelming preeminence of U.S. naval power in the Western Pacific plus the ability and will of the United States to use that power effectively to thwart Chinese measures against Taiwan. The 1996 crisis showed that the United States was prepared and able to intervene swiftly, forcefully, and decisively.

The confrontation also clarified U.S. policy on the eventuality of a cross-Strait war. Speaking in New York on 17 May 1996, Secretary of State Christopher said that following the confrontation Washington "reaffirmed" that "our 'one China' policy is predicated on the PRC's pursuit of a peaceful resolution of issues between Taiwan and Beijing."[1] In other words, and stated with undiplomatic bluntness, were Beijing to actually attack Taiwan, U.S. pledges "acknowledging" Beijing's claim to Taiwan would be in abeyance. While this implication can be found in U.S. policy statements tracing back to 1971, this was the first time it was stated so baldly and officially. This significantly raises the PRC stakes in cross-Strait war.

Clarification of U.S. policy may have a positive effect on Sino-American relations, leading to increased mutual understanding. But such clarity also means loss of psychological influence over Taiwan for Beijing. Taiwan's greater confidence in U.S. protection will not necessarily lead to reckless actions by Taiwan; U.S. representatives will certainly explain to Taiwan's leaders that U.S. guarantees are not categorical and do not cover situations created by Taiwan's own adventurism. Still, Taiwan's leaders and people will be substantially more confident that if they encounter Chinese attack primarily as a result of their continued refusal to accept Beijing's terms, they can count on effective U.S. protection. That is not advantageous to Beijing's strategy of "peaceful reunification." It also vastly increases the anticipated costs of nonpeaceful reunification. Beijing must now base its calculations on the assumption that a nonpeaceful effort will very probably involve war with the United States.

The cost of the 1996 confrontation to U.S.-PRC relations was great. In retrospect it may rank with the Beijing Massacre of June 1989 in terms of China's standing in U.S. public opinion. The Massacre sharply increased Americans' perception of China as a brutally repressive regime. The Strait Crisis repositioned China as a power the United States may have to fight. The effects of such a shift in perceptions could be substantial, influencing U.S. decisions on such issues as MFN, Intellectual Property Rights (IPR), and WTO entry. It is doubtful that China's leaders and their advisors assign much weight to the vague, amorphous influence of

American public opinion. A more objective understanding rooted, perhaps, in a closer knowledge of the U.S. political system leads independent scholars, it seems to me, to a rather different conclusion.

Most broadly the 1996 crisis has increased the probability that China and the United States will enter a more confrontational, less cooperative relationship. While the military leaders in both countries had previously considered the possibility of war, its likelihood seemed so remote that little was done beyond contingency planning. Prudent leaders will now have to rank such a possibility much higher. Shortly after the crisis there were media reports that China was retargeting part of its nuclear missile force against the United States. Those reports may have been apocryphal, but they illustrate the sort of moves that are likely on both sides. On the U.S. side, intervention to block a Russian sale of SS-18 missile technology (which occurred in May 1996 shortly after the crisis) became more likely. After all, with the probability of war ranked higher, prudence requires such caution. The greatest cost to China may have been endangering the supportive approach of the United States toward China's long-term modernization effort.

China's Strait brinkmanship did not inoculate any country against transgressing Beijing's "principles" on Taiwan. The few countries that had been willing to transgress those "principles" before the 1996 crisis (e.g., France, Germany, and the Netherlands, by selling or considering the sale of weapons to Taiwan) had been forced by other, less drastic sorts of pressure to reverse themselves. It is not clear that West European countries will now be less willing to transgress Beijing's "principles"—indeed, it may work the other way. Beijing's threats against Taiwan brought thousands of foreign reporters to Taiwan in the weeks and days before the 23 March presidential election. Their broadcasts back to their home countries of news about Taiwan's democratization and Beijing's threatening exercises increased sympathy for a small country daring to adhere to democratic ways while under threat of attack by a large, powerful dictatorship. Beijing's efforts to isolate Taiwan will henceforth be more difficult.

Shifts in Japan's Taiwan policy were also costly to China. Since the 1970s a major PRC objective has been to keep Japan out of the Taiwan issue. As a result of the 1996 crisis, Tokyo began to speak out on the modalities of cross-Strait unification and relations and on the value of Taiwan's internal democratization. It seems fair to conclude that China's own actions brought about a result it sought to avoid.

In the Asia-Pacific region Beijing's willingness to resort to military means to achieve its objectives led to increased respect for and fear of its growing military might. Economic and political considerations will no longer be considered a deterent to military force, should Beijing judge the stakes to be high enough. Other Asian governments will rate more highly the risks associated with crossing Beijing and will view with greater apprehension China's growing military power. Capitals throughout the region will ask whether their own countries might become targets for Chinese military forces, what Beijing's long-term objectives are, and whether China could dominate the entire region militarily.

China's coercion of Taiwan in 1996 will probably make other Asian-Pacific countries desire a balance of power which will check and constrain China. This may result in the formation of multilateral security arrangements among neighbors and involvement of extraregional powers. Again, this would be antithetical to China's policy interests. China has long sought to prevent the coalescence of such a regional balance of power. It attempted to keep the regional situation open and fluid, under a relatively benign and gradually declining U.S. presence, while Chinese power slowly expanded. The effort to bludgeon Taiwan into submission threatened this important interest.

In terms of cross-Strait relations, the costs of Beijing's coercive exercises were heavy. Movement in the direction of Taiwan independence is less likely now, but so too is Taiwan's acceptance of the "one country, two systems" arrangement. The impact of Beijing's exercises on Taiwan's political situation was nothing less than a fundamental realignment to the benefit of forces Beijing described as open and undisguised secessionists. Prior to the intensification of PLA pressure, the key issues in Taiwan's electoral politics were internal: the involvement of criminals in and the disproportionate influence of money upon politics; social problems such as poverty and child prostitution; the environment; governmental corruption; and a general weariness associated with rule by the same party for forty-five years. With an election fought in terms of domestic issues, the KMT's prospects were not rosy. Its steady and growing setbacks in elections between 1992 and the December 1995 Legislative Yuan elections were testament to this. Shortly after the December 1995 elections the DPP and the New Party—occupying opposite wings of the political spectrum—orchestrated a legislative alliance on domestic policy issues. Had the presidential campaign of March 1996 been waged under those conditions, Lee Teng-hui's prospects would not have been good.

In early 1996 Lee's objective was to win a majority of the popular vote in March. There was a good chance he would fail and assume office as a minority president.

That was not to be. As Taiwan's political landscape was rapidly rearranged by Beijing's escalating pressure in February and March, the incipient anti-KMT alliance between the DPP and the New Party was aborted. Pressure from the PRC recast the election as a referendum on the "unification/independence question" (*tong du wenti*), and the two opposition parties quickly moved to their natural opposite poles over that issue. Rhetoric and symbolism associated with the "unification/independence question" increasingly dominated the campaign. The theme of the New Party's major rally in Taipei on the last campaign day before the election, for example, was "uphold peace and oppose war." In context, that meant opposition to Lee Teng-hui's "provocative" moves that had brought Taiwan to the brink of war with China. One slick New Party brochure widely distributed at that rally attacked Lee Teng-hui's "pragmatic diplomacy" as lacking in cool analysis. Lee's visit to the United States, for instance, had not improved Taiwan's actual relations with the United States, but had "caused" cross-Strait relations to worsen. His application for UN membership for Taiwan was also unlikely to succeed and should be made a priority. Taiwan's security could be guaranteed only by paying attention to Beijing's reactions. Taiwan should not rely on the United States, the strength of which was declining. Besides, the United States needed to cooperate with Beijing on many issues and therefore would not come to Taiwan's assistance. The similarity of such New Party views to those of Beijing was one reason why the New Party was Beijing's favorite in the election. It was also a reason why potential New Party supporters swung their votes to Lee Teng-hui.

Chinese pressure also prompted DPP supporters to begin shifting en mass to Lee Teng-hui's camp. Lee was attacked not only by the Chinese Communists, but also by Taiwan politicians, not for economic and social policies unpopular with voters, but for international moves that had won considerable voter support. Lee was also in the enviable centrist position on the "unification/independence question." To his left was the DPP calling for "independence." To his right was the New Party calling for "unification." In the center stood Lee Teng-hui. Once the "unification/independence question" superseded domestic issues, Lee's standing was bound to increase.

There was considerable sympathy among native Taiwanese for Lee

Teng-hui as Taiwan's first Taiwanese president. As the PLA threatened to attack because of Lee's "pragmatic diplomacy"—which was highly popular with native Taiwanese voters—and New Party politicians echoed Beijing's criticisms, Lee's popularity rocketed. His campaign propaganda stressed the need for unity in the face of external threat. One television ad that played repeatedly in the days before the election showed two hands breaking a single chopstick above a map of Taiwan and the adjacent China mainland coast. A voice stated that something standing alone was easy to break. Another hand then added several more chopsticks, and the two hands tried unsuccessfully to break them. The message: a vote for Lee gave an additional increment of unity and strength.

The election resulted in a landslide 54 percent vote for Lee Teng-hui, far exceeding KMT expectations. The DPP's candidate, Peng Ming-min, received 21 percent of the vote. Given that Beijing's actions had recast the election as a referendum on the "unification/independence question," that meant that 74 percent of the electorate was opposed to "unification." The New Party, Beijing's favorite, received only 14 percent of the vote. Lee Teng-hui took office with the strongest support possible under a democracy. In his electoral camp were the proindependence forces. These results, which were almost a direct result of China's own actions, marked a major setback for Beijing's efforts to weaken Taiwan politically so as to better compel it into submission.

Beijing's coercive exercises will probably lead to further strengthening of Taiwan's defenses. As Taiwan began the transition to democracy at the end of the 1980s, criticism of its large defense budget grew strong. Many civilians concluded that the threat of PLA attack was bogus and was used by the KMT to prop up its authority. Calls for cuts in defense spending mounted.[2] Lee Teng-hui and the KMT were able to fend off that pressure by cutting defense spending as a percent of GNP from 6.8 percent in 1987 to 4.3 percent in 1994, although increasing it in absolute terms, from about NT$175 billion in 1987 to about NT$235 billion in 1994.[3] Throughout the early 1990s pressure to cut defense spending continued, mostly from the DPP. Because of its hatred of KMT authoritarianism and its belief that the KMT manipulated a bogus PRC threat for its own purposes, the DPP routinely adopted antimilitary positions. That began to change before 1996, but the confrontation of that year produced a major perceptual shift, as DPP leaders became ardent advocates of a strong defense against the PRC. Because of shifts in U.S. policy, Taiwan's money was better able to buy the high-technology weaponry it needed to counter the PLA. During the crisis, for example, the U.S. government approved the sale of Stinger antiaircraft missiles to Taiwan. A short while later it was disclosed that U.S. Patriot antimissiles were also to be sold to Taiwan. Other similar sales will probably follow. United States willingness to transfer a higher level of military technology to Taiwan to allow it to strengthen its defenses is another part of the price of the 1996 crisis to Beijing.

This list of Chinese losses is the work of an American professor, undoubtedly influenced by personal values and beliefs. So, too, would be a Chinese analysis. Policy failure is extremely difficult for its authors to recognize. The beliefs and convictions that led to a decision continue to operate after its implementation and structure the cognition of its results, skewing perceptions toward success and filtering out or minimizing evidence of failure. There is a strong tendency for subordinates to structure their analyses to conform to the known beliefs and convictions of their superiors. It is typically easier to switch personnel than to change beliefs and perceptions. Democratic systems have the advantage of being able to periodically install new leaders who will bring with them a new set of advisors. In nondemocratic systems the same set of people may be in control of policy for very long periods. In such an environment it may be extremely difficult for a government to accurately assess the gains and losses of its policies.

This may well be the case with Beijing's appraisal of its coercion of Taiwan. According to a Hong Kong report, at the end of March 1996 the CCP Politburo held an enlarged meeting to evaluate the results of the three recent waves of exercises. The conclusion "fully confirmed" those exercises: they punctured the arrogance of the Taiwan independence forces, reduced the proportion of votes won by the DPP, and restrained to some extent the arrogance of the people in power in Taiwan advocating Taiwan independence.[4] Subsequent Chinese media commentary on the exercises fits with this positive appraisal. A spokesman for the Taiwan Affairs Office of the CCP Central Committee told Xinhua News Agency about three months after the confrontation that China's exercises had been a great success. They had "fully shown the determination and capability of the Chinese people, the Communist Party of China, and the Chinese Government to safeguard China's sovereignty and territorial integrity, and they have heavily cracked down on the splittist forces in Taiwan which attempted to achieve 'Taiwan independence.' "[5]

Regarding the international reaction to the March confrontation, a researcher at the Taiwan Institute of the Chinese Academy of Social Sciences (CASS) found that "many countries held a mild, understanding, and even positive attitude to these military exercises." In response to U.S. congressional criticism of China's exercises, for example, UN Secretary General Boutros-Ghali called on Western countries not to interfere in China's internal affairs. "This represented the views of most countries, and was a more international voice," according to the CASS researcher. "Virtually all countries around the Asia-Pacific region held the same attitude" as Boutros-Ghali. This included Japan, Korea, Singapore, and the Philippines, among others. The PLA paper *Jiefang junbao* (Liberation daily) deemed the exercises successful because they demonstrated the capabilities of the PLA in high-tech warfare.[6]

The Politburo "conclusion" of late March spoke highly of the "patriotic enthusiasm" aroused by the exercises among people across the nation. This popularity of the government's firm line is important to note. The government was perceived as having punished Taiwan's traitors to the Han race and foreign interventionists trying to keep China weak. It did not fear U.S. gunboat diplomacy and had refused to cower before U.S. bullying. It struck a blow for the unification of the motherland while demonstrating to the world China's resolute, principled firmness. Government propaganda played those themes to the hilt during the crisis. They struck a resonant chord, and public opinion rallied around the Party. For a regime struggling to find a way out of a deep legitimacy crisis, this was a major gain.

The gap between China's and the outside world's perception of the consequences of China's coercive exercises is one of the most dangerous aspects of the Taiwan situation. China's actions are seen as threatening by foreign governments and publics, but China cannot understand how this could be so. When foreigners respond to China's actions with criticism or countervailing measures, China's leaders see this as proof of hostility to China. The consequent Chinese response may well be even tougher policies. After all, those firm policies worked in 1996.

15 / Conclusions

Democratization of Taiwan's political system is deeply troubling to Beijing. From the CCP's perspective, democratization is tantamount to "all-out Westernization" and will inevitably take Taiwan toward the West and away from China. Here a bit of background is useful. Shortly after the Taiwan Strait confrontation of August 1958, the CCP adopted major changes in its Taiwan policy. No longer would it seek to seize the KMT-held offshore islands of Jinmen and Mazu. Instead, those islands would be left in KMT hands until Taiwan itself passed to CCP control. Keeping the KMT on those offshore islands would maintain a link between Taiwan and the mainland, thereby helping to foil U.S. schemes to create two Chinas. One expression of that new approach was a letter to "Taiwan compatriots" calling on the KMT to oppose the United States' "two China" scheme and promising them "a way out" (*chu lu*) if they did. In a talk to provincial and municipal CCP secretaries in February 1959, Mao explained the rationale of the new approach:

> At this point, our choice in Taiwan is between Hu Shi and Chen Cheng or Chiang Kai-shek. Which is better? Faced with this choice, I think that Chiang Kai-shek is better. Chen Cheng and Hu Shi have more connections with the United States and therefore Chiang Kai-shek is better.[1]

Hu Shi, a leading early twentieth-century intellectual, was a forceful advocate of Western civilization's rationalistic method and ethos. Hu was the foremost Chinese advocate of American philosopher John Dewey's pragmatism, having taken his doctorate in philosophy under Dewey at Columbia University in the 1910s. Hu argued against the notion that China occupied some sort of special position in the world and in favor of China's assimilation of the rational, skeptical method and spirit promoted by the West. While eschewing both politics and sweeping political prescriptions, he was critical of dictatorship and sympathetic to constitutional democracy. When Mao made his comments, Hu was head of Academia Sinica, an influential government-sponsored think tank in Taiwan. Chen Chang was one of Chiang Kai-shek's more competent military officers, having served under Chiang since the early 1920s. He was one of the Nationalist officers favored by Chiang's U.S. military advisors Generals Joseph Stilwell and Albert Wedemeyer. Chen was certainly no liberal politically, but during the 1950s as Taiwan's premier he served as protector of and advocate for a group of technocrats who, along with U.S. aid advisors, engineered Taiwan's agricultural, industrial, and commercial modernization. That transformation was achieved in close association with a large-scale U.S. aid program and with the objective of turning Taiwan into an open-market economy and, ultimately (so U.S. advisors hoped), a liberal system politically. Chen Cheng, in other words, was an instrument of the westernization of Taiwan's economic sphere, just as Hu Shi was of its political-intellectual sphere. Economically, Chiang Kai-shek tended toward a statist orientation; politically he favored an authoritarian dictatorship. Chiang detested liberal democracy for a number of reasons, not the least of which was that it would, he believed, interfere with the "sacred mission" of liberating the mainland from Communist rule.

Mao preferred Chiang because his rule would create political conditions propitious to unification. Continued authoritarian rule would prevent unpatriotic voices, such as those advocating Taiwan independence, from speaking out. It would keep the public mind focused on the objective of unification. Granted the conditions for that unification were to include destruction of the CCP regime, but that was a wild dream. In the meantime Chiang's rule would keep alive Chinese nationalism. Authoritarian rule on Taiwan also left open the possibility that the leaders of the CCP and the KMT might reach a deal without too much regard for popular sentiment on Taiwan. After all, the CCP and the KMT had cooperated twice before for the benefit of the nation. Rule by Hu Shi and Chen Cheng would allow the sprouting of "evil weeds," one of the most noxious of which was Taiwan independence. Bourgeois democratization would create obstacles to a deal by the top leaders of Taiwan and the mainland disposing of Taiwan over the heads of the people of that island. Beijing's dilemma in 1996 was that "Hu Shi and Chen Cheng" had won the struggle for Taiwan.

Beijing has few positive incentives with which to entice Taiwan to accept the "one country, two systems" plan. Tyranny, even in its milder nontotalitarian and postcommunist variants, has little appeal to the people of Taiwan, who have completed a long, difficult march to freedom and democracy and see little to be gained and much potentially to be lost by associating with the PRC. Taiwan citizens are put off by the continuing backwardness of the mainland: pervasive inefficiency, lack of a sense of individual responsibility, corruption, and so on. There is also the huge gap between living standards on Taiwan and the mainland. Appeals to pure Chinese nationalism succeed with a small minority in Taiwan, but with the negative side effect of stimulating countervailing, and more powerful, Taiwanese nationalist sentiments. Economic incentives associated with expanded cross-Strait cooperation are powerful and may ultimately prove to be Beijing's most effective instrument. Taiwan might eventually be persuaded that special access to the China market should be secured by entering into a special but loose political relationship.

Negative sanctions and coercion seem to offer a simple, immediately effective solution, but that sword would cut both ways. Chinese actions restricting Taiwan business operations on the mainland could adversely affect China's development drive. Economic sanctions would have diminishing effectiveness. In response to sanctions, Taiwan businesses would begin shifting investment to Southeast Asia. Each new sanction would accelerate this shift, reducing Taiwan's dependence on the mainland and the effectiveness of subsequent sanctions.

With military sanctions, too, Beijing's *political* problems are immense. In many ways Beijing's situation is similar to that of other governments that have had to deal with revolutionary or national independence movements. Throughout history governments have tried to break those movements by military force, only to find that application of force stimulated even greater opposition: the Boston Massacre of 1770 in the American Revolution; Bloody Sunday of January 1905 in the Russian Revolution; the Jallianwala Bagh firing of 1919 in the Indian independence movement; the firing on demonstrators in Tehran by the Shah's police in late 1978. Historians of those movements typically point to such episodes of bloodshed as critical points in the psychological transition to a collective identity that defines itself as separate from the authority ordering the repression. That incomplete repression only makes matters worse seems to be understood by CCP leaders, at least those of Deng Xiaoping's generation, and is one reason why the repression applied in June 1989 was so overwhelming. Beijing may have restricted itself to nonbloody military coercion in 1996 not only because such tactics reduced the likelihood of early and effective U.S. intervention, but they also minimized injury to what Chinese refer to as *minzu qingjie,* the sentimental knot that binds an ethnic group together. If this logic is correct, the implication is that when the CCP decides to cross the threshold and apply bloodshedding military coercion, it will do so on a massive scale designed to overwhelm opposition swiftly and completely.

Some people, including many Chinese analysts, would object strongly to the proposition that the 1996 confrontation was about Taiwan's democratization. They would argue that what Beijing found objectionable was not the fact that Lee Teng-hui and other Taiwanese leaders were now elected through the contrivances of Western-style democracy, but their various policy actions. The Chinese government has said repeatedly and authoritatively that is it willing to accept any form of self-rule that the people of Taiwan deem appropriate as long as that does not entail efforts to establish Taiwan in the international community as a state separate from the PRC.

Yet accepting these propositions at face value does not settle the issue. The actions objectionable to Beijing were linked to deep political-psychological transitions underway in Taiwan. The tectonic forces that are currently destabilizing the more than two-decade-old status quo on the Taiwan issue are linked to transitions underway in Taiwan. Concepts of collective self-identity, views of one's group and of significant "other" groups, are rapidly changing on Taiwan. The fact that possession of political power is now substantially a function of appealing to changing collective identities creates strong incentives for leaders to cater to these identities. The pernicious actions objectionable to Beijing arose directly out of the increasingly competitive nature of Taiwan's political process. Although the CCP may not wish at present to dismantle Taiwan's new democratic processes, it clearly seeks to place major limits on them. It has also made clear its conviction that "bourgeois democratic" institutions have no place on China's soil.

The 1996 crisis was fraught with the danger of Sino-U.S. conflict. The next crisis over Taiwan may be even more dangerous. In 1996 the stakes were high for both Beijing and Washington. For Beijing the question was nothing less than whether Taiwan would become, someday, a part of the PRC. For the United States it was U.S. credibility in Asia and, beyond that, whether the United States would remain a major power in East Asia. The United States repeatedly said, in diplomatic parlance, of course, that it would help defend Taiwan against unprovoked PRC attack. If it failed to do so, what Asian nation would again believe U.S. promises of assistance? Japan might begin to rethink its reliance on U.S. protection. The result would be the greatest erosion of U.S. credibility in Asia since the mid-1970s, coming at a time when China was becoming increasingly powerful and assertive. For a great power with voluntary allies, credibility is an important commodity.

By 8 March both sides were locked into an escalating confrontation. Beijing announced its first wave of exercises. Washington responded with one aircraft carrier deployment. Beijing proceeded with its exercises and announced a second round. Washington ordered a second carrier to the scene. Both sides were acutely aware that their prestige was now committed, and that the costs would be very high if they were perceived to back down. Both were determined to stand firm and show no weakness. Powerful internal factors operated in both China and the United States to severely constrain government flexibility. In China the requirements of regime legitimacy and succession to Deng Xiaoping mandated that leaders show firmness. They could not afford politically to appear to back down before the gunboat diplomacy of U.S. hegemonists. On the U.S. side, Bill Clinton's reelection strategy and the Democratic Party's hope of reversing the "Republican revolution" of November 1994, as well as the Republican Party's hope of sustaining that "revolution," dictated firmness. On neither side could top leaders operate in a dispassionate atmosphere of pure national interest. On both sides leaders were under strong domestic pressures to demonstrate toughness.

A small power in the middle of the U.S.-PRC confrontation—Taiwan— also held a critical initiative, thereby increasing risks. Unfortunately, great-power wars have sometimes been touched off by minor actors. Serb nationalist Gavrilo Princip shot Austro-Hungarian crown prince Francis Ferdinand in June 1914 with the intent of sparking a European war that would liberate the South Slav peoples from Austria's domination. Advocates of Taiwan independence understood that the United States would not endorse Taiwan independence except, perhaps, under extraordinary circumstances, such as U.S.-PRC war. Fortunately, Lee Teng-hui was not Gavrilo Princip. Would some other Taiwanese leader have come closer to filling Princip's shoes? Or might some ardent pro-independence field commander in Taiwan's military forces take the initiative in creating circumstances he believed would free his nation? The fact that the critical third actor in the 1996 crisis was a small power that might have benefited from conflict between the two larger powers increased uncertainty.

While the 1996 crisis carried a genuine risk of a Sino-U.S. conflict, it was far less dangerous than it might have been. In important ways, the confrontation was a stable crisis. Neither the PRC nor the United States felt that its objectives would be well-served by war with the other, and both knew that the costs of such a war would be extremely high. Both acted cautiously even while demonstrating firmness. United States carriers did not transit the Taiwan Strait and kept well away from PLA exercise areas. The PLA did not send missiles, submarines, or warplanes in the direction of the U.S. battle groups as it had done during the Yellow Sea confrontation of October 1994. Both sides sought to limit and control the confrontation. Because war was anticipated by neither side, there was no incentive to strike first to get the upper hand in the coming conflict.

The next crisis over Taiwan will probably be less stable. Beijing will anticipate and plan for U.S. intervention. Psychological and material preparations will contribute toward Chinese escalation once the United States intervenes. Once preparations have been made to confront the United States, failure to carry them forward can be taken as evidence of irresolute leadership. Anticipation of intervention is a step toward anticipation of war, and once leaders conclude that war is inevitable a new logic begins to operate. The logic of preemption becomes far more persuasive. Who would deny, for example, that one of Saddam Hussein's mistakes was to allow U.S. forces free use of Saudi Arabia's ports during the buildup in the months prior to Desert Storm?

There is also a "falsely crying wolf" effect at work regarding China's use of nonbloody coercion, which forces China's military actions to ever higher levels. Everyone knows the story of the little boy who falsely cried "wolf" so many times that when the wolf finally appeared and the boy again cried "wolf," no one came to his rescue. Similarly, each time China deploys its military forces to threaten Taiwan but sheds no blood and destroys no property, the subsequent repetition of that action loses its effect. To have an appropriate psychological effect, the next action must carry the threat to a higher level. Thus in 1993 and 1994 the PLA conducted maneuvers along the central China coast adjacent to Taiwan. Repetition of similar exercises in 1995 would have met a blasé response in Taiwan; thus the mid-1995 missile tests of northern Taiwan and larger exercises later in the year. For the same reason, the missile demonstrations of 1996 were brought closer to and bracketed Taiwan and were backed up by large-scale combined forces exercises. Next time Beijing decides to intimidate Taiwan, it will have to go still further.

Taiwan's democratization has enhanced U.S. interests in Taiwan and will make more dangerous the next confrontation over the island. The proposition that the United States has interests in Taiwan arising from democratization is only beginning to seep into the consciousness of the U.S. policy elite. A 1993 policy paper by the Atlantic Council of the United States and the National Committee on United States–China Relations is a case in point.[2] That blue-ribbon report "assesses U.S. interests; and makes specific recommendations for American policies upon which to base a long-term relationship" between the United States and the People's Republic of China, Taiwan, and Hong Kong. It was intended to educate elite opinion in the United States regarding China policy. The report says: "With respect to Taiwan, America's *overriding interest* is that the future relationship between Beijing and Taipei be determined by them peacefully. Washington should make it clear to various forces in Taiwan that the autonomy that is now enjoyed would be jeopardized if the people of Taiwan declared de jure independence" (emphasis added). "The interests of the United States" require that the relationship between Beijing and Taipei "be resolved peacefully (by the people on both sides of the Taiwan Strait without U.S. mediation or pressure.)" Regarding the exact nature of U.S. interests regarding Taiwan, the report merely says that "American interests in and connections to Taiwan are extensive," noting such things as economic and cultural exchanges. It is presumably those economic and cultural interests that underlie insistence on peaceful resolution of the conflict between Beijing and Taipei.

Insistence on the peaceful resolution of the Beijing-Taipei dispute would seem to be a policy, not an interest. Policies serve interests—they do not create them. The Atlantic Council–National Committee report says not a word about any important political interest the United States might have in Taiwan's secure evolution as a democratic, liberal capitalist polity. The report notes that "although the United States no longer has any formal defense alliance with Taipei, the 1979 Taiwan Relations Act (TRA) makes clear U.S. interest in Taiwan's security and calls on the President of the United States to assure that the United States helps maintain Taiwan's capacity to defend itself." The only "U.S. interests" mentioned, however, are economic and cultural exchanges. The reason for that is suggested by the observation that "it will serve neither the interests of the United States nor the welfare of the people of Taiwan or Hong Kong for the United States to call into question the principles upon which U.S. policy toward China has been based for many years"—

the three communiqués and the TRA. In the realm of diplomacy this is undoubtedly true. But to confuse analysis of U.S. interests with the particular policies used to promote those interests leads not to clarity but to confusion. The most important U.S. interest in Taiwan is related not to trade, investment, and cultural exchanges, but to political concern that the liberal, democratic polity that has emerged on Taiwan is not snuffed out by the CCP. Taiwan has emerged as a vibrant, liberal, and democratic state. The CCP government of the PRC, on the other hand, is one of the world's few remaining Leninist regimes. It has repeatedly demonstrated its firm opposition to individual freedom and democracy. Were Taiwan brought under its control, Taiwan's political development would likely be redirected along the lines of the CCP's core political beliefs. The United States has an interest in seeing that this does not happen. Public discussion of these issues may cause tension with Beijing, but failure to discuss them leads to muddled thinking.

A 1995 report by another blue-ribbon independent task force sponsored by the Council on Foreign Relations came several steps closer to recognizing the U.S. interest in preserving a democratic Taiwan.[3] Written two and a half years after the Atlantic Council–National Committee report and in the aftermath of the PLA missile tests of 1995, this report affirmed the U.S. interest in promoting democratic institutions in East Asia. It also recognized that "Taiwan has evolved from an authoritarian state to a representative democracy, and its human rights record now compares favorably with other nations in the region."[4] Yet the report does not combine those two propositions and conclude that the United States has an interest in preventing the forcible destruction of Taiwan's democracy. The reasons for this omission may well be political expediency having to do with the drafting of what is intended to be an influential policy report. The drafters of the Council on Foreign Relations report were concerned with not signaling Taiwan that the United States would support Taiwan even if it unilaterally and explicitly declared its independence of China. Achievement of this required a degree of calculated ambiguity that renders U.S. support for Taiwan contingent on various scenarios. In terms of policy, such calculated silence and ambiguity may well make sense, but it does not contribute to a clear understanding of U.S. interests.

The emergence of a democratic Taiwan was a result of the sustained use of U.S. power and influence over a period of several decades. Throughout the Cold War, the United States encouraged the evolution of Taiwan's polity along democratic lines. National Security Council policy statements of 1955 and 1957 listed that as the second-ranking U.S. objective vis-à-vis Taiwan. The United States sought, the memoranda said, "an increasingly efficient Government of the Republic of China (GRC), evolving toward responsible representative government, capable of attracting growing support and allegiance from the people of mainland China and Taiwan, and serving as the focal point of the free Chinese alternative to Communism."[5] The particular concerns were specific to the 1950s confrontation with the PRC, but the overriding objective of U.S. policy—promotion of democracy—corresponded to a broader U.S. interest.

From 1950 through 1965 Taiwan was one of the leading recipients of U.S. economic and military assistance. U.S. officials regularly and deliberately used that assistance as leverage to move Taiwan toward liberal and democratic forms. U.S. advisors in all fields flooded Taiwan, dispensing along with their technical advice exhortations about greater democracy. Hundreds of thousands of students from Taiwan passed through U.S. universities and many returned home with U.S. style political ideas, which seeped through Taiwan society at both the elite and popular levels. More basically, of course, U.S. military power prevented Taiwan from being drawn into the cataclysm of Mao Zedong's centrally planned economy, agricultural collectivization, vast campaigns of repression, and Gulag of concentration camps. While it is indisputable that the people of Taiwan shaped their own political destiny, it is equally clear that United States policy sought a liberal, democratic Taiwan and that its efforts were ultimately successful. Now the United States has an interest in seeing that the product of its sustained effort is not destroyed.

Taiwan's contemporary polity is arguably the freest and certainly the most democratic state to emerge in the long history of Chinese civilization. The impact of the first Chinese democracy on the future political evolution of China itself may conceivably be significant, but even if it is not, the core beliefs of the United States give it an interest in preventing that democracy from being forcibly destroyed—even by bloodless coercion. Hitler's destruction of Czechoslovak democracy in 1938 was also bloodless.

Lack of clarity about the nature of U.S. interests could have serious detrimental consequences in the event of a Sino-U.S. war precipitated by PRC efforts to subordinate Taiwan. Were another confrontation of the 1996 sort to escalate into such a war, for what purposes would the American people be called upon to endanger the lives of their sons and daughters? Trade and investment? Peace? Both the Atlantic Council–National Committee and the Council on Foreign Relations reports view regional stability—peace—as the overriding U.S. interest in East Asia. If this is the case, it would seem to follow that the United States should do whatever is necessary to avoid war, even to the extent of sacrificing Taiwan. As any student of the 1930s and 1940s knows, such an argument for fighting for peace can be cogently made. And as any student of the 1960s and 1970s knows, such an argument provides an extremely risky political foundation upon which to build popular support for a U.S. war effort.

Firm popular U.S. support for a war with China over Taiwan can be built only on the basis of some broader, transcendent moral objective. But moral principle must be grounded in the realities of national security defined in terms of power. Such an integrated framework is provided by use of U.S. power to sustain the democratic polities that have emerged along the western littoral of the Pacific Ocean over the past half century. For many decades U.S. power has been used to help bring about the emergence of these polities. Their survival guarantees U.S. security in the Pacific region in a fundamental sense well into the next century. Use of U.S. power in this fashion accords with the highest moral principles inspiring the American people. It accords also with the geopolitical realities of power in the Pacific and the security of the United States of America confronted by the emergence of a powerful, assertive, and antidemocratic China.

Notes

ABBREVIATIONS USED IN THE NOTES AND BIBLIOGRAPHY

AFP   Agency France Press
FBIS, DRC   *Foreign Broadcast Information Service, Daily Report, China*
FBIS, EAS   *Foreign Broadcast Information Service, Daily Report, East Asia*
FEER   *Far Eastern Economic Review*
PNA   Philippine News Agency

Sources included in the Bibliography are listed here in abbreviated form.

1 / THE SIGNIFICANCE OF THE 1996 CRISIS

1. Winkler, "Institutionalization and Participation."

2. Huntington, *The Third Wave.*

3. Michael D. Swaine calls these people "conservatives" and locates them in "various party and government advisory bodies, especially those with links to major figures among China's gerontocracy" (Swaine and Henry, *China,* pp. 50–54). Allen S. Whiting also calls them "conservatives" but locates them in the Chinese Communist Party's (CCP) propaganda-ideological apparatus. Whiting too credits them with support from several elders (Whiting, "Chinese Nationalism and Foreign Policy After Deng").

4. Wang Jisi, "How and Why Things Went Wrong in Sino-American Relations, 1989–1992," p. 49. Sutter, *Sino-U.S. Relations.*

5. Michael Swaine says that the influence of this perspective is "increasing, but has not (yet) eclipsed the mainstream" point of view (*China,* p. 52). Allen Whiting says that ideological influence peaked in late 1991 and declined after Deng Xiaoping's southern tour in early 1992 ("Chinese Nationalism," p. 304).

6. *Japan Digest,* vol. 6, no. 145 (25 Aug. 1995), p. 1.

7. Chanda et al., "Territorial imperative"; Richburg and Mufson, "Saber-Rattling."

8. See Whiting, "ASEAN Eyes China."

9. Ibid., p. 12.

10. Ibid., pp. 26–27.

11. Prime, "China's Economic Progress"; Prime, "The Economy in Overdrive."

12. Mansfield and Snyder, "Democratization and the Danger of War."

13. Ibid., p. 29.

2 / TAIWAN'S "DRIFTING AWAY"

1. "Chinese Embassy Position."
2. Ash and Kueh, "Economic Integration within Greater China."
3. Lin Chong-pin, "Beijing and Taipei."
4. *A Bridge for Chinese.*
5. This important point is made by Yu-shan Wu ("Taiwan in 1993," p. 52), a professor at National Taiwan University.
6. This is the central point of Jackson, *Quasi-states.*
7. Winkler, "Institutionalization and Participation."
8. Cheung, "Talk Soft, Carry Stick."
9. Lee's interview with Ryotaro was originally published in *Hei bai xinwen zhoukan* (Black and white news weekly) (Taipei), 29 May–4 June 1994. It was later included in a compilation of Lee Teng-hui's writings titled *Jingying da Taiwan* (Managing great Taiwan).
10. Cheung, "Talk Soft, Carry Stick."
11. Li Jiaquan, "Two Fallacies on 'Taiwan Independence.' "
12. Ibid.
13. Bai, "Deng Xiaoping Is Worried That Taiwan May Be Lost."
14. On 24 September 1994 the Thai newspaper *New China Post* carried a report on Lee's discussions with Hsu. This meeting was brought to my attention and a summary of the Thai report provided by an acquaintance at the Contemporary International Relations Institute in Beijing.
15. Li Jiaquan, "Two Fallacies on Taiwan Independence."

3 / TAIWAN'S "PRAGMATIC DIPLOMACY"

1. On the origin and result of these talks, see *A Resume of the Koo-Wang Talks.*
2. The "White Paper" was reprinted in *Zhongguo shibao* (China times), 6 July 1994 (trans. in *FBIS, DRC,* 11 July 1994, pp. 50–59).
3. Xinhua, 12 July 1994; and Beijing radio, 19 July 1994 (trans, in *FBIS, DRC,* 18 July, pp. 92–93; and 20 July 1994, pp. 34–35).
4. *Asia 1991 Yearbook* (Hong Kong: Far Eastern Economic Review, 1991), pp. 6–7.
5. *Free China Journal,* 13 Aug. 1993, p. 1.
6. Yu-shan Wu, "Taiwan in 1993," pp. 53–54.
7. *Free China Journal,* 6 Jan. 1996, p. 7.
8. "Bidding High," *Free China Review,* Dec. 1994, pp. 36–37.
9. *Free China Journal,* 2 June 1995, p. 1.
10. Philip Lu, "Golf Ball Diplomacy."
11. *Liaowang,* 25 September 1995 (trans. in *FBIS, DRC,* 25 Oct. 1995, pp. 89–91).
12. See Yu-shan Wu "Taiwan in 1994," p. 67.

4 / BEIJING'S OBJECTIONS TO U.S. POLICY

1. For the texts of the 1972, 1978, and 1982 communiqués, see Harding, *A Fragile Relationship,* p. 384.

2. Regarding China's arms acquisitions program, including deals with the former USSR, see Gill and Kim, *China's Arms Acquisitions from Abroad.*

3. Xinhua (trans. in *FBIS, DRC,* 3 Sept. 1992, p. 1).

4. *New York Times,* 11 Sept. 1994, p. 9.

5. Regarding Chinese elite perceptions of the United States, see Shambaugh, *Beautiful Imperialist.*

6. Harding, *A Fragile Relationship,* p. 363.

7. This point is made in Chu, "National Unity, Sovereignty and Territorial Integration."

8. House Bill 2333, 103rd Congress, 2nd Session.

9. Nicholas Kirstof, "More Than One Way to Squeeze China," *New York Times,* 22 May 1994, p. E5.

10. Sutter, *Taiwan.* Members of Congress had been pushing the Clinton administration to go substantially further by allowing Taiwan to use the title "Republic of China," endorsing Taiwan's membership in the UN, sending senior U.S. officials to Taiwan, allowing Taiwan's senior officials to visit the U.S., and providing for the sale of advanced weapons to Taiwan.

11. *New York Times,* 8 Sept. 1994, p. A5.

12. *New York Times,* 9 Sept. 1994, p. A3; 11 Sept. 1994, p. A9.

13. Press release of PRC Mission to the UN, 16 Feb. 1995.

14. *Free China Journal,* 18 Nov. 1994, p. 3.

15. Lee Teng-hui, address to the National Unification Council, Taipei, 8 April 1995. Copy of speech provided by SEF, Taipei.

16. *China Daily* (Beijing), 18 July 1995, p. 1.

17. Xinhua (trans. in *FBIS, DRC,* 31 Jan. 1996, pp. 75–76).

5 / THE TAIWAN ISSUE IN CHINESE DOMESTIC POLITICS

1. Richard Baum, *Burying Mao.*

2. Deng Liqun served in a series of ideological-propaganda posts during the 1950s and 1960s. During the 1980s he was director of the Central Committee propaganda department and head of the leading group for CCP cadre education. Following the Beijing massacre in 1989 he was a leading advocate of the doctrine of "peaceful evolution" and a critic of Deng Xiaoping's program of opening and reform.

Hu Qiaomu served as Mao Zedong's secretary in the 1940s, and in a number of propaganda, educational, and legal positions in the 1950s–1980s. In the 1980s he was author of several major polemics against liberalization on the ideological front.

3. Zhao Ziyang served as Party secretary of Guangdong Province in the early

1960s. In 1976 he was posted as first secretary of Sichuan Province, where he pioneered agricultural decollectivization. He was promoted to the Politburo in 1979 and became head of the State Council in 1980. He was a primary architect of reform throughout the 1980s.

Hu Qili was a protégé of Hu Yaobang in youth work in the 1950s. In 1980 he was appointed secretary of the Young Communist League, and in 1982 became director of the General Office of the Central Committee. He was an important member of the liberal reform group in the 1980s, and was reputedly the only prominent member of that group to refuse to repudiate Zhao Ziyang after the Beijing massacre.

Tian Jiyun was involved in financial work during the 1950s and 1960s and emerged in the 1980s as a key engineer of economic reform from his post as deputy secretary general of the State Council. Tian entered the Politburo in 1985. Basic biographical information is available in Wolfgang Bartke, *Who's Who in the People's Republic of China,* 2nd ed. (New York and München: K. G. Saur, 1987).

4. Regarding these events see Garver, "The Chinese Communist Party and the Collapse of Soviet Communism"; and Garver, "China, German Unification, and the Five Principles of Peaceful Coexistence."

5. Whiting, "Chinese Nationalism and Foreign Policy After Deng."

6. Baum, *Burying Mao.* See also Suisheng Zhao, "Deng Xiaoping's Southern Tour."

7. Recent scholarly attempts to assess this phenomenon are presented in Unger, ed., *China Nationalism.* See also Jisi Wang, "Pragmatic Nationalism"; and Forney, "Patriot Games."

8. Ye Jianying was a veteran of the Whampoa Military Academy who played a principle role in executing the Long March. During the 1930s and 1940s he was one of the CCP's major military leaders. He served as defense minister during the crucial period around Mao's death and helped accomplish the arrest of the radical Maoists led by Jiang Qing (Madame Mao). Throughout the 1980s he was one of China's most senior elders.

9. Li Peng was orphaned by the KMT execution of his parents and adopted by Zhou Enlai in 1937. Sent to study electrical engineering in Moscow in 1948, he returned to China to fill a number of increasingly prominent roles in the energy sector during the Maoist era. During the 1980s he was a leader in the energy and electronics sectors. Elected to the Politburo in 1985, he played a key role in effecting the military solution to the political crisis of early 1989.

Qiao Shi rose through a series of state and Party positions during the 1950s and 1960s. From 1978 to 1983 he served as deputy head and then head of the CCP's International Liaison Department, one of China's overseas intelligence organs. He became director of the CCP's organizational department in 1984 and entered the Politburo in 1985.

After being purged as a "rightist" in 1957, Zhu Rongji reemerged in the 1980s to become an important architect of economic reform.

Li Peng, Qiao Shi, and Zhu Rongji all are about thirty years younger than Deng Xiaoping, Chou Yun, and Ye Jianying.

10. Shirk, *The Political Logic of Economic Reform in China.*

11. Regarding Jiang's effort to court the PLA, see Shambaugh, "China's Commander in Chief."

12. Huang, "The Chinese Navy's Offshore Active Defense Strategy."

13. A forceful presentation of this argument by Andrew J. Nathan precipitated a major exchange of opinions in the July 1996 issue of the *China Journal* (Nathan, "China's Goals in the Taiwan Strait"; see also the replies to Nathan's thesis by others in that issue). My own view is that the narrow security concerns outlined by Nathan are indeed quite close to the hearts of China's military leaders, but that even they, and even more so other Chinese leaders, *think* primarily in more nationalist terms along the lines suggested by Chih-yu Shih's contribution to that debate ("National Security Is a Western Concern").

14. This came up repeatedly in discussions in China, and is also frequently alluded to by Hong Kong reporters.

15. Allen S. Whiting covers much of the same ground as the rest of this chapter in his recent article "Chinese Nationalism and Foreign Policy After Deng." A caveat is necessary concerning the account given in the rest of this chapter, much of which is based on reports in the Hong Kong press. While some such reports have proved to be true, others have proven false. In this case, however, Hong Kong media reports of PLA discontent with the central government's Taiwan policy are generally corroborated by members of the Western diplomatic and journalistic communities in Beijing who have spoken with well-connected Chinese, and by visiting Western academics (including this author during the summer of 1995) who have interviewed such people. While declining to confirm or deny reports about particular letters, meetings, or decisions, Chinese frequently confirmed that the military had been critical of what it felt was a weak policy on the Taiwan issue. This evidence substantiates the over-all direction of Hong Kong press reports, if not each particular incident reported.

16. Shu, "The Hands Held by China and the United States." See also Cheng Chenchun, "The Conservatives Are Fanning an Anti-U.S. Wind."

17. Wu Qingwen, "The Chinese Military Reacts." According to Dr. Paul Frandano of the U.S. National Intelligence Council, *Xin bao* (New daily) is one of the more highly regarded and reliable of the Hong Kong publications (personal communication with the author, 11 Sept. 1995).

18. Cheng Chenchun, "Conservatives Are Fanning an Anti-U.S. Wind."

19. Shu, "The Hands Held by China and the United States."

20. Tian, "Foreign Ministry's Secret Report on Sino-U.S. Relations."

21. Ren, "CPC Makes New Policy Decision."

22. Ming, "New Elements in the CPC's Taiwan Policy."

23. Lo and Li, "One Hundred and Sixteen Generals."

24. Ibid.

25. Ren, "The CPC Intensifies Its Peace Offensive against Taiwan."

26. Ren, "CPC Decides to Adjust Strategy toward United States."

27. Lo and Li, "One Hundred and Sixteen Generals."

28. Ibid.

29. Lo Ping, "Notes on northern journey." This bit of information was reportedly supplied by an NPC delegate.

30. Ibid.

31. Ibid.

32. Ren, "China Insists Foreign Countries Should Accord Li Peng Equally Courteous Reception."

33. Ibid. Circumstantial evidence lends credence to these reports of criticisms of challenges to Qian Qichen's handling of foreign affairs at this juncture. Shortly after Jiang Zemin's public endorsement of Qian's work, Xinhua reported that Qian had delivered a report surveying China's diplomacy to a joint meeting of the Central Committee Propaganda Department and "other departments" (Xinhua, 10 June 1994, trans. in *FBIS, DRC*, 10 June 1994). Such a report would certainly have required Politburo approval—and debate. About this time "well informed sources in Beijing" also reported that Qian Qichen would soon resign as foreign minister (*Xingdao ribao*, 10 June 1994, trans in *FBIS, DRC*, 10 June 1994, pp. 26–27). This report was denounced by an MFA spokesman as "sheer fabrication" (*FBIS, DRC*, 13 June 1994, p. 14).

34. Li Qiqing, "Deng meets Chen."

35. *Xin bao*, 6 Sept. 1994 (trans. in *FBIS, DRC*, 7 Oct. 1994, pp. 33–34).

36. Ting, "Hawks Dominate China's Policy toward Taiwan."

37. Xinhua, 29 May 1995 (trans. in *FBIS, DRC*, 30 May 1995, pp. 82–83).

38. Special dispatch by Beijing staff reporter, "Infuriated by Lee Teng-hui's Visit, CPC Hardliners Call for Re-explanation of Jiang's Eight Point Proposal to Curb Taiwan Independence Forces," *Lianhe bao* (United daily) (Hong Kong), 26 May 1995 (trans. in *FBIS, DRC*, 26 May 1995, pp. 5–6). See also *New York Times*, 1 Aug. 1995, p. A2; and Lam, "Taiwan Gamble Pays Off for Jiang."

39. Ting, "Hawks Dominate."

40. Joffe, *China After the Gulf War;* Liu, *Reflections on the Gulf War.*

41. See Gurtov and Hwang, *China Under Threat;* and Whiting, *The Chinese Calculus of Deterrence.*

42. Whiting, *Chinese Calculus of Deterrence.*

43. Mansfield and Snyder, "Democratization."

44. Baum, *Burying Mao.*

45. Perhaps the best hope for the development of genuine competitive elections in China is through Chinese recognition that submission of elite disputes over policy and power to the masses for resolution, rather than to the paramount leader, elder veterans, or the military, offers a more solid guarantee of stability.

6 / THE U.S. VISA DECISION AND BEIJING'S REACTION

1. *New York Times*, 9 April 1996, p. A6.

2. *Congressional Quarterly Weekly Report*, 1995, pp. 125, 1342.

3. Editorial, "Taiwan Insulted Again, U.S. Prefers Terrorist over Friend," *FEER*, 23 March 1995, p. 5.

4. *New York Times*, 8 Sept. 1994, p. A5.

5. *China Daily*, 24 May 1995, p. 4.

6. *New York Times,* 29 July 1995, p. 3.

7. Gordon Chang, *Friends and Enemies;* Mayers, *Splitting the Monolith.*

8. Personal communication, Beijing, spring–summer 1995.

9. Beijing Xinhua (in English), 23 May 1995 (in *FBIS-DRC,* 23 May 1995, pp. 3–5).

10. "Taiwan's Actions Delay Meeting," *China Daily* (Beijing), 17 June 1995, p. 1.

7 / BEIJING'S PROBING OF U.S. INTENTIONS

1. Xinhua, 31 July 1995 (trans. in *FBIS, DRC,* 1 Aug. 1995, pp. 21–23).

2. Marshal Green, "Omens of Change," in Green, Holdridge, and Stokes, *War and Peace with China.*

3. The three communiqués and various unilateral statements are available in Harding, *A Fragile Relationship,* pp. 373–90.

4. The text of the TRA is in Downen, *The Taiwan Pawn in the China Game.*

5. See Garver, "Arms Sales, the Taiwan Question, and Sino-U.S. Relations."

6. *Wall Street Journal,* 14 Sept. 1995, p. A15; *South China Morning Post,* 9 Sept. 1995, p. 7.

7. *New York Times,* 13 July 1995, p. A8.

8. *South China Morning Post,* 1 Aug. 1995 (trans. in *FBIS, DRC,* 1 Aug. 1995, p. 5).

9. *New York Times,* 29 July 1995, p. A3.

10. On behalf of this author, U.S. senator Sam Nunn's office asked the State Department for a copy of Clinton's letter to Jiang. Senator Nunn was told that the letter was not available for public distribution.

11. *Dagong bao* (Hong Kong), 3 Aug. 1995 (trans. in *FBIS, DRC,* 8 Aug. 1995, pp. 4–5).

12. *New York Times,* 2 Aug. 1995, p. A3.

13. "Taiwan and the United Nations." Testimony by Kent Wiedemann, deputy assistant secretary of state for East Asian and Pacific affairs, before the House International Relations Committee, 3 Aug. 1995.

14. *New York Times,* 28 Aug. 1995, pp. A1, 2.

15. Xinhua, 29 Aug. 1995 (trans. in *FBIS, DRC,* 30 Aug. 1995, p. 1).

16. *New York Times,* 29 Aug. 1995, p. A8.

17. *New York Times,* 23 Sept. 1995, p. A4.

18. *Free China Journal,* 11 Aug. 1995, p. 1.

19. *U.S. Department of State Dispatch,* 23 Oct. 1995, vol. 6, no. 43, pp. 773–75.

20. Xinhua, 24 Oct. 1995 (trans. in *FBIS, DRC,* 24 Oct. 1995, p. 14).

21. Trans. in *FBIS, DRC,* 25 Oct. 1995, pp. 88–89.

22. The U.S. side described it as "very good," the "best of the three meetings" thus far held between Jiang and Clinton (*New York Times,* 25 Oct. 1995, p. 1). The Chinese side described it as "candid, amicable, positive and useful" (Xinhua, 24 Oct. 1995, trans. in *FBIS, DRC,* 27 Oct. 1995, p. 1).

23. Xinhua, 24 Oct. 1995 (trans. in *FBIS, DRC,* 27 Oct. 1995, p. 1).

24. This important point was not mentioned by Assistant Secretary Winston

Lord in his press briefing following the Jiang-Clinton summit. Indeed, Lord did not mention Taiwan at all, but stressed areas of common interest and cooperation, and the U.S. commitment to cooperation with China ("The U.S. and China: Working Together Toward a Stable Relationship," *United States Department of State Dispatch*, 6 Nov. 1995, vol. 6, no. 45, p. 816). Nor did any of the Chinese coverage of the summit mention Clinton raising such a point. Had he, Beijing's propaganda almost certainly would have criticized it.

25. *Guang jiao jing* (Hong Kong), 16 Nov. 1995 (trans. in *FBIS, DRC*, 29 Nov. 1995, pp. 93–95).

26. This was the main theme of Nye's boss, Secretary of Defense William Perry, in a speech to the Washington State China Relations Council on 30 October, shortly before Nye's visit to China (Xinhua, 31 Oct. 1995, in *FBIS, DRC*, 31 Oct. 1995, pp. 3–4).

27. *New York Times*, 18 Nov. 1995, p. A3; 7 Feb. 1996, p. A3.

28. East Asia Wireless File, British Broadcasting Corporation, 14 Dec. 1995, p. 28.

29. *New York Times*, 4 Aug. 1995, p. 4; *Facts on File* (New York: Facts on File Inc., 1995), p. 644.

8 / THE DECEMBER LEGISLATIVE YUAN ELECTIONS

1. Copper, *Taiwan's 1995 Legislative Yuan Election*. Unless otherwise indicated, this chapter follows Copper's excellent study.

2. Christopher Bodeen, "Lee's U.S. Visit Supported by Big Majority in Taiwan," *China Post* (international ed.), 6 June 1995, p. 1 (cited in Copper, *Taiwan's 1995 Legislative Yuan Election*, p. 8).

3. Lt. General (Ret.) Zhou Shifu, *Shei ze shei: Chanshu Li Hao ju san* (Who blames whom: Narrative of the joining together and falling out of Lee [Teng-hui] and Hau [Pei-tsun]) (Taipei: Zhou Shifu, circa 1996).

4. Ibid.

5. *Asiaweek*, 8 Sept. 1995, p. 28 (cited in Copper, *Taiwan's 1995 Legislative Yuan Elections*, p. 9).

6. Julian Baum, "Up and Running," *FEER*, 7 Sept. 1995, p. 14 (cited in Copper, *Taiwan's 1995 Legislative Yuan Elections*, p. 10).

7. Cited in Copper, *Taiwan's 1995 Legislative Yuan Elections*, p. 10.

8. Ibid., pp. 18–23.

9. Xinhua, 18 Oct. 1995 (trans. in *FBIS, DRC*, 19 Oct. 1995, pp. 21, 25); *Sankei shimbun* (Tokyo), 11 Nov. 1995 (trans. in *FBIS, DRC*, 13 Nov. 1995, p. 30).

10. Beijing, Xinhua domestic service, 25 Nov. 1995, and *Pingguo ribao* (Hong Kong), 27 Nov. 1995 (trans. in *FBIS, DRC*, 27 Nov. 1995, pp. 23–25).

11. *Wenhui bao*, 27 Nov. 1995 (trans. in *FBIS, DRC.*, 28 Nov. 1995, p. 72).

12. Copper, *Taiwan's 1995 Legislative Yuan Elections.*, pp. 19–23.

13. From Zeng Liang-ping, *Leap Month of August 1995: T Day—The Warning of Taiwan Strait War* (Taipei: Business Weekly, Aug. 1994) (trans. in *FBIS, Daily Report Supplement*, 31 Jan. 1996 [FBIS-CHI-96–021-S]). It should be noted that Zeng speci-

fied several other "zero days" on which it would make sense for the CCP to attack. Regarding the impact of the bestseller, see Julian Baum, "A Case of Nerves."

14. Copper, *Taiwan's 1995 Legislative Yuan Elections,* pp. 25–34.

15. Ibid., p. 3.

9 / THE CONFRONTATION

1. East Asian Wireless File, British Broadcasting Corporation, 14 Dec. 1995, pp. 25–33.

2. *New York Times,* 27 and 31 Jan. 1996, pp. A4, A2.

3. *Facts on File, 1996,* p. 46.

4. Letter submitted by President Bill Clinton to a member of Congress on 27 Nov. 1995, in *Taiwan International Review* (published by Taiwan's DPP), vol. 1, no. 3 (Nov.–Dec. 1995), p. 14.

5. "U.S. Policies Toward Beijing Increasingly Rankle GOP."

6. *United States Department of State Dispatch,* 3 April 1995, vol. 6, no. 14, pp. 273–78.

7. *New York Times,* 7 Feb. 1996, p. A3.

8. Office of Naval Intelligence, *Chinese Exercises.*

9. Japanese defense ministry information in *Nihon keizai shimbun,* 13 March 1996 (trans. in FBIS, DRC, 14 March 1996, p. 4).

10. Office of Naval Intelligence, *Chinese Exercises,* p. 6.

11. *Guang jiao jing,* 16 March 1995 (trans. in FBIS, DRC, 21 March 1996, pp. 31–34).

12. *Ming bao* (Hong Kong), 7 March 1996 (trans. in FBIS, DRC, 7 March 1996, pp. 40–41).

13. Xinhua, 4 March 1996 (trans. in FBIS, DRC, 5 March 1996, p. 68).

14. Beijing Radio International Service, 5 March 1996 (trans. in FBIS, DRC, 6 March 1996, p. 1).

15. Office of Naval Intelligence, *Chinese Exercises,* p. 7.

16. Dept. of Defense news briefing, Secretary William J. Perry, 8 March 1996, Defenselink, <http://www.pentagon.mil>.

17. Dept. of Defense news briefing, 12 March 1996, Defenselink, <http://www.pentagon.mil>.

18. Office of Naval Intelligence, *Chinese Exercises,* p. 7.

19. *Wenhui bao,* 5 March 1996 (trans. in FBIS, DRC, 11 March 1996, p. 15).

20. Television transcript of Tim Russert interview with Secretary of State Warren Christopher, *Meet the Press.* Datatimes Corporation f.6, "Burrelle's TV Transcripts."

21. Reuter, Taipei, Taiwan, 12 March 1996. From "In the News," America On-line, 14 March 1996.

22. Department of Defense news briefing, 12 March 1996, Defenselink, <http://www.pentagon.mil>.

23. Xinhua, 12 March (trans. in FBIS, DRC, 13 March 1996, p. 1).

24. Zhongguo Tongxunshe (Hong Kong), 13 March 1996 (trans. in FBIS, DRC, 14 March 1996, pp. 3–4).

25. The number fifty is from *Guang jiao jing,* 16 Apr. 1996 (trans. in *FBIS, DRC,* 17 May 1996, pp. 27–32).

26. Office of Naval Intelligence, *Chinese Exercises,* p. 8.

27. *Guang jiao jing,* 16 April 1996 (trans. in *FBIS, DRC,* 17 May 1996, p. 28).

28. The coordinates for the exercise area are in Xinhua, 15 Mar. 1996 (trans. in *FBIS, DRC,* 15 March 1996, p. 42).

29. Office of Naval Intelligence, *Chinese Exercises,* p. 9.

30. *Guang jiao jing,* 16 April 1996 (trans. in *FBIS, DRC,* 17 May 1996, p. 29).

31. Ibid.

32. Office of Naval Intelligence, *Chinese Exercises,* p. 9.

33. *Guang jiao jing,* 16 April 1996 (trans. in *FBIS, DRC,* 17 May 1996, p. 29).

34. Geoffrey Crothall, "Li Peng Warns U.S. 'Not to Interfere' in Taiwan," *South China Morning Post,* 18 March 1996 (in *FBIS, DRC,* 18 March 1996, p. 5).

35. *Wenhui bao,* 20 March 1996 (trans. in *FBIS, DRC,* 20 March 1996, pp. 5–7).

36. *Dagong bao,* 12 March 1996 (trans. in *FBIS, DRC,* 12 March 1996, pp. 11–12).

37. *Dagong bao,* 13 March 1996 (trans. in *FBIS, DRC,* 13 March 1996, pp. 9–11).

38. *Wenhui bao,* 14 March 1996 (trans. in *FBIS, DRC,* 14 March 1996, p. 17).

39. Li Xiangwen, "Special Article: United States Should Warn Lee Teng-hui," *Wenhui bao,* 14 March 1996 (trans. in *FBIS, DRC,* 14 March 1996, pp. 5–6).

40. Zeng Shuwan, "Beijing Military Observer Analyzes That PLA Is Entirely Capable of Dealing with Foreign Aircraft Carriers Should They Start Trouble," *Wenhui bao,* 21 March 1996 (trans. in *FBIS, DRC,* 21 March 1996, pp. 30–31). Of course, the United States had not actually considered sending troops to Chechnya.

41. McVadon, "PRC Exercises, Doctrine, and Tactics toward Taiwan."

42. Hong et al., *Zhong mei junshi zhongtu,* pp. 462–65.

10 / WERE CHINA'S LEADERS SURPRISED BY U.S. INTERVENTION?

1. The author was in Beijing during that time and spoke with acquaintances who participated in some of these activities.

2. Wang Fei-ling, "Shiyong zhuyi zhudaoxiade Meijun celue—Fenxi Meijun jieru Tai hai zhanzheng de kenengxing" (American military strategy under the guidance of realism—An analysis of the probability of U.S. military intervention in a Taiwan Strait war), *Mingbao yuekan* (Mingbao monthly) (Hong Kong), Aug. 1995, pp. 24–26.

3. Chanda, "Collateral Damage."

4. Lu, "Beijing's Near and Medium Policies toward Taiwan."

5. Robert Jervis, *Perception and Misperception in International Politics* (New Jersey: Princeton University Press, 1976).

6. *Pingguo ribao* (Hong Kong), 19 March 1996 (trans. in *FBIS, DRC,* 20 March 1996, p. 5).

7. *Xin bao,* 8 March 1996 (trans. in *FBIS, DRC,* 8 March 1996, pp. 2–3).

11 / PRC STRATEGY

1. Lin Chong-pin, "The Military Balance in the Taiwan Strait."
2. *Guang jiao jing* (Hong Kong), 16 Feb. 1993 (trans. in *FBIS, DRC,* 1 March 1993, pp. 65–66.
3. This distinction was suggested by Lin Chong-pin, director of the Graduate Institute of Political Science of National Sun Yat-sen University, Kaohsiung, Taiwan.
4. Wang Feiling, "Shiyong zhuyi . . ."
5. Bitzinger and Gill, *Gearing Up for High-Tech Warfare?*
6. Allen, Krumel, and Pollack, *China's Air Force Enters the 21st Century,* pp. 31–34, 118.
7. McVadon, "PRC Exercises, Doctrine, and Tactics toward Taiwan."
8. Lin Zhenghong, "Di wu zongdui qitu ansha hoxuanren."
9. *Lianhe bao,* 22 March 1996, p. 1; "Sooner or Later, Taiwan Pays the Price of Cross-Strait Tension," *FEER,* 28 March 1996, pp. 58–59.

12 / NUCLEAR COERCION WITH CHINESE CHARACTERISTICS

1. Godwin, "Chinese Military Strategy Revised"; Godwin, "Changing Concepts."
2. Lin Chongpin, quoted in Holloway, "A Chill Wind."
3. Xinhua, 25 Mar. 1996 (trans. in *FBIS, DRC,* 26 March 1996, p. 31).
4. *Pingguo ribao,* 18 Aug. 1995 (trans. in *FBIS, DRC,* 23 Aug. 1995, p. 30); *Ming bao,* 16 Aug. 1995 (trans. in *FBIS, DRC,* 18 Aug. 1995, pp. 27–28).
5. Tyler, "As China Threatens Taiwan, U.S. Listens."
6. *Lianhe zaobao* (United morning daily) (Singapore), 11 Jan. 1996 (trans. in *FBIS, DRC,* 2 Feb. 1996, pp. 12–13).
7. "China Fires Mobile Missile," *South China Morning Post,* 1 June 1995, p. 1; Holloway, "A Chill Wind."
8. Ding, "Beijing's Moratorium on Nuclear Tests."
9. Jim Wolf, "PRC gave nuclear warning to U.S.: Lord," Reuters Press Agency, *The China Post* (Taipei), 19 March 1996, p. 1.
10. Shao and Zhang, *Ezhi Tai du.*
11. Ibid., pp. 330–31.

13 / THE INTERNATIONAL EFFECT OF THE CRISIS

1. *United States Security Strategy for the East Asia–Pacific Region.*
2. *FBIS, EAS,* 5 March 1996, p. 13; 6 March 1996, p. 9.
3. MOFA press conference, 13 March 1996 (trans. in *FBIS, EAS,* 13 March 1996, pp. 7–10); Kyodo Press Agency, 6 and 11 March 1996 (trans. in *FBIS, EAS,* 7 March 1996, p. 10; 11 March 1996, p. 21).

4. *Sankei shimbun,* 18 March 1996 (trans. in *FBIS, EAS,* 21 March 1996, p. 8).

5. Agency France Press, Hong Kong, 7 March 1996 (trans. in *FBIS, EAS,* 7 March 1996, pp. 10–11).

6. *Sankei shimbun,* 18 March 1996 (trans. in *FBIS, EAS,* 21 March 1996, p. 8).

7. *Sankei shimbun,* 14 and 18 March 1996 (trans. in *FBIS, EAS,* 15 March 1996, pp. 7–8; 21 March 1996, pp. 8–9).

8. *Sankei shimbun,* 14 and 18 March 1996 (trans. in *FBIS, EAS,* 12 and 15 March 1996, pp. 6–7, 8–9); *Asahi shimbun,* 24 March 1996 (trans. in *FBIS, EAS,* 25 March 1996, pp. 12–13).

9. *Asahi shimbun,* 24 March 1996 (trans. in *FBIS, EAS,* 25 March 1996, p. 13).

10. *Mainichi shimbun,* 24 March 1996 (trans. in *FBIS, EAS,* 25 March 1996, p. 11).

11. MOFA press conference, 26 March 1996 (trans. in *FBIS, EAS,* 27 March 1996, p. 3).

12. Regarding the Ikeda-Qian talks, see Kyodo, 31 March 1996 (trans. in *FBIS, EAS,* 1 April 1996, pp. 16–17); *Yomiuri shimbun,* 1 and 2 April 1996 (trans. in *FBIS, EAS,* 3 April 1996, pp. 14–15; and 4 April 1996, pp. 8–9).

13. *Yomiuri shimbun,* 2 April 1996 (trans. in *FBIS, EAS,* 4 April 1996, pp. 8–9).

14. "Other States Shouldn't Interfere in Taiwan Issue, Qian Stresses," *Japan Times* (Tokyo), 1 April 1996, pp. 1, 3.

15. Kyodo, 1 April 1996 (trans. in *FBIS, EAS,* 1 April 1996, p. 18).

16. Kyodo, 1 and 2 April 1996 (trans. in *FBIS, EAS,* 1 and 2 April 1996, pp. 9, 18).

17. MOFA Press Conference, 13 March 1996 (trans. in *FBIS, EAS,* 13 March 1996, pp. 11–12).

18. Freeman, "The End of Taiwan."

19. *Sankei shimbun,* 17 March 1996 (trans. in *FBIS, EAS,* 19 March 1996, p. 1).

20. *Sankei shimbun,* 18 March 1996 (trans. in *FBIS, EAS,* 20 March 1996, p. 2).

21. "United States–Japan Joint Declaration on Security Alliance for the Twenty-first Century," 17 April 1996, dist. by Pacific Forum CSIS, Honolulu, <http://www.pacforum@lava.net>.

22. Ibid.

23. *Yonhap* (Seoul), 15 March 1996 (trans. in *FBIS, EAS,* 15 March 1996, p. 37).

24. *Yonhap,* 13 March 1996 (trans. in *FBIS, EAS,* 14 March 1996, p. 20).

25. KBS-1 television, 13 March 1996 (trans. in *FBIS, EAS,* 14 March 1996, p. 21).

26. *Korea Herald,* 2 March 1996 (in *FBIS, EAS,* 5 March 1996, pp. 50–51).

27. *Yonhap,* 9 March 1996 (trans. in *FBIS, EAS,* 11 March 1996, p. 57).

28. *Korean Update,* Information Office, Embassy of the Republic of Korea, Washington, D.C., 1 April 1996.

29. *Yonhap,* 13 March 1996 (trans. in *FBIS, EAS,* 14 March 1996, p. 20).

30. *Yonhap,* 15 and 26 March 1996 (trans. in *FBIS, EAS,* 15; 26 March 1996, pp. 37, 34).

31. *China's Foreign Relations,* p. 174.

32. AFP, Hong Kong, 8 March 1996 (trans. in *FBIS, EAS,* 8 March 1996, p. 60).

33. PNA, 11 March 1996 (trans. in *FBIS, EAS,* 12 March 1996, p. 75).

34. PNA, 12 March 1996 (trans. in *FBIS, EAS,* 13 March 1996, p. 55).

35. Quezon television, 12 March 1996, and *Manila Standard* (trans. in *FBIS, EAS,* 12 March 1996, pp. 75–76; 15 March 1996, p. 58).

36. *Business World* (Manila), 18 March 1996 (in *FBIS, EAS,* 20 March 1996, p. 73); Quezon radio, 12 March 1996 (trans. in *FBIS, EAS,* 12 March 1996, p. 77).

37. *FBIS, EAS,* 5 March 1996, p. 84; 13 March 1996, p. 57.

38. *Thailand Times* (Bangkok), 27 March 1996 (in *FBIS, EAS,* 27 March 1996, p. 72).

39. *Business Times* (Singapore), 4 March 1996 (in *FBIS, EAS,* 6 March 1996, pp. 48–49).

40. *Straits Times* (Singapore), 14 March 1996 (trans. in *FBIS, EAS,* 14 March 1996, pp. 28–29).

41. Xinhua, 21 March 1996 (trans. in *FBIS, DRC,* 22 March 1996, p. 8).

42. *Zhongguo duiwai jingji maoyi nianjian 1994* (Yearbook of China's foreign economic relations and trade 1994) (Beijing: Zhongguo Shehui Chubanshe, 1994), pp. 468–75.

43. Su Dai Bingran, "Strategic Basis of the Sino-European Relations in the Post Cold War Period"; and Li Qingsi, "The European Union and Its Relations with China," papers presented at the Conference on China and Europe toward the 21st Century, at People's University of China, Beijing, 19–21 July 1995.

44. "Mercedes-Benz Seals $1 Billion China Deal," *International Herald Tribune,* 13 July 1995, pp. 1, 7. In April 1996 China concluded a $1.5 billion deal with a European aerospace consortium to produce passenger planes. Boeing, the U.S. aerospace company, was the major competitor against the Europeans for the contract (*New York Times,* 11 April 1996, pp. 1, 6).

45. Rühe's comments came in an interview with the newspaper *Flensburger Tageblatt* (19 March 1996). Regarding other German criticism of China's actions, see "Seiters Kritisent China's Politik," *Frankfurter Allgemeine,* 23 March 1996, p. 4; "Chinapolitik, 'Reiner Zynismus,'" *Der Spiegel,* no. 14 (April) 1996, p. 21.

14 / APPRAISING THE GAINS AND COSTS OF BEIJING'S COERCIVE EXERCISES

1. William T. Pendley, "Taiwan: Getting It Right." Pacific Forum, Center for Strategic and International Studies, Pac Net no. 21, 24 May 1996. <http://www.csis.org>.

2. Tai Ming Cheung, "Still Gung-ho," *FEER,* 18 May 1989, p. 23.

3. Bitzinger and Gill, *Gearing Up for High-Tech Warfare?,* p. 33.

4. *Xingdao ribao,* 29 April 1996 (trans. in *FBIS, DRC,* 29 April 1996, pp. 31–32).

5. Xinhua, 22 June 1996, (trans. in *FBIS, DRC,* 24 June 1996, pp. 66–67).

6. *Jiefang junbao* (Beijing), 21 March 1996 (trans. in *FBIS, DRC,* 27 March 1996, pp. 26–27).

15 / CONCLUSIONS

1. Chen Dunde, *Mao Zedong yu Jiang Jieshi* (Mao Zedong and Chiang Kai-shek) (Beijing: Ba Yi Chubanshe, 1993), pp. 302–6.

2. *United States and China Relations at a Crossroads,* policy paper by the Atlantic

Council of the United States and the National Committee on United States–China Relations, Barber B. Conable and John C. Whitehead, co-chairs; David M. Lampton and Alfred D. Wilhelm, Jr. co-rapporteurs, Washington, D.C. February 1993.

3. "Managing the Taiwan Issue: Key Is Better U.S. Relations with China," report of an independent task force sponsored by the Council on Foreign Relations, November 1995.

4. Ibid., p. 8.

5. NSC 5503, "U.S. Policy Toward Formosa and the Government of the Republic of China," approved by President Dwight D. Eisenhower on 15 Jan. 1955; NSC 5723, with the same name, approved on 4 Oct. 1957 (*Foreign Relations of the United States*, 1955–57, vol. 2, pp. 30–34; vol. 3, pp. 119–623).

Bibliography

Allen, Kenneth W., Glenn Krumel, and Jonathan D. Pollack. *China's Air Force Enters the 21st Century*. Project Air Force. Santa Monica, Calif.: RAND, 1995.

Ash, Robert F., and Y. Y. Kueh. "Economic Integration within Greater China: Trade and Investment Flows Between Hong Kong and Taiwan." In *Greater China: The Next Superpower?*, David Shambaugh, editor, pp. 82–93. New York: Oxford University Press, 1995.

Bai, Xingliang. "Deng Xiaoping Is Worried That Taiwan May Be Lost." *Guang jiao jing*, 16 February 1993 (trans. in *Foreign Broadcast Information Service, Daily Report China* [*FBIS, DRC*]), 1 March 1993, pp. 65–66).

Baum, Julian. "A Case of Nerves." *Far Eastern Economic Review* (*FEER*), 20 July 1995, p. 26.

Baum, Richard. *Burying Mao: Chinese Politics in the Age of Deng Xiaoping*. Princeton, N.J.: Princeton University Press, 1994.

Bitzinger, Richard A., and Bates Gill. *Gearing Up for High-Tech Warfare? Chinese and Taiwanese Defense Modernization and Implications for Military Confrontation Across the Taiwan Strait, 1995–2005*. Washington, D.C.: Center for Strategic and Budgetary Assessments, 1996.

A Bridge for Chinese. Taipei: Straits Exchange Foundation, August 1994.

Caldwell, John, and Paul Godwin. "China's Force Projection Potential: An Assessment of the PLA's Conventional Military Capability, 1994–2005." Paper presented at American Enterprise Institute and Thompson, Mickle, Imbot Asia Ltd. conference on the PLA, Coolfont, W.Va., September 1995.

Chanda, Nayan. "Collateral Damage." *FEER*, 28 March 1996, pp. 16, 18.

———, et al. "Territorial Imperative." *FEER*, 23 February 1995, pp. 14–16.

Chang, Gordon. *Friends and Enemies: The United States, China, and the Soviet Union, 1948–1972*. Stanford University Press, 1990.

Chang Parris H. "Don't Dance to Beijing's Tune." *China Journal*, no. 36 (July 1996), pp. 103–6.

Chen Dunde. *Mao Zedong yu Jiang Jieshi* (Mao Zedong and Chiang Kaishek). Beijing: Ba Yi Chubanshe, 1993.

Chen Tian. "Foreign Ministry's Secret Report on Sino-U.S. Relations." *Zheng ming* (Hong Kong), 1 November 1992 (trans in *FBIS, DRC*, 3 November 1992, pp. 5–7).

Cheng Chenchun. "The Conservatives Are Fanning an Anti-U.S. Wind." *Cheng-ming*, 1 Oct. 1992 (trans. in *FBIS, DRC*, 1 Oct. 1992, pp. 9–11).

Cheng, Li, and Lynn White. "The Army in the Succession to Deng Xiaoping." *Asian Survey*, vol. 33, no. 8 (1993), pp. 758–59.

Cheung, Tai Ming. "Talk Soft, Carry Stick." *FEER*, 18 October 1990, p. 37.

Chu Shulong. "National Unity, Sovereignty and Territorial Integration." *China Journal,* no. 36 (July 1996), pp. 98–102.

Chuang Meng. "Deng Puts Forward New 12-Character Guiding Principle for Internal and Foreign Policies." *Jing bao,* no. 172 (5 November 1991), pp. 84–86 (trans. in *FBIS, DRC,* 6 November 1991, pp. 28–30).

China's Foreign Relations, A Chronology of Events (1949–1988). Beijing: Foreign Languages Press, 1989

"Chinese Embassy Position, U.S. Should Honor Its Commitments by Deeds." *Congressional Digest,* Aug.–Sept. 1995, pp. 201, 224.

Copper, John F. *Taiwan's 1995 Legislative Yuan Election.* Occasional Papers/Report Series in Contemporary Asian Studies (School of Law, University of Maryland), no. 1–1992 (132).

Ding, Arthur S. "Beijing's Moratorium on Nuclear Tests: An Evaluation of Mainland China's Nuclear Weapons." *Issues and Studies,* vol. 32, no. 7 (July 1996), pp. 131–33.

Downen, Robert L. *The Taiwan Pawn in the China Game: Congress to the Rescue.* Washington, D.C.: Georgetown University, Center for Strategic and International Studies, 1981.

Forney, Mat. "Patriot Games." *FEER,* 3 Oct. 1996, pp. 22–26.

Freeman, Chaz. "The End of Taiwan." *New York Times,* 15 February 1996, p. 16.

Garver, John W. "Arms Sales, the Taiwan Question, and Sino-U.S. Relations." *Orbis,* Winter 1993, pp. 999–1035.

———. "China, German Reunification, and the Five Principles of Peaceful Coexistence." *Journal of East Asian Affairs,* vol. 7, no. 1 (Winter–Spring 1994), pp. 135–172.

———. "China's Push Through the South China Sea: The Interaction of Bureaucratic and National Interests." *China Quarterly,* no. 132 (December 1992), pp. 999–1102.

———. "The Chinese Communist Party and the Collapse of Soviet Communism." *China Quarterly,* no. 133 (March 1993), pp. 1–26.

Gill, Bates, and Taeho Kim. *China's Arms Acquisitions from Abroad, A Quest for Superb and Secret Weapons.* Stockholm International Peace Research Institute Research Report no. 11. London: Oxford University Press, 1995.

Godwin, Paul H. B. "Changing Concepts of Doctrine, Strategy, and Operations in the Chinese People's Liberation Army, 1978–87." *China Quarterly,* no. 112 (December 1987), pp. 57–90.

———. "Chinese Military Strategy Revised: Local and Limited War." *Annals of the American Academy of Political and Social Science, China's Foreign Relations* (Allen S. Whiting, special editor), volume 519 (January 1992), pp. 197–98.

Green, Marshal, John H. Holdridge, and William N. Stokes, ed. *War and Peace with China: First Hand Experiences in the Foreign Services of the United States.* Bethesda, Md.: DACOR Press, 1994.

Gurtov, Melvin, and Byong-Moo Hwang. *China Under Threat; The Politics of Strategy and Diplomacy.* Baltimore: Johns Hopkins University Press, 1980.

Harding, Harry. *A Fragile Relationship: The United States and China since 1972.* Washington, D.C.: Brookings Institution, 1992.

Harris, Stuart. "The Taiwan Crisis: Some Basic Realities." *China Journal,* no. 36 (July 1996), pp. 129–34.

Holloway, Nigel. "A Chill Wind." *FEER,* 15 June 1995, pp. 15–16.

Hong Yonghong et al. *Zhong Mei junshi zhongtu, qian qian, hou hou* (Record of Sino-American military conflict). Beijing: Zhongguo Shehui Chubanshe, 1996.

Huang, Alexander Chieh-cheng. "The Chinese Navy's Offshore Active Defense Strategy, Conceptualization and Implication." *Naval War College Review,* vol. 47, no. 3 (Summer 1994), sequence 347, pp. 7–32.

Huang, Yasheng. "Commentary: Taiwan Strait Crisis and Sino-U.S. Relations." *Journal of Asian Business,* vol. 12, no. 3 (1996), pp. 87–90.

Huntington, Samuel P. *The Third Wave: Democratization in the Late Twentieth Century.* Norman Ok.: University of Oklahoma Press, 1993.

Jackson, Robert H. *Quasi-states: Sovereignty, International Relations and the Third World.* London: Cambridge University Press, 1990.

Jia, Qingguo. "Reflections on the Recent Tension in the Taiwan Strait." *China Journal,* no. 36 (July 1996), pp. 93–97.

Joffe, Ellis. "China after the Gulf War: The Lessons Learned." Paper presented at seminar on the Gulf War and the Far East, Center for National Security Studies, Los Alamos National Laboratory, Los Alamos, New Mexico, Nov. 1991.

Kristof, Nicholas. "More Than One Way to Squeeze China." *New York Times,* 22 May 1994, p. E5.

Lam, Willy Wo-Lap. "The Factional Dynamics in China's Taiwan Policy." *China Journal,* no. 36 (July 1996), pp. 116–18.

———. "Taiwan Gamble Pays Off for Jiang." *South China Morning Post,* 5 August 1995, p. 7.

Lee Teng-hui. *Jingying da Taiwan* (Managing great Taiwan). Taipei: Yuanliu Chuban Gongsi, Jan. 1995.

Li Jiaquan. "Two Fallacies on 'Taiwan Independence Are the Same Strain." Beijing radio, 6 February 1996 (trans. in *FBIS, DRC,* 8 February 1996, pp. 70–73).

Li Qiqing. "Deng Meets Chen; They Reach 8 Point Understanding." *Zheng ming,* 1 Sept. 1994, pp. 22–23 (trans. in *FBIS, DRC,* 6 September 1994, pp. 37–38).

———, and Li Zuqing. "One Hundred and Sixteen Generals Write to Deng Xiaoping on Policy toward United States." *Zheng ming,* 1 June 1993 (trans. in *FBIS, DRC,* 2 June 1993, pp. 33–35).

———. "Salvation Meeting Between Chen Yun and Deng Xiaoping," *Zheng ming,* 11 November 1991 (trans. in *FBIS, DRC,* 15 November 1991, pp. 24–27).

Lin, Bainiao. "CPC Formulates New Policy Towards United States." *Zheng ming,* no. 170, 1 Dec. 1991, pp. 17–19 (trans. in *FBIS, DRC,* 2 Dec. 1991, pp. 6–9).

Lin, Chong-pin. "Beijing and Taipei: The Dialectics in Post-Tiananmen Interactions." *China Quarterly,* no. 136 (Dec. 1993), pp. 770–804.

———. "Chinese Military Modernization: Perceptions, Progress, and Prospects." *Security Studies,* vol. 3, no. 4 (Summer 1994), pp. 718–53.

———. "The Military Balance in the Taiwan Straits." Paper presented at Hong Kong Conference on the PLA toward 2000, 13–15 July 1995.

Lin Zhenghong. "Di wu zongdui qitu ansha hoxuanren, wuqian tugong shanto zaoyao zuoluan" (Fifth column is planning to assassinate candidates, five thousand agents have been infiltrated to spread rumors and disorder). *Xin Taiwan* (New Taiwan) (Taipei), 21 March 1996, no. 2, pp. 17–19.

Liu Jinlin. "Reflections on the Gulf War and Lessons Drawn from It." Paper presented at seminar on the Gulf War and the Far East, Center for National Security Studies, Los Alamos National Laboratory, Los Alamos, New Mexico, Nov. 1991.

Lo Ping. "Deng and Chen Have a Secret Talk in Hangzhou." *Zheng ming,* no. 210 (1 July 1994), pp. 11–12 (trans. in *FBIS, DRC,* 26 July 1994, pp. 14–15).

———. "Notes on Northern Journey; CPC Military Attacks Ministry of Foreign Affairs." *Zheng ming,* 1 July 1994 (trans. in *FBIS, DRC,* 26 July 1994, pp. 33–36).

——— and Li Zuqing. "One Hundred and Sixteen Write to Deng Xiaoping on Policy toward United States." *Zheng ming,* 1 June 1993 (trans. in *FBIS, DRC,* 2 June 1993, pp. 33–35).

Lu, Philip. "Golf Ball Diplomacy." *Free China Review,* May 1994, p. 30.

Lu Ren. "Beijing's Near and Medium Policies toward Taiwan. *Qing bao* (Hong Kong), 1 January 1996 (trans. in *FBIS, DRC,* 11 January 1996, pp. 82–86).

Managing the Taiwan Issue: Key Is Better U.S. Relations with China. Report of an independent task force sponsored by the Council on Foreign Relations (Stephen Friedman, chairman). New York: Council on Foreign Relations, 1995.

Mansfield, Edward D., and Jack Snyder. "Democratization and the Danger of War." *International Security,* vol. 20, no. 1 (Summer 1995), pp. 5–38.

Mayers, David Allan. *Splitting the Monolith: U.S. Policy Against the Sino-Soviet Alliance, 1949–1955.* Baton Rouge, La.: Louisiana State University Press, 1986.

McVadon, Adm. (Ret.) Eric. "PRC Exercises, Doctrine, and Tactics toward Taiwan: The Naval Dimension." Paper presented at conference on the PLA, 6–8 Sept. 1996, Coolfont, W. Va., sponsored by American Enterprise Institute.

Meng Lin. "Generals Jointly Sign Petition on *Yinhe* Incident." *Jing bao,* no. 10 (5 October 1993), p. 54 (trans. in *FBIS, DRC,* 13 October 1993, pp. 41–42).

———. "Hu Qiaomu Criticizes Pro-American Faction Inside CCP." *Jing bao,* no. 169 (5 August 1991), p. 54–55 (trans. in *FBIS, DRC,* 7 August 1991, pp. 17–18).

Ming Li. "New Elements in the CPC's Taiwan Policy." *Qing bao,* 5 May 1993, (trans. in *FBIS, DRC,* 12 May 1993, pp. 66–67).

Nathan, Andrew J. "China's Goals in the Taiwan Strait." *China Journal,* no. 36 (July 1996), pp. 87–93.

Office of Naval Intelligence, U.S. Navy. *Chinese Exercises Strait 961: 8–25 March 1996.* May 1996.

Pollack, Jonathan D. "China's Taiwan Strategy: A Point of No Return." *China Journal,* no. 36 (July 1996), pp. 111–16.

Prime, Penelope B. "China's Economic Progress: Is It Sustainable?" In William Joseph, ed., *China Briefing 1997.* New York and Boulder: Asia Society and Westview Press, 1997.

———. "The Economy in Overdrive: Will It Crash?" *Current History,* vol. 29, no. 575 (Sept. 1993), pp. 260–64.

Ren Huiwen. "Background to China's 'Four Nots' Policy Towards the United States." *Xin bao,* 17 Sept. 1993, p. 24 (trans. in *FBIS, DRC,* 17 Sept. 1993, pp. 1–3).

———. "China Insists Foreign Countries Should Accord Li Peng Equally Courteous Reception." *Xin bao,* 8 July 1994 (trans. in *FBIS, DRC,* 13 July 1994, pp. 1–2).

———. "CPC Decides to Adjust Strategy toward United States." *Xin bao,* 21 May 1993 (trans. in *FBIS, DRC,* 24 May 1993, pp. 6–7).

———. "The CPC [Communist Party of China; same as CCP] Intensifies Its Peace Offensive against Taiwan." *Xin bao,* 14 May 1993 (trans. in *FBIS, DRC,* 18 May 1993, pp. 81–82).

———. "CPC Makes New Policy Decision on Army Participation in Government and Political Affairs." *Xin bao,* 11 Dec. 1992 (trans. in *FBIS, DRC,* 14 Dec. 1992, pp. 28–30).

A Resume of the Koo-Wang Talks. Taipei: Straits Exchange Foundation, December 1993.

Richburg, Keith, and Steven Mufson. "Saber-Rattling in Spratlys Raises Risks of Asian Conflict." *International Herald Tribune,* 6 June 1995, p. 4.

Shambaugh, David. *Beautiful Imperialist: China Perceives America, 1972–1990.* Princeton, N.J.: Princeton University Press, 1991.

———. "China's Commander in Chief: Jiang Zemin and the PLA." Paper presented at American Enterprise Institute and Thompson, Mickle, Imbot Asia Ltd. conference on the PLA, 9–11 June 1995, Coolfont, W.Va.

———. "Growing Strong: China's Challenge to Asian Security." *Survival,* Summer 1994, pp. 43–59.

———. "The Insecurity of Security: The People's Liberation Army's Evolving Doctrine and Threat Perceptions Towards 2000." *Journal of Northeast Asian Studies,* vol. 13, no. 1 (Spring 1994), pp. 3–25.

Shao Weizhong and Zhang Shan. *Ezhi Tai du: Bu chengnuo shifang wuli* (Curbing Taiwan independence: Not promising to abandon military force). Beijing: Zhongguo Shehui Chubanshe, 1996.

Shi, Yan. "He Xin Submits Written Statement to CPC Leadership to Expose U.S. 'Vigorous Attempt to Turn China into Chaos, Subjugate and Dissect China.' " *Bai xing,* no. 244 (16 July 1991), pp. 3–4 (trans. in *FBIS, DRC,* 24 July 1991, pp. 9–11).

Shih, Chih-Yu. "National Security Is a Western Concern." *China Journal,* no. 36 (July 1996), pp. 106–10.

Shirk, Susan L. *The Political Logic of Economic Reform in China.* Berkeley: University of California Press, 1993.

Shu Zu. "The Hands Held by China and the United States in Their Contest." *Zheng ming,* 1 October 1992 (trans. in *FBIS, DRC,* 15 October 1992, pp. 5–9).

Sutter, Robert G. *Sino–U.S. Relations: Status and Outlook—Views from Beijing.* Office of Senior Specialist memorandum. Washington, D.C.: Library of Congress, 15 August 1994.

———. "Taiwan: Recent Developments and U.S. Policy Choices." Congressional Research Service brief no. 1394006, 12 September 1994.

Swaine, Michael D. *The Military and Political Succession in China: Leadership, Institutions, Beliefs.* Santa Monica, Calif.: RAND, 1992.

———, and Donald P. Henry. *China: Domestic Change and Foreign Policy.* Santa Monica: RAND, 1995.

Tian Chen. "Foreign Ministry's Secret Report on Sino-U.S. Relations." *Zheng ming,* 1 Nov. 1992 (trans. in *FBIS, DRC,* 3 Nov. 1992, pp. 5–7).

Ting Chenwu. "Hawks Dominate China's Policy toward Taiwan." *Xin bao,* 14 March 1996 (trans. in *FBIS, DRC,* 21 March 1996, pp. 11–13).

Tyler, Patrick E. "As China Threatens Taiwan, U.S. Listens." *New York Times,* 24 Jan. 1966, p. A3.

Unger, Jonathan., ed. *Chinese Nationalism.* Armonk, N.Y.: M. E. Sharpe, 1996.

United States and China: Relations at a Crossroads. Barbara B. Conable, Jr., and John C. Whitehead, cochairs; David M. Lampton and Alfred D. Wilhelm, Jr., co-rapporteurs. Policy paper. Washington, D.C.: Atlantic Council of the United States and National Committee on United States–China Relations, February 1993.

United States Security Strategy for the East Asia-Pacific Region. Washington, D.C.: U.S. Department of Defense, Office of International Security Affairs, February 1995.

"The U.S. and China: Working Together Toward a Stable Relationship." *United States Department of State Dispatch,* 6 November 1995, vol. 6, no. 45, p. 816.

"U.S. Policies Toward Beijing Increasingly Rankle GOP." *Congressional Quarterly, Weekly Report,* 10 February 1996, p. 360.

Van Ness, Peter. "Competing Hegemons." *China Journal,* no. 36 (July 1996), pp. 125–28.

Wang Feiling. "Shi yong zhuyi zhudaoxiade Meijun celue—Fenxi Meijun jieru Tai hai zhanzheng de kenengxing" (American military strategy under the guidance of realism—An analysis of the probability of U.S. military intervention in a Taiwan Strait war). *Mingbao yuekan* (Mingbao monthly) (Hong Kong), 1995, no. 8, pp. 24–26.

Wang, Jisi. "How and Why Things Went Wrong in Sino-American Relations, 1989–1992." *New Ideas and Concepts in Sino-American Relations.* Report on conference sponsored by American Enterprise Institute and Shanghai Institute for International Studies, 18–20 November 1992.

———. "Pragmatic Nationalism: China Seeks a New Role in World Affairs." *Oxford International Review,* Winter 1994, pp. 28–30, 51.

Whiting, Allen S. "ASEAN Eyes China: The Security Dimension." Paper presented at U.S. Army War College Annual Strategy Conference "China into the 21st Century: Strategic Partner and/or Peer Competitor," April 1996.

———. *The Chinese Calculus of Deterrence: India and Indochina.* Ann Arbor: University of Michigan Press, 1975.

———. "Chinese Nationalism and Foreign Policy after Deng," *China Quarterly,* no. 142 (June 1995), pp. 295–316.

Winkler, Edwin A. "Institutionalization and Participation: From Hard to Soft Authoritarianism?" *China Quarterly,* no. 99 (Sept. 1994), pp. 481–99.

Wu Qingwen. "The Chinese Military Reacts Strongly Against U.S. Fighter Plane Sales to Taiwan." *Xin bao,* 15 October 1992 (trans. in *FBIS, DRC,* 19 October 1992, pp. 4–6).

Wu, Yu-shan. "Taiwan in 1993: Attempting a Diplomatic Breakthrough." *Asian Survey,* vol. 36, no. 1 (January 1994).

————. "Taiwan in 1994: Managing a Critical Relationship." *Asian Survey,* vol. 35, no. 1 (January 1995).

You, J. "Taiwan in the Political Calculations of the Chinese Leadership." *China Journal,* no. 36 (July 1996), pp. 119–25.

Yue Shan. "Central Advisory Commission Submits Letter to CCP Central Committee Opposing 'Rightist Tendency.'" *Zheng ming,* no. 175 (1 May 1992), pp. 13–14.

————. "Wang Zhen Takes Advantage of Winning to Curse Deng Xiaoping." *Zheng ming,* no. 171 (1 January 1992) (trans. in *FBIS, DRC,* 10 January 1992, pp. 23–24).

Zeng Lanhai. "CCP Decides on Its International Archenemy." *Zheng ming,* no. 195 (1 January 1994), pp. 16–18 (trans. in *FBIS, DRC,* 25 January 1994, pp. 4–6).

Zhao, Suisheng. "Deng Xiaoping's Southern Tour: Elite Politics in Post-Tiananmen China." *Asian Survey,* vol. 33, no. 8 (1993), pp. 739–56.

Index

Adams, Gerry, 69
Adulyadej, Bhumibol, 31
Antihegemonists, 6, 7, 167*n5*
ASEAN. *See* Association of Southeast Asian Nations
Association of Southeast Asian Nations (ASEAN), 6

Baum, Richard, 47, 65
Beijing massacre, 38–39, 50, 150, 169*n2* (ch. 5), 170*n3*
Bo Yibo, 59
Boutros-Ghali, Boutros, 31
Bush, George: sale of fighter planes to Taipei, 35, 48, 51–54; renewal of MFN, 37, 51–52; administration of, 38

Carter, Jimmy, 98, 108. *See also* Normalization negotiations of 1978–79
CCP. *See* Chinese Communist Party
Chen Cheng, 90, 157–58
Chen Li-an, 90–92
Chen, Stephen, 82
Chen Yun: reform ideas of, 47; as "second generation" CCP leader, 50; opposition to political deals, 53–54; response to aircraft sales to Taiwan, 54; criticism of weak U.S. policy, 56; eight-point agreement with Deng Xiaoping, 59; mentioned, 60, 65
Chi Haotian: on aircraft sales to Taiwan, 54; speech threatening force, 74; reunification stressed by, 102; mentioned, 58, 82. *See also* Coercive campaign of 1996
Chiang Ching-kuo: as opponent of PRC, 16; and martial law, 17, 22; po-

litical transition under, 22, 157–58; "one China" under, 28; mentioned, 23, 27, 89, 91, 119
Chiang Kai-shek: politics on offshore islands, 3; as opponent of PRC, 16; death of, 22, 38; "one China" under, 28; and campaign for UN membership, 30; mentioned, 86, 89, 119
Chiang Wei-kuo, 90
China threat: reverse of U.S. opinion on, 5; U.S. policy toward, 6, 7, 70–71; and disputed airspace, 8–9; and transition from communism, 10–11; use of force mentioned, 74; view of U.S. as hostile, 78; U.S. concessions, 79–80; toward Taiwan, 85–88; of military action against Taiwan and nuclear attack on U.S., 97, 128–29, 131; U.S. allies concern toward, 134, 139, 141, 156. *See also* Antihegemonists; Coercive campaign of 1996; Military power; Sanctions
China-U.S. relations. *See* Sino-U.S. relations
Chinese Communist Party (CCP), 21
Chou Yun, 170*n9*
Christopher, Warren: and U.S. Congress, 69–70; and visa controversy, 78–82 *passim;* response to expelling of Air Force officers from China, 87; and "one China," 150; mentioned, 101. *See also* Coercive campaign of 1996
Clinton, Bill: and Lee Teng-hui visa, 13, 78–80; stance on MFN, 37–38, 39; lectured by Jiang Zemin, 67; attacked by U.S. Congress, 68; and China's advance against Taiwan,